CONTENTS

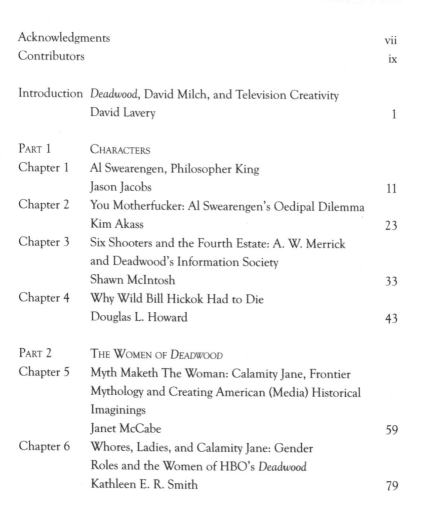

READING
DEADWOOD

Reading Contemporary Television

Series Editors: Kim Akass and Janet McCabe
janetandkim@hotmail.com

The *Reading Contemporary Television* series aims to offer a varied, intellectually groundbreaking and often polemical response to what is happening in television today. This series is distinct in that it sets out to immediately comment upon the TV *Zeitgeist* while providing an intellectual and creative platform for thinking differently and ingeniously writing about contemporary television culture. The books in the series seek to establish a critical space where new voices are heard and fresh perspectives offered. Innovation is encouraged and intellectual curiosity demanded.

Published and Forthcoming:

READING
DEADWOOD

A WESTERN TO SWEAR BY

Edited by **DAVID LAVERY**

I.B. TAURIS
LONDON · NEW YORK

Published in 2006 by I.B.Tauris & Co Ltd
6 Salem Road, London W2 4BU
175 Fifth Avenue, New York NY 10010
www.ibtauris.com

In the United States of America and in Canada distributed by
Palgrave Macmillan, a division of St Martin's Press
175 Fifth Avenue, New York NY 10010

ISBN 10: 1 84511 221 0
ISBN 13: 978 1 84511 221 9

A full CIP record for this book is available from the British Library
A full CIP record for this book is available from the Library of Congress

Library of Congress catalog card: available

Typeset in Goudy Old Style by Steve Tribe, Andover
Printed and bound in Great Britain by TJ International Ltd, Cornwall

ACKNOWLEDGMENTS

Like *Reading* The Sopranos, a contemporaneous I.B.Tauris project, the timeframe under which this collection was developed was challenging, to say the least. Without the incredible cooperation and critical acumen of its authors, Jason Jacobs, Kim Akass, Shawn McIntosh, Doug Howard, Janet McCabe, Kathleen Smith, Amanda Klein, Joe Millichap, Sean O'Sullivan, David Drysdale, Paul Wright, Hai Lin Zhou, Christopher Williams, Erin Hill, and Scott Diffrient, this book would have never made it to the thoroughfare.

Once again, cheers to Philippa Brewster at I.B.Tauris, and Janet and Kim, the *Reading Contemporary Television* series editors, who kept me on schedule and yet gave me the leeway needed to pull this off.

Thanks as well to Marc Leverette and Doug Howard for special assistance in the rush to complete the book.

This book is dedicated to a woman who does an amazing Calamity Jane imitation and remains, after 25 years, someone (to quote another de-mythologizing Western of the day) I don't know how to quit and never will.

CONTRIBUTORS

Kim Akass has co-edited (with Janet McCabe) and contributed to *Reading Sex and the City* (I.B.Tauris, 2004), *Reading Six Feet Under: T.V. To Die For* (I.B.Tauris, 2005) and *Reading The L Word: Outing Contemporary TV* (I.B.Tauris, 2006). She is currently researching representations of the mother and motherhood in American TV Drama and is one of the founding editors of *Critical Studies in Television* (MUP), as well as (with McCabe) series editor for *Reading Contemporary Television* for I.B.Tauris.

David Scott Diffrient recently earned his Ph.D. from UCLA's Department of Film, TV, and Digital Media, and is currently a Visiting Lecturer in the University of Michigan's American Culture Program and Screen Arts and Cultures Department. He has published articles in several journals, including *CineAction* and *Cinema Journal*, and his essays can be found in such anthologies as *Horror Film: Creating and Marketing Fear*, *Beyond Life is Beautiful: Comedy and Tragedy in the Cinema of Roberto Benigni*, *South Korean Golden Age Melodrama: Gender, Genre, and Nation*, and *New Korean Cinema*. His essays on television series appear in the forthcoming volumes *Dear Angela: Remembering My So-Called Life* and *Watching Teen TV: Text and Culture*.

David Drysdale currently teaches and conducts research at the University of Northern British Columbia, where he is completing his graduate work. In the past he has presented on *Unforgiven* as well as the figure of Wyatt Earp in *Doctor Who* and *Star Trek*. Currently he is working on an extended study of Wyatt Earp in Cold War western film.

Erin Hill is a graduate student in the Critical Studies Program in the Department of Film, Television and Digital Media at UCLA's School of Theatre, Film and Television. She co-founded *Mediascape*, UCLA's online visual culture journal.

Douglas L. Howard is Assistant Chair in the English Department at Suffolk County Community College. His work has appeared in *Literature and Theology*, *The Chronicle of Higher Education*, *PopPolitics*, *The Gothic Other* (co-editor and contributor), *This Thing of Ours: Investigating* The Sopranos, and *Reading* The Sopranos.

Jason Jacobs teaches screen history and aesthetics in the School of Arts, Media and Culture at Griffith University in Brisbane, Australia. He is the author of *The Intimate Screen: Early British Television Drama* (Clarendon Press, 2000) and *Body Trauma TV* (British Film Institute, 2003), and he is editor of screenaesthetics.com.

Amanda Ann Klein is a Ph.D. candidate in film studies at the University of Pittsburgh. Her dissertation reconceives classical theories of genrification and cycle formation through a case study of the 1990s gangsta cycle. Her publications include forthcoming essays in *The Quarterly Review of Film and Video* and an article in an anthology on images of deviance in the media. She has also published online essays in *Critical Quarterly* and *Reality Blurred: Exposed*.

David Lavery will soon become chair in Film and Television at Brunel University, London. He is the author of over one hundred published essays and reviews and author/editor/co-editor of eleven books, including *Full of Secrets: Critical Approaches to* Twin Peaks and *Reading* The Sopranos: Hit TV from HBO. He co-edits the e-journal *Slayage: The Online International Journal of Buffy Studies* and is one of the founding editors of the new journal *Critical Studies in Television: Scholarly Studies of Small Screen Fictions*.

Janet McCabe is Research Associate in TV Drama at Manchester Metropolitan University. She is author of *Feminist Film Studies: Writing the Woman into Cinema* (Wallflower, 2004), and is co-editor of *Reading* Sex and the City (I.B.Tauris, 2004), *Reading* Six Feet Under: *TV To Die For* (I.B.Tauris, 2005) and *Reading* The L Word: *Outing Contemporary Television* (I.B.Tauris,

2006). She is managing editor of the new television journal *Critical Studies in Television* (MUP) as well as (with Akass) series editor of *Reading Contemporary Television* for I.B.Tauris.

Joseph Millichap is Professor Emeritus of English at Western Kentucky University. His publications on American literature, film, and culture include *Steinbeck and Film*, *Robert Penn Warren: A Study of the Short Fiction*, and *Dixie Limited: Railroads, Culture, and the Southern Renaissance*.

Shawn McIntosh is co-author of *Converging Media: Introduction to Mass Communication*, a textbook for undergraduate media courses, and is a lecturer in the Strategic Communications Program at Columbia University's School of Continuing Education. He has been an editor and freelance writer for ten years for various newspapers and magazines in the UK, USA, and Japan.

Sean O'Sullivan is an Assistant Professor of English at the Ohio State University. He is the author of *Mike Leigh* (forthcoming in the University of Illinois Press' *Contemporary Film Directors* series). His work addresses British cinema and television, serial fiction across media, and narrative connections between the visual and verbal arts. His next project is *The Portrait and the Plot*, a study of Jacques-Louis David, Charles Dickens and Alfred Hitchcock.

Kathleen E. R. Smith is the Clyde Bostick Professor of Social Studies and Associate Professor of History in the School of Social Sciences, Northwestern State University of Louisiana. She is the author of *"God Bless America": Tin Pan Alley Goes to War* (University Press of Kentucky, 2003) and *Lieutenant Colonel Emily U. Miller: A Biography* (Northwestern State University of Louisiana Press, 1984). She is the Editor of *Zwolle, Louisiana: Our Story; Portrait of a Small Town* (Town of Zwolle, Louisiana and the Louisiana Endowment for the Humanities, 2000).

G. Christopher Williams is an Assistant Professor of English at the University of Wisconsin-Stevens Point. His work has appeared in *Film Criticism, Post Script, Popular Culture Review, Gothic Studies*, and *Atenea*. He is a regular contributor to the multimedia reviews section at popmatters.com.

Paul Wright took his doctorate in Comparative Literature from Princeton University. He has taught at Princeton and Osaka University in Japan and currently teaches at Villanova University as a post-doctoral fellow in Core Humanities. His main area of research is Renaissance cultural history, including humanism, Machiavelli, and Milton. He is at work on a book-length study of Machiavelli's *Florentine Histories*, and continues to insist that Al Swearengen and Machiavelli are both misunderstood civic founders.

Hailin Zhou, a native of Shanghai, China, took her doctorate in Comparative Literature from Waseda University, Japan. Her research interests include Chinese and Japanese literature between the world wars, including the phenomenon of Chinese collaboration with Japanese occupiers of China in this crucial period. She currently teaches at Villanova University, where she offers courses on Chinese and Japanese language, literature, cuisine, and film. She continues to insist that her spouse should watch less television, and his reply that "It's not TV, it's HBO" seems oddly unoriginal.

"They's developments that need interpretatin' on every front."

Dan Dority, "Complications" (2.5)

"We'll hire some great minds to do the heavy lifting."

Maddie, "A Lie Agreed Upon," Part 2 (2.2)

DEADWOOD, DAVID MILCH, AND TELEVISION CREATIVITY

DAVID LAVERY

David had more miles on him the day I met him than I'll probably have the day I die. He'll wrestle his demons forever, but I've never known anyone else who has learned to put his demons at his service in quite the way he has. I think that's his real genius. And David is a genius in the literal definition of that word. He is truly unique, truly original. *NYPD Blue* allowed him to exorcise some of his demons or, certainly, to turn a light on in the room where they reside. None of this was done from a distance. He took on addiction, alcoholism, racism—things that are just so fundamental to our nature and things that are dangerous in society he found a way to explore cold-bloodedly. In a medium that is utterly fearful, he has been a fiercely brave writer.

Steven Bochco (Singer 197)

In a documentary ("How It All Began") on the Season One DVDs of *Seinfeld*, co-creator Jerry Seinfeld reminisces about the conception of the tremendously successful NBC sitcom named after him. As is so often the case in the medium, it seems in retrospect highly unlikely that such a phenomenal series ever happened. *Seinfeld* (1990-1998) might have been *sui generis*. "The idea that you have two guys [Seinfeld, Larry David] who have never written a show, being run by a network executive that had never had a show, leading to a show that has a unique and unusual feel—this is a model that all the networks subsequently ignored and never did again—except for HBO." In order to produce its branded "Not TV" television, HBO has developed a new method of engendering shows, one Seinfeld thinks, perhaps grandiosely, he helped to originate. For HBO "hires people that they like and says that's the end of their job. We like you; do what you think you should do, and it leads to much more distinctive programming."

The matchless, "hideously beautiful" (McCabe, p. 63 below), astonishing, "filthy joy" (Jacobs, p. 11 below) of a television series this book considers came into the world when its creator David Milch (*Hill Street Blues*, *NYPD Blue*) was invited by HBO to propose a project for their consideration. Similar, unrefusable offers to long-time network veteran David Chase (*The Rockford Files*, *I'll Fly Away*, *Northern Exposure*) and film screenwriter Alan Ball (*American Beauty*) had brought about the stupendously successful *The Sopranos* (1999–2007) and the one-of-a-kind *Six Feet Under* (2000–2005) respectively. In collaboration with the influential producer Steven Bochco, Milch had reimagined the ensemble drama with *Hill Street Blues* (NBC, 1981–1987). Working again with Bochco on the tremendously controversial *NYPD Blue* (1993–2005), a series that may have resurrected the sixty-minute drama, he expanded the parameters of network television narrative, introducing profane language and posterior nudity and making an alcoholic, racist cop, modeled after Milch's own father, the series' central character.[1] Along the way, he had won numerous awards for his work, including multiple Emmys and Humanitas Prizes.[2] Milch seemed a perfect candidate to create a show on the censorship-free premium cable channel.

A former Yale University creative writing professor who had left academe to seek his fortune in Hollywood because an Ivy League salary could not sufficiently support his heroin addiction, alcoholism, and gambling habits, Milch has long felt a certain experiential affinity for the symbiotic relationship of cop and criminal and understandably pitched HBO another police drama,[3] this one set not in Los Angeles or New York, but in Rome—at the time of Nero (AD 54–68), a series that, Milch confirms in several interviews, would have begun with the arrest of St Paul. Already committed to the new series *Rome*, an innovative new joint production with the BBC that would air in the USA in 2005, HBO declined, but Chris Albrecht and Carolyn Strauss invited another proposal from Milch—perhaps one that would explore similar themes in a different setting. *Deadwood* was the result.

Milch is credited as writer of only two of *Deadwood*'s twenty-four episodes (the pilot and Part 1 of "A Lie Agreed Upon," 2.1), while a largely invisible team of a dozen writers, several of whom had worked with Milch on earlier series, authored the other twenty-two.[4] The official authorship credits do not seem to reflect the unique nature of *Deadwood*'s creation as depicted in various news accounts (Wolk, Havrilesky, Singer, D'Alessandro) and in the documentaries ("The New Language of the Old West," "An Imaginative Reality") and episode commentaries on the Season One DVDs.

It is not unusual, of course, for a network or cable series with a team of writers to work together with a creator/executive producer/showrunner who gets to review the final draft of virtually every script: Chris Carter on *The X-Files*, Chase on *The Sopranos*, Joss Whedon on *Buffy the Vampire Slayer*—all exemplify such a process, each seeking to maintain, given this singular opportunity for quality control in a medium usually considered more conducive to the writer's craft than the movies, his creation's signature voice.

Unlike most creators, Milch has never directed a single episode of *Deadwood* (or of any of his earlier series for that matter), but his influence is not limited to the script. We know that he prepares his actors at rehearsal in a manner comparable to that of the great directors—as Molly Parker and Keith Carradine acknowledge in their commentary on "Here Was a Man." In *Entertainment Weekly*'s insightful report on "How the West is Run," we catch a glimpse of Milch carefully modulating—directing?—Mr. Wu's "cocksuckers," asking for the expletive to be "more plaintive than angry" (Wolk 68).

Wolk reports, too, that *Deadwood*'s actors listen to "long preparatory lectures about context and subtext, dappled with historical metaphors to explain the many levels he's aiming for" (70). Singer speaks of the "typical Milchian riff, a garrulous but lucid stream of subtextual information—intellectually daunting, digressive, arcane, wittily profane..." (192). According to Ian McShane (Al Swearengen), the subject of the "polymathic" (Wolk 70) former college professor's impromptu orations is more likely to concern "nineteenth-century Germany economics" than the upcoming scene.

Wolk describes Milch's "blitzkrieg form of creativity" in which "scenes are written the day before shooting, leaving his cast and crew as dizzily uncertain about their futures as a frontiersman in an untamed land" (68-9). As validation of his own creative method, he quotes fondly, on several occasions, his father's admonition, "If you want to hear God laugh, tell him your plans"; Milch prefers to work without them:

> Script outlines, preplanned story arcs: It's all anathema to Milch,
> whose last-minute, improvisatory writing style is a conscious decision
> to write unconsciously. ... When he dictates a scene,[5] he has no
> endgame in mind—he simply begins with a situation, then channels
> the characters, letting them speak through him. ... But once he's
> finally imagined a scene, he'll never start over, as this would be an
> untenable slight against his imagination.
>
> (Wolk 69)

In his insightful conversations with Carradine on the Season One DVDs,
Milch speaks fervently, with a tone that might be deemed pious, about the
sense of privilege he feels in taking "part in a sacrament" ("New Language"),
insisting that "the muse knows where to find me every morning."[6]

And yet Milch does not operate under any Romantic notion that if
"Poetry comes not as naturally as the Leaves to a tree it had better not come
at all" (Keats 318). With characteristic erudition, he cites ("An Imaginative
Reality") the famous example of the German chemist Kekule who, after years
of study and research, came by a solution to the long-standing question of
the structure of the benzene molecule in a dream (Koestler 169–71) and
insists that "visions come to prepared spirits."[7] His immediate preparation
for Deadwood included reading virtually every issue of The Black Hills Pioneer,
steeping himself in the history of the American West, the gold rush, and
Deadwood itself, and revisiting the Western genre, with which he had only a
passing familiarity prior to creating Deadwood.

In his conversation with Heather Havrilesky, Milch admits his relative
ignorance of the genre. Having grown up, uninterested in the Western, in
the days of Hopalong Cassidy and the Cisco Kid, he managed to "remain
innocent of the classical Westerns" that followed. His latter-day research into
the form in his preparation for Deadwood led him to a typically Milchian
complex understanding of the cultural forces at work in the genre. The
Western film "had everything to do with what Hollywood was about at that
time, and nothing to do with what the West was about." The Western as we
know it was "really an artifact of the Hays Production Code of the '20s and
'30s" and not about the West. Heavily influenced by "middle-European Jews
who had come out to Hollywood to present to America a sanitized heroic
idea of what America was ... an America disinfected and pure."

"Working in network television," Milch tells Havrilesky, was very like working under the Hays Code. "You can spend your time pissing and moaning about the strictures within which you're forced to work, or you can try and find ways to neutralize the distorting effect of those strictures, which is to develop personalities [or] characters whose own internal process winds up at the same place as the external strictures, but for internal reasons." Milch's extraordinary creation Andy Sipowicz, *NYPD Blue*'s alcoholic, racist detective, who, in the series' twelve years on the air struggles to become a worthwhile human being and acquire a soul (Lavery), exemplifies such a narrative strategy. Because "every storyteller works within the conventions of his time," however, the Hays Code produced a different result: "stoic characters who lived by a code and then a kind of justifying dramatic structure which validated that."

Milch's preparations to make "reality come alive" in his imagination so he might make *Deadwood* didn't just include his very professorial research into history and context. "I've spent decades learning my craft," he tells Carradine. The influence of Robert Penn Warren (beautifully articulated in Joe Millichap's contribution to this book), his eclectic reading (in interviews Milch routinely makes reference to a wide variety of writers and books, from the Bible to Shakespeare, Hawthorne, Santayana, William and Henry James, Nathanael West), his work on *Hill Street Blues* and *NYPD Blue*, even his numerous failed series (*Capital News, Big Apple, Brooklyn South*)—all made *Deadwood* possible.

Milch's creation is rich in character-based humor (the oleaginous E. B. Farnum might be funnier than any sitcom character now on TV); scatological (what other show has depicted the passing of kidney stones, the suppression of a "digestive crisis," the "situating" of phlegm?); macabre (Woo's Pigs are extremely well fed); articulately profane (see John Allan Bridge's consideration of *Deadwood*'s language on the book's website);[8] unpredictably observant (receiving a blowjob from Dolly, Al exclaims, looking down, "Do you dye your hair?"); wonderfully Shakespearean (the series is full of monologues and soliloquies: Al's to Dolly, the Chief; E. B.'s to the imbecilic Richardson and a blood-stained floor; Charley's and Jane's to the grave of Wild Bill); graced by minor and mid-major characters (Ellsworth, Dan Dority, Jewel, Johnny Burns, Mr. Wu, Tom Nuttal, Con Stapleton, Silas Adams, Blazanov, Andy Cramed) beautifully realized and three dimensional; rudely, crudely, and perfectly in keeping with both the era and Milch's worldview,[9] not politically correct (racism, Indian-hating, anti-Semitism, sexism, in word and brutal deed, are all *Deadwood* realities, part of its "reckless verisimilitude"—see the Ellroy epigraph to Wright and Hailin Zhou's essay in this volume). In its elaborate, intricate, "cold-blooded" reconnoitering of a place and a time, *Deadwood* reminds this viewer at least of the work of William Faulkner, who once scrawled on a map (included in *Absalom, Absalom* [1936]) of his brainchild, the "fictional" Yoknapatawpha County, "William Faulkner, Sole Owner & Proprietor." Given the collaborative nature of television creativity, the world of a series can never be solely owned, but make no mistake: David Milch is *Deadwood*'s proprietor.

"It's not by any virtue that I have received a gift," Milch insists. "It's an accident. But the crime would be not to be respectful of it" ("An Imaginative Reality"). Cast and crew on the films of the late Federico Fellini spoke of "the daily miracle" (*Fellini: I'm a Born Liar*) of working with the constantly improvising "Maestro." By all reports, the creation of *Deadwood*, Milch's masterpiece, decades in the making, has been similarly miraculous.

ABOUT THIS BOOK

In full agreement with the ever-observant Dan Dority and the conniving Maddie (see the epigraphs to the book, p. xiii above), I have assembled a variety of "great minds" in order to do the "heavy lifting" necessary to address those many developments in *Deadwood* in need of "interpretatin'."

Part 1, "Characters", examines several of the camp's inhabitants. Both Jason Jacobs ("Al Swearengen, Philosopher King") and Kim Akass ("You Motherfucker: Al Swearengen's Oedipal Dilemma") offer perspectives on Deadwood's most fascinating and powerful citizen. Shawn McIntosh ("Six Shooters and the Fourth Estate: A. W. Merrick and Deadwood's Information Society") scrutinizes the editor of the camp's newspapers and contextualizes him both in the Western genre and in history. And Douglas Howard ("Why Wild Bill Hickok Had to Die") considers the central (though short-lived) role of the famous gunfighter in the series.

"The Women of *Deadwood*," Part 2, continues to focus on residents of the camp, this time its women. Janet McCabe ("Myth Maketh The Woman:

Calamity Jane, Frontier Mythology and Creating American (Media) Historical Imaginings") reflects on the differences between the "real," mythic, and HBO versions of Jane Cannary, and Kathleen E. R. Smith ("Whores, Ladies, and Calamity Jane: Western Gender Roles and the Women of HBO's *Deadwood*") offers not only a second take on Calamity Jane but historically grounded analyses of Alma Garrett, Martha Bullock, Miss Isringhausen, Trixie, and Joanie Stubs as well.

Part 3, "*Deadwood* and Genre," offers three essays seeking to pinpoint *Deadwood*'s generic allegiances. Amanda Klein ("'The Horse Doesn't Get a Credit': The Foregrounding of Generic Syntax in *Deadwood*'s Opening Credits") begins at the beginning in her examination of the series' establishing montage. Joseph Millichap ("David Milch, Robert Penn Warren, and the Literary Contexts of *Deadwood*") takes into consideration the powerful influence of a great American writer on the series' creator. And Sean O'Sullivan ("Old, New, Borrowed, Blue: *Deadwood* and Serial Fiction") finds surprising resonances between literary and televisual episodic narrative.

Part 4, "The Fabric of Society in *Deadwood*," includes three essays. David Drysdale ("'Laws and Everything Other Damn Thing': Authority, Bad Faith, and the Unlikely Success of *Deadwood*") seeks to explain the implicit social and political appeal of the series in the Bush era. G. Christopher Williams ("Pimp and Whore: The Necessity of Perverse Domestication in the Development of the Western") contemplates the relationship of Al Swearengen and Trixie as a mirror of the development of community in *Deadwood*. Paul Wright and Hai Lin Zhou ("Diving the 'Celestials': The Chinese Subculture of *Deadwood*") explore the anything but peripheral role of Deadwood's Asian immigrants.

The earthy corporeality of the series is the focus of Part 5, "The Body in *Deadwood*," which offers essays by Erin Hill ("Body Crises in *Deadwood*") and David Scott Diffrient ("*Deadwood* Dick: The Western (Phallus) Reinvented").

Two appendices—a guide to the series' episodes, writers, and directors and a comprehensive encyclopedia of all things *Deadwood*—complete the book.

Additional essays and a hyperlinked version of the *Deadwood* Encyclopedia are available at the book's website: http://www.davidlavery.net/Deadwood.

PART 1
CHARACTERS

CHAPTER 1

AL SWEARENGEN, PHILOSOPHER KING[1]

Jason Jacobs

And further, I said, let us agree that they are lovers of all true being; there is no part whether greater or less, or more or less honorable, which they are willing to renounce; as we said before of the lover and the man of ambition.

Plato, The Republic

May I venture to indicate one last trait of my nature which creates for me no little difficulty in my relations with others? I possess a perfectly uncanny sensitivity of the instinct for cleanliness, so that I perceive physiologically—smell—the proximity or—what am I saying?—the innermost parts, the entrails, of every soul ... I have in this sensitivity psychological antennae with which I touch and take hold of every secret: all the concealed dirt at the bottom of many a nature, perhaps conditioned by bad blood but whitewashed by education, is known to me almost on first contact.

Nietzsche, Ecce Homo

With his grubby long johns visible beneath the Prince Albert suit, Ian Mc-Shane's Al Swearengen can hardly be accused of cleanliness; but he is central to the filthy joy of *Deadwood*. Those watery, unblinking blue eyes bespeak a fierce unrelenting intelligence that can morph, adapt, and swoop to whatever promises his advantage in the camp; fierceness that recruits, but is not tempered by, strategic charm, no less strategic for being naturally available, no less charming for being at the service of greed. The dramatic centrality of Swearengen's active being is felt most strongly in its absence, particularly in those early episodes of Season Two when, after a savage battle with Seth Bullock, he sickens and becomes comatose. These episodes, vivid as they are, lack the compelling quality, even when off-screen, of Swearengen's knowing, planning, gaze. There are several aspects that characterize this compelling presence, not least his deftness in *smelling* the "entrails" of those he meets.

His first conversation with Seth Bullock is instructive here ("Deadwood," 1.1). Bullock and his partner Sol Star enter the Gem Saloon in order to negotiate the buying of the lot where they have set up their temporary hardware store:

Seth:	We'd like to make an offer on that lot we're rentin'.
Al:	*(Pouring them whiskey shots)* Sell my back teeth for the right money.
Seth:	Six hundred get the job done?
Al:	I guess before I name a price I wanna know if you boys have unnamed partners.
Seth:	*(CU, annoyed)* Why?
Al:	I think specifically Wild Bill Hickok. Didn't you and Hickok act together in the street this morning?
Sol:	We just met Wild Bill Hickok.
Seth:	*(To Sol)* What business of that is his?
Al:	You mean what business of mine is that.
Bullock:	*(Furious)* Don't tell me what the fuck I mean.
Al:	*(Calm, meeting Bullock's gaze evenly)* Not a tone to get a deal done.

The scene begins with Al teasing Bullock about his killing, with Hickok, of Ned Mason, which Bullock takes as an insulting accusation that he is a loose gun. Here Swearengen provokes the revelation of the essence of Bullock's character: his barely contained propensity for violence even when it sabotages his interests. Questioning his motives and his honesty before apparently correcting his grammar is enough to send him over the edge. David Milch has described Bullock in terms that evoke Nietzsche as much as Swearengen himself:

> Darwin wrote about accidents of evolution—he called them
> "sports"—species which turned out to be superadaptive in whatever
> environment they discovered themselves in. In social terms, those
> are civilizers.
>
> (Singer 196)[2]

At first sight, Al appears the opposite of a civilizer but he provides the essential means by which the miners slake their fatigue and anxiety: the provision of sex, drugs, and gambling; these services offer the transient pleasures of losing the self in acts that, ultimately, destroy the self. Al's insight is into the darkness of men's appetites rather than their aspiration for joy; into the primitive, sometimes brutal, urges of men rather than their hopes for a better life. Like a catfish in an aquarium, Swearengen is a bottom dweller, who feeds off the labor and detritus of others; this parasitic economy is presented with clarity early in the same episode when veteran prospector Whitney Ellsworth presents some recently prospected gold to the Gem's owner in exchange for gambling, sex and booze:

| Ellsworth: | Inform your dealers and whores of my credit and pour me a drink. |
| Swearengen: | Honor and a pleasure my good man. |

As the miners rape the Indian land for gold, Al feeds on what remains at the end of the day with his whores' blowjobs an apt act for the sucking dry of the last of their day's energy, money, and pride. But like Ellsworth ("I wouldn't trust you as far as I could throw ya") everyone knows Swearengen's game: his superadaptivity is underlined by his winning charm, his ability to shape shift and therefore communicate with the full range of Deadwood's inhabitants from the limited pantomime of conversation with Mr. Wu ("Cocksuka! Swergin!"), and his negotiations with General Crook ("Sold Under Sin," 1.12), to his sly manipulation of George Hearst ("Boy the Earth Talks To," 2.12).

In part, this advantage is genetic, positioning him as an amalgam of voices, styles, and gestures; it gives him an attractive mongrel quality that is supported by McShane's voice, which exploits the full resonance of chest, exploring the deepness of it not only for commanding attention but also making wit and sarcasm constantly available amidst the same rich vibrancy. Later in the same scene with Ellsworth we get a hint of this adaptive mixture:

Ellsworth:	Now with that limey damn accent of yours, are these
	rumors true that you're descended from English nobility?
Swearengen:	I'm descended from all those cocksuckers.
Ellsworth:	*(Raising his shot glass)* Well here's to you, your Majesty.

Unlike the spineless English aristocracy, Swearengen seems more akin to a gamekeeper-cum-poacher, giving the impression of a bastard son of an aristocrat; he who controls the grounds, the mansion, and the Lady, not by his kingly visibility, but underhandedly, watching, calculating, planning, and earning.

Swearengen's ability to "smell out" a situation clearly enables his control of lesser intelligences such as the weasely E. B. Farnum and Johnny Burns; but his keen apprehension of the diversity of human nature and aspiration is also a match for those whose outward status and savvy should be beyond the clutches of a mere brute. A. W. Merrick would no doubt imagine himself to be Al's intellectual superior, but when Merrick's newspaper office and printing press are vandalized by Cy Tolliver's henchmen, Al, in a private meeting with the despairing Merrick, provides solace through admonition:

> Pain or damage don't end the world, or despair or fuckin' beatin's. The world ends when you're dead. Until then, you got more punishment in store. Stand it like a man—and give some back.
>
> ("E. B. Was Left Out," 2.7)

The casting is crucial here. It is important that Al is both squarely of the camp but also before and beyond it. McShane is doubly removed. First of all, as an Englishman he hails from the North, born in Lancashire and raised in Manchester before training at the Royal Academy of Dramatic Arts in London. Before *Deadwood*, he was probably best known for the title role in the BBC television series *Lovejoy* (BBC, 1986; 1991–1994), in which he played a lovable rogue antique dealer. Even there Lovejoy is an outsider: the series was set in East Anglia, where Lovejoy stands out as a Londoner with nous and an eye for rare antiques. This gentle comedy-mystery employed McShane's swarthy charm to humanize the rather seedy namesake of

Jonathan Glazer's novels on which the series was based. McShane is also known for his portrayal of villains, and his menace is exemplified in the role of Teddy Bass in *Sexy Beast* (2000).

Bass is depicted in Glazer's film as a top-of-the-food-chain villain, but is given little depth or humanity; a heavily made-up McShane is shot in a way that *asserts* his villainy rather than attempting to grasp it. As we shall see, it is this tendency in British film and television—and part of a tradition in British literary output—to assert a single dimension of a character rather than unpacking his humanity in all its complexity that *Deadwood* transcends. McShane's Swearengen represents a radical and sophisticated departure from this approach and, in part, *Deadwood*'s power depends on it.

Swearengen is not only a can-do fixer who adapts to situations, but also one who can adapt environmental contingency to suit his business. He can play the one-on-one with intimate menace but is also able to work a full room with theatrical relish. In the pilot episode, when news of the Metz family massacre reaches the Gem, Swearengen realizes that fear of Indian attack will dampen the customers' appetites for booze and sex; playing the spokesman for righteous justice, Al responds to the mood of fear, nurturing it and then turning it back on itself, through the promise of righteous and profitable revenge (but) the next day, while more earthy—and, for him, profitable—pleasures continue to be available right now:

> I guess when it starts pissin' rain in here we'll know who to blame.
> [Dan has just fired his gun at the ceiling in order to gain everyone's attention.] I know word's circulating Indians killed a family on the Spearfish road. Now it's not for me to tell anyone in this camp what to do, much as I don't want more people getting their throats cut, their scalps lifted, or any other godless thing that these godless bloodthirsty heathens do—or even if someone wants to ride out in darkest night—but I will tell you this: *I'd use tonight to get myself organized*—ride out in the morning, *clear-headed*—and, starting tomorrow morning, I will offer a personal fifty dollar bounty for every decapitated head of as many of these godless heathen cocksuckers as anyone can bring in, tomorrow—with no upper limit! That's all I say on that subject—except, next round's on the house. (*Cheers.*) And God rest the souls of that poor family! And pussy's half-price, next fifteen minutes.

Here McShane stands in the Gem's main bar and uses it as a stage, working through the mood of his clients by shaping it to his own ends. Never did fearful and selfish procrastination sound so sensible and noble.

Swearengen's obvious rival in the camp is Cy Tolliver, who offers a more up-market brothel and gambling house and has all the trappings of status and wealth. Yet Powers Boothe's extraordinary performance constructs a character whose fundamental brutality is present, even when he is at his most charming. So, while both men commit or have committed extraordinary violence, each act is predicated on very different motivations.

In "Suffer the Little Children" (1.8), Cy Tolliver's torture and killing of the two thieves, Flora and Miles Anderson, is both a recognition and acting out of his weaknesses, as well as a punishment for their source: his love for Joanie Stubbs. After the young thieves attempt escape, Tolliver has them beaten and then bound in chairs inside the Bella Union. He toys with them both before killing them as a way of making plain to Joanie the extent of his rage at being emotionally captive to her needs; it is a lesson as much for her as for him; their relationship is reflected in the beaten and bloody young people dying before them:

> (To Flora, half-unconscious) You bust somethin' up there, sweetheart? (Cy starts hitting her on the head several times) Does that fuckin' hurt you? You fuckin' understand me? See, that upsets Joanie now. "Oh, Cy, do up the boy. My God, I can't stand to see the other." You want me to see to the boy, Joanie? 'Cause you know I'm clay in your hands.

> (To Miles) Fuck it, Miles! You're found fuckin' guilty of bein' a cunt. I'm hereby passin' judgment for you lettin' this little bitch push you around and tellin' you what to do. When you were supposed to be a man and showin' her the fuckin' rules! (Slaps Miles) You hear me, Miles, and for bein' the cunt you are now, before you could have been a man, (points gun at Miles) done your fuckin' part, you little piece of shit. (Shoots and kills Miles.)

The potential loss of Joanie provokes acute distress, which Tolliver projects in a brutal murder, whereas Trixie's abandonment of Swearengen has a very different impact. Al's anger at Trixie for fucking the "Jew bastard" Sol

Star—because, crucially, she desires him—is articulated through a deep and nasty sulk. Al appears to be philosophical about the whole thing, despite the evident cost to him emotionally:

> (To Sol) Don't think I don't understand. I mean what can any one of us every really fucking hope for, huh? Except for a moment here and there with a person who doesn't rob, steal or murder us? At night it may happen. Sun-up, one person against the fucking wall, the other may hop on the fucking bed, trusted each other enough to tell half the fucking truth. Everybody needs that. It becomes precious to 'em. They don't want to see it fucked with.
>
> ("Jewel's Boot Is Made for Walking," 1.11)

But the cost to Al if he is seen *caring* about such an 'ideal' being 'fucked with' overcomes any possibility of personal revenge, despite this implied threat to Sol. The episode begins with Swearengen, anxious about the warrant out on him for the murder he committed in Chicago, calling Trixie back to bed—just as he describes to Sol—but it ends with Trixie lost to him. Once again, Al adapts in the midst of what must be painful rejection. His solution is not to beat Trixie (as he did in the pilot, merely for killing a client), but to seek out her replacement and subjugate that whore with the rule that denies intimacy and reduces her to the merely functional. And yet it is in this scene that Swearengen begins to tell the unnamed whore who fellates him in the bedroom adjoining his office what we've never seen him tell Trixie: about his past, his youth, and perhaps his motivation.

The sequence comes at the end of the episode and progresses from Swearengen standing fully dressed to his orgasm lying on his bed. His monologue provides the continuity; it is both a restatement of his integrity as a tough guy but also his reflection on the circumstances that have literally brought him to *this instant*, this orgasm, in this way. On Al's mind is not only the desertion of Trixie, and the warrant for his arrest, but also the suffering of Reverend Smith, who he has seen from the balcony of the Gem exhibiting increasing pain and humiliating madness. Somewhat bizarrely, given its content, the scene stands as one of the poetic moments in the series.

The most prominent aspect of the sequence is Swearengen's exploitation of the whore, and the cuts to wide shots constantly remind the viewer during his monologue that this is the case. He wants to rub her face in the reality of the situation while at the same time pondering the tender oddness of recruiting (rescuing?) her from the very same orphanage he was imprisoned in. However, Swearengen's theatrical *assertion* of tough dominance—do this, do that, don't talk, etc—is undercut by the oddness of his recollection—the way in which it directly contradicts his claim not to "look back." "Don't look back" means not being bothered by shit that clouds one's judgment: and yet as human beings we are sometimes plagued and tormented by visions and voices from the past that we cannot help but turn over and over in our minds. One could say this is just Milch using style to cover himself; insulating the scene against the accusation of theatrical soliloquy by juxtaposing the imminence of orgasm with a recollection of abuse. Swearengen even sees humor in the "some chance" of breaking the cycle he must now realize he is a part of: perhaps his mother became a mayor, as he is—at least unofficially. As much as Swearengen would like to be the director, would like to control noise, gesture, sound, attitude—he cannot prevent the uncanny realization of the cyclic patterns of repetition that go beyond irony. His mother sold him to Mrs Anderson, the owner of the orphanage, who sold *the whore* to him; or in *Deadwood*'s favored patois, a cocksucker sells him to a woman who will sell him another cocksucker, and *this* understood, laid out, as he has his cock sucked by that very whore. And this in a scene where the imagery of using, consumption, abuse, and emotional brutality are acute.

If the above scene demonstrates both the danger and the cruelty of introspection (in vivid contrast to the therapeutic sessions that contemporary ideology tell us are so necessary for self-realization), they at the same time demonstrate the way that Swearengen is both subject to, but also commander of, his impulses. This puts him in contrast to, say, Tony Soprano (James Gandolfini), for Swearengen is not prone to indolence, or hostage to his impulses and compulsions: his vigilance and aliveness to his world is total. From the morning's first piss to the day's last blowjob, his eyes watch, and study. Those eyes, unlike Tony's, however, are vulnerable to their own panoptic grasp.

The first episode of Season Two ("A Lie Agreed Upon," Part 1, 2.1) begins with Al ruffled by the prospect of Governor Pennington's attempt to read his response to the threat of installing multiple commissioners adjacent to the camp. Sitting in his office, Silas Adams and Dority watch as he holds out the Governor's letter, and then he comments on the large magnifying glass he has to use in order to read it: "Yes, it has fallen to this." Swearengen is far-sighted. After reading the letter, he leaves his office, whiskey bottle in hand and goes out to the balcony and spies workmen in the distance erecting new telegraph poles. His grasp of the town depends on his reliable vision—he has to see everything—and the balcony offers a perfect vista from which to view the entire camp. But he cannot see telegraph signals hidden in a wire: "Messages from invisible sources, what some people think of as progress," he declaims with disdain. Dority suggests it does no harm, and Swearengen again invokes the way in which the telegraph problematizes his clear view of the unfolding world: "Ain't the state of things cloudy enough? Don't we face enough fuckin' imponderables?"

Faced with this, Swearengen looks down at aspects of the camp he *can* grasp and provokes the fight with Bullock mentioned above, for Bullock and his temper are within his understanding and control. He is alive to the temptations of self-deception as much in others as in himself. Watching from the Gem balcony with Dority and Adams as Seth emerges from an energetic sex session with Alma Garrett, Swearengen is unimpressed with the way this blinds Bullock to himself and the purpose Al has set out for him:

> He don't even know if he's breathin' or takin' it in through fucking gills. He is *that* fucking cuntstruck. They're afloat in some fairy fuckin' bubble—lighter than air—him, her snatch, and his stupid fuckin' badge.

Al watches him as he attends to the four guards on the stagecoach that is securing Alma's money:

> Self-deceiving cocksucker I am—I thought when America took us in, Bullock would prove a resource. Look at him—striding out like some randy maniac bishop.

I've written elsewhere of Tony Soprano's ability to act strategically on impulses that ultimately suit his ambitions;[3] similarly, after Seth is called to deal with trouble at Nuttall's bar, Al effectively, and instinctively, acts to "lance the boil" of Bullock's "cuntstruckness":

> (*Calling down to Bullock, who stops in his stride*) Sheriff! About his duties
> to the camp. Lucky trouble didn't jump out earlier, huh, Bullock?
> Might have found you mid-thrust at other business?

Mortified by this loud public insult, Bullock glares up back at Al, who seals
his invitation to battle with a direct challenge:

> What is it? Taken by a vision? *You* would not want to be staring like
> that at *me*.

When Bullock returns, Swearengen attempts to reason with him ("Jesus
Christ. *Bullock*. The world abounds in cunt of every kind—including hers"),
Bullock's fury is beyond words. Their eventual battle ends with Al pulling
a knife on the prone Bullock, but he hesitates as he notices a boy—in fact
Bullock's adopted son, William—watching from a recently arrived carriage.
His panoptical vision is also a weakness, making him vulnerable to sudden
sights the world throws his way. (He later remarks, "Cow-eyed kid looking
from that coach—that's what fuckin' unmanned me.")

According to an interview with McShane, "[if] Al ever had a day off from
the Gem, he'd go up to his balcony, and still be looking down the street! You
know, Al's always looking—what's happening in this town, what am I missing?
So that's why you never see him out of the town."[4] The balcony is the major
space from which Swearengen monitors the Deadwood camp; it represents
his distance, his authority, and his purview of power. The balcony should
provide distance and objective sight, but, as in his catching sight of William,
we see that sight involves too. It is from the balcony he witnesses the Reverend
Smith in the final throes of his illness and has to turn away at the sight of
it ("Jewel's Boot Is Made for Walking") as he jibbers through the crowd still
praising God. In the final episode of Season Two ("Boy the Earth Talks To")
we see Al hovering on the balcony of the Gem, eager to avoid being *seen* to be
looking—being seen to be interested in the festival of community that is the
wedding celebration of Alma Garrett and Whitney Ellsworth. The impulse
toward community that is at the heart of the interest of the series is shown
here, ironically, in Swearengen's curiosity. As he tells his only interlocutor,
the severed head of an Indian in a box, "They dance on, Chief, however
much at home, as at yours and mine, comfort and love await."

Swearengen's swarthy brute-ness and intelligent charm clearly relates him to some famous literary figures, most obviously *Wuthering Heights'* Heathcliff but also *Oliver Twist's* Bill Sikes. In casting McShane, *Deadwood* acknowledges this heritage physically: compare him, for example, with Robert Newton or Oliver Reed playing Sikes in *Oliver Twist* (Lean, 1948) and *Oliver!* (Reed, 1968). However, these figures, while not exactly one-dimensional, do not have the complexity of Swearengen. As David Ellison argues, it is important to acknowledge that Swearengen represents a "fusion of characteristics that Dickens could only distribute across characters. In other words, Swearengen is Sikes in all of his brute menace but he is also Fagin—a super-adaptive, improvisational opportunist with a dab line in self-parody." In this way, one of the major achievements of *Deadwood* lies in Milch's discovery of McShane's ability to nuance a British kind of villainy: one that references but also transcends (Americanizes?) the binary tic of Victorian psychology that opposes, say, Heathcliff against Edgar, Jekyll/Hyde, Picture/Dorian, Jack the Ripper/Prince Albert.[5] In this way, the fortuitous casting of McShane (the real Al was born in Iowa) allowed David Milch to articulate and realize a depth to Swearengen that not only enhanced the vividness of a real historical character but was also to overcome one of the pervasive oddities of nineteenth-century British literary characterization. In this respect, Al Swearengen, as played by McShane, is a philosophic intervention into the nature of characterization itself.

CHAPTER 2

YOU
MOTHERFUCKER

AL SWEARENGEN'S OEDIPAL DILEMMA

KIM AKASS

Of one thing we can be sure, Al Swearengen is a bit of a bastard. Towards the end of Season One of *Deadwood* we are treated to a rare moment of self-disclosure during his drunken soliloquy to a whore ("Jewel's Boot Is Made for Walking," 1.11). Much has upset Al over the course of this day, but the catalyst for this particular outburst is his discovery that Trixie, his number one whore and confidante, has visited Sol Star for an illicit fuck "on the house." Swearengen's revenge is to summon Star to the Gem and, forcing Trixie to witness the transaction, order the bewildered man to pay him $5 for the pleasure of sex with his favorite whore. Humiliating Trixie publicly is not enough retribution, however, and he sends her packing saying, "Tonight you sleep with your own." In the privacy of his bedroom, his full rage erupts as he demands anonymous, disconnected sex, bluntly expressed to a wretched, unnamed whore:

> I was fuckin her and now I'm going to fuck you if you don't piss me
> off or open your yap at the wrong fuckin' time. The only time you're
> supposed to open your yap is so I can put my fuckin' prick in it.
> Otherwise you shut the fuck up.

As the owner of the Gem and all the whores in it, Al is clearly somebody who can take his pick of women without sentimentality, and yet his naked contempt for the woman in his bed remains shocking. Angry at her vocal affirmation of him, Swearengen tells the unfortunate prostitute, "Shut the fuck up. You suck my dick and shut the fuck up."

In many ways Swearengen's emotive response to Trixie's infidelity seems like an overreaction. She may have dented his sense of sexual prowess and knocked his masculinity, but he has had to weather worse storms than this: he has a price on his head throughout most of Season One; his saloon has had to survive competition in the form of rival Cy Tolliver's up-market Bella Union; and he is only just managing to maintain a shaky hold over his business dealings in Deadwood. The Reverend Smith's gradual descent into madness and the re-emergence of an old Chicago warrant on Swearengen's head may have upset him more, but it is surely Trixie's illicit fuck that has led Al to this particular emotional juncture. An unnerving moment in the narrative, it is the emotional catharsis of this scene, as I shall argue, that not only reveals much about this paradoxical character but also exposes a particular brand of misogyny peculiar to twenty-first-century representational forms.

"MY CHERRY'S INTERFERING WITH MY WORK"

Karen Horney's investigation into male sexuality suggests that one of the causes of psychological problems in the male originates in his dread of woman "as a sexual being" (Horney 116). Building upon Sigmund Freud's formulation of the castration complex, Horney argues that "the male has to entrust his genitals to the female body, that he presents her with his semen and interprets this as a surrender of vital strength to the woman, similar to his experiencing the subsiding of erection after intercourse as evidence of having been weakened by the woman" (116–17). Swearengen's extreme reaction to Trixie's infidelity is arguably because her visit to Star has implied a sexual desire not satisfied by his own outward virility and sexual confidence. Already made vulnerable by his attachment to Trixie, Al's masculinity certainly seems to have been affected by a "dread of not being able to satisfy the woman" (126) as well as a more general sense of betrayal. He may have a cocksure demeanor and power in the town, but his reaction to Trixie's "house call" exposes a vulnerability, one that bares itself in anger projected onto the unnamed woman in his bed and in his very physical and sexual silencing of her.

Horney's work has long been overlooked but here it seems to offer a persuasive account of the troubling misogyny at work in *Deadwood*. Convinced that Freud's "controversial postulate of the Oedipus complex" is a stage of development "that every child has to go through" (125), she suggests that much male insecurity stems from an earlier age when he "felt himself to be a man, but was afraid his masculinity would be ridiculed." Adding "traces of this insecurity will remain more frequently than we are inclined to admit, frequently hidden behind an overemphasis on masculinity as a value in and of itself." (127) It may be that Trixie's illicit orgasm has opened a chink in Swearengen's emotional armor and reveals much about the fragility of his masculinity. Horney's thesis allows us insight into the trauma experienced by Swearengen as his sense of masculinity collapses so totally in the face of Trixie's infidelity.

IT'S LIKE DOING ONE THING AND MEANING A MOTHER

This peek at Swearengen's unconscious and his character's motivation is nothing compared to the revelations that follow. He may tell the prostitute, "Don't be sorry, don't look fuckin' back because, believe me, no-one gives a fuck," but this is exactly what he does over the course of the next few minutes. Launching into the sorry tale of his early life and setting the pace of the blowjob to match the narrative thrust of his story, Swearengen reveals the source of his misery—that his mother sold him to "Mrs. fat-ass fucking Anderson"—the same woman that now supplies Al with women for the Gem. That this is the root cause of his rampant misogyny is evidenced by Swearengen's rising vitriol and heightened sexual arousal as his story unfolds. It may be the "seven dollars and sixty-odd fucking cents" that she left him with "on her way to sucking cock in Georgia" that fuels his outrage, but the fantasy he weaves around his mother's life exposes a torment at the heart of Swearengen's sense of masculinity. Postulating that she probably became "a mayor or some other type of success story unless by some fucking chance she wound up as a ditch for fucking come" Swearengen uses this maternal fantasy to achieve his own orgasm. Telling the woman in his lap, "Now. Fucking. Go. Faster..." he ejaculates, seemingly adding his own ejaculatory fluid to the "ditch" that is his mother.

If Horney is to be believed, men's problems are indeed the result of their early relationship with the mother since she is "usually entrusted with the care of the infant." "[I]t seems," she continues, "to be very difficult to fully free oneself from these early experiences" (126). Swearengen's orgasmic rendering of this last memory of his mother—the return of the repressed—perfectly illustrates Horney's hypothesis and serves as a prime example of the direct link between the sins of the mother revisited in the son. By abandoning him to the care of "Mrs. fat-ass fucking Anderson," Swearengen's mother has not only committed one of society's greatest maternal crimes (short of infanticide) but also left her son to negotiate his own upbringing under the protection of an indifferent caretaker and ruthless businesswoman, one that supplies children to brothels. If it is true that "at puberty a boy's task is obviously not merely to free himself from his incestuous attachment to his mother, but more generally, to master his dread of the whole female sex" (140-1), then Swearengen's path to mature masculinity was clearly fraught with difficulty. And it does not take much to equate this drunken, ill-humored, ejaculating man with the specter of an abused childhood.

So far, so damaged. This brief and, some might say, myopic analysis of Swearengen's blowjob argues that he is certainly much more of a "motherfucker" than a "cocksucker." But is this not a pointless exercise? Surely this is a good time to remind ourselves that Al Swearengen is the fictionalization of a real character who resided in Deadwood in 1876.

FRONTIER LIFE—FACT OR FICTION?

Al Swearengen (sometimes spelled Swearingen or Swerengen) reportedly did "move to Deadwood in the summer of 1876" and was "one of the earliest non-mining men in the area" ("Legends of America," March 2005). History tells us that he was the owner of the Gem Variety Theater, which provided entertainment for the men of the community in the form of boxing prize-fights, comedians, dancers, and singers. Of course this was just a front for the serious business of selling women for sex and the saloon "soon gained a reputation for its debasement of the women who were pressed into service there" (March 2005). Swearengen and his staff were notorious for brutality and "The Gem had a reputation for the most vile entertainment featuring the debasement of women in a generally violent and wide open town" (Fall 2005). Swearengen's callous attitude toward women is well documented, and creator David Milch has obviously carefully considered the background of his character despite the infamously untrustworthy nature of the frontier's history. What then prompted Milch (other than narrative efficacy), to divert from Al Swearengen's "real" story into yet another tale woven from poetic and dramatic license? What do we make of Swearengen's maternal abandonment issues when it is revealed that the actual Al was one of twin brothers and "the oldest of eight children, raised by parents Daniel and Keziah Swerengen until they were adults in Iowa" (March 2005)? In the light of a relatively stable upbringing, it appears that the dramatic license taken here may tell us more about the demands of the Western genre and our own cultural preoccupations than my initial investigation into this character's sexual peccadilloes would suggest.

Moreover, what are we to make of the fictionalization of Swearengen's domestic circumstances? G. J. Barker-Benfield, the historian of American nineteenth-century sexual politics, is useful here, suggesting that pioneer couples "have not captured American myth" anything like the lone hunter with "the promise of total mobility because he was free of women" (2000: 8). It may not actually matter to the development of the narrative that in reality Swearengen was married three times, arriving in Deadwood with his first wife, Nettie, who soon left him and later divorced him citing spousal abuse. His violence towards Trixie in "Deadwood" (1.1) for killing a punter in self-defense quickly and effortlessly establishes Swearengen's attitude to women, dispensing with the need for a huge back-story and instigating a narrative arc that culminates in his drunken blowjob. What is most interesting about this particular revelation is that it adds another, more contemporary layer to the legend of the lone frontiersman that, Barker-Benfield suggests, "was largely a creation of the eastern imagination" (8)—possibly not unlike that of the East Coast-based HBO. The excision of Nettie from the narrative removes any threat of a civilizing force traditionally symbolized by the frontier wife. It also serves to bolster the already well-established myth of the "cold, implacable pioneer" (6) that still haunts our postmodern imaginations.

Returning to the woman in Swearengen's bed is informative in the light of such insights—especially when we consider that the real Swearengen recruited his women from the East and, being a peddler of dreams, promised to make them performers at his theater. Once the women had arrived courtesy of a one-way ticket paid for by him, they found themselves stranded "with little choice other than to work for the notorious Swearengen or be thrown into the street. Some of these desperate women took their own lives rather than being forced into a position of virtual slavery" (2003–2005). Compare this to Milch's fictional Swearengen whose whores

> are bought at the same orphanage where he was raised, including a cripple who has absolutely no use to him at any pragmatic level. He is constantly presenting himself as a pure pragmatist, yet to insist on getting your whores at one particular orphanage is at once an impulse to take revenge on women, and also to rescue women.
>
> *(salon.com 2005)*

Unsurprisingly, it seems the real Swearengen shared none of our Al's irrational impulses to rescue women, but this particular twist to the tale is as revealing as Swearengen's blowjob confession. The contradictory emotional pull Milch invests in his character is obviously itself a pragmatic decision, and there is a certain neatness to the cause and effect nature of taking revenge on women while also rescuing them.

But the question remains: why does he need to take revenge on them at all? Karen Horney may shed some light here; she argues that men "have never tired of fashioning expressions for the violent force by which man feels himself drawn to the woman, and side by side with his longing, the dread that through her he might die and be undone" (134). She adds, "[may] not this be one of the principal roots of the whole masculine impulse to creative work—the never-ending conflict between the man's longing for the woman and his dread of her?" (135). Maybe this is a question that could be leveled at the writers of *Deadwood*. Especially in light of Swearengen's real back-story, revealing no particular motivation for his brutality towards women, just the result of a "cold" and "pitiless" attitude towards the push Westwards with "the demands of this struggle [affecting] the attitude of the American male toward his wife and family" (Barker-Benfield, 5).

If *Deadwood*'s representation of Swearengen owes more to post-Freudian and post-feminist thinking than a nineteenth-century sensibility, what do we make of our twenty-first-century Swearengen's misogyny? As a media-literate audience, we are smart enough to know that, among other things, visual fictions often demand the compression of many characters into one, a series of events into a single action-packed day, and the suspension of disbelief in order to allow the drama to work. It should not matter to us that the real Swearengen was, by all accounts, more of a brutal misogynist than the one portrayed in *Deadwood*. It is vital that viewers find him, as the central character of the series, engaging enough to care about and yet realistic and compelling enough to watch week after week. In fact, is it not remarkable (blowjob aside) that compared to other portrayals of masculinity in the show, Swearengen is positively agreeable? Cy Tolliver is a good example. Beating Flora and Miles Anderson to near-death in public in order to "make an example of them" proves his implacable attitude towards women and children (or teenagers). He shows no remorse for forcing his favorite whore, Joanie Stubbs, to shoot Flora to "put her out of her misery" after he has shot her brother ("Suffer the Little Children," 1.8) and evokes Alexis de Tocqueville's description of the frontier man as someone who is "a cold and insensible being" (quoted in Barker-Benfield 6). And, to this extent, Tolliver better embodies the nineteenth-century American frontier male as "hard, closed off from the feelings regarded ... as "natural to the heart" (quoted in Barker-Benfield 7) than Swearengen.

If Tolliver is a more reliable representation of nineteenth-century masculinity (interestingly there is no real Cy Tolliver to compare him to), then it is not surprising that Swearengen is a more sympathetic and complex character than his ancestor. After all, if a contemporary audience is to identify with and have sympathy for a man capable of appalling acts of brutality and rampant misogyny, then we must be given sufficient motivation. With an eye to post-feminism, and in order to wreak his revenge on women, what better justification can he be given than a mother that abandoned him to a terrible fate? After all, if Horney is to be believed, the dread of woman is so powerful that "the grotesque nature of the anxiety, as we meet with it in the symbolism of dreams and literary productions, points unmistakably to the period of early infantile fantasy" (141). Not Swearengen's early infantile fantasy of course, especially now that we know the "true story" behind his characterization, but the projection of this dread onto a fictional character.

THE DREAD OF WOMAN

Returning to Swearengen's blowjob scene should be instructive in light of the above. The grotesque nature of the dread of woman (or the anxiety surrounding it) seems to be so threatening to the creators of *Deadwood* as to insinuate itself onto Swearengen's drunken climax. Horney may reassure us that, despite man's attitude toward motherhood being a "large and complicated chapter. ... [even] the misogynist is obviously willing to respect woman as a mother and to venerate her motherliness under certain conditions" (114). But there is little evidence of this within *Deadwood*, and particularly in this scene, as the absence of respect is replaced by degradation and humiliation. In fact, by applying a modern-day cause-and-effect sensibility to the character of Swearengen—as an alibi for his terrible misogyny—an even more sinister dread of woman emerges, one that is evidenced by the sexualizing of the mother to achieve climax and one that obviously haunts the creators of *Deadwood*. This terrible dread is usually only alluded to and, further, is one that the male has "many strategic reasons for keeping ... quiet" (136).

Horney argues that for men the real dread of woman is not due to the castrating mother, or the castrated mother as theorized by Freud, but the "dread of his own inadequacy, of being rejected and derided" because as a boy his "penis is too small for his mother's genital" (142). Thankfully she assures us that this is all an unconscious process, but nevertheless argues that, since "it is the mother from whom we receive not only our earliest experience of warmth, care, and tenderness, but also our earliest prohibitions" (126), the resulting power over her son means he is hit "in a second sensitive spot—his sense of genital inadequacy, which has presumably accompanied his libidinal desires from the beginning" (142). The result of this is, for Horney at least, "of vital importance" as the boy's frustration "by his mother must arouse a twofold fury in him: first through the thrusting back of his libido upon itself, and secondly, through the wounding of his masculine self-regard." She thus concludes that "the impulses take on a sadistic tinge" (143). If Swearengen's blowjob is a purely fictional twenty-first-century fantasy, then what are we to make of the sadistic tinge contained within?

Barker-Benfield's investigation into the history of sexual politics may prove illuminating here, as he suggests that in the nineteenth century "there was a uniquely extreme distinction between sexual roles in America" (2000: 20). His thesis argues that "white American men's experience of the increasingly democratic society was one of unrelenting pressure, and that their sexual beliefs and their treatment of women were shaped very largely by that pressure" (liv). Citing "westward expansion, the economic pattern of boom and bust, the separation of the sexes associated with industrialization, and increasing democracy" (xiv), Barker-Benfield is concerned with how nineteenth-century values are reflected in gender roles, especially the evidence that "male attitude[s] ... demanded not only that two styles of life, male and female, be separate, but that women should remain subordinate, and in the home" (20–1). His overriding concern is that "the pressure these circumstances generated led American men to view their own sexuality and women in a particular and negative way" (xiv). And he suggests that we are still suffering the damaging effects of this formulation in American society today.[1]

It is not too surprising that *Deadwood*, screened as it is on HBO, the underbelly of the networks and purveyor of the darker side of life, enters into a dialogue with the sex wars raging in America at this present time. Surely, and in this age of self-help and therapeutic confession as seen on TV, the creators of the series are enlightened enough to realize the impact of a scene like this? And, surely something as powerful as Swearengen's maternal fantasy while climaxing into a whore's mouth should not disappear into the ether without so much as the blink of an eye? Given the length of the sequence, and the sheer audaciousness of it, it is surprising that the scene is overlooked in online reviews, commentaries and even on the HBO website episode guide. Is it possible that the nature of this trauma and the dread it invokes is so terrible that the existence of it has to be totally repressed?

Horney again sheds more light on an ever-present resentment towards women that finds its inception in the child's early years. It is worth reminding ourselves that Horney was writing this some seventy years ago, but I would ask the question, has anything really changed when we hear that men's "resentment expresses itself, also in our times, in ... distrustful defensive maneuvers against the threat of women's invasion of their domains; hence their tendency to devalue pregnancy and childbirth and to overemphasize male genitality" (115). That Swearengen's blowjob does all this within the space of minutes leads me to echo Karen Horney's words:

> Is it not really remarkable (we ask ourselves in amazement), when one considers the overwhelming mass of [this] transparent material, that so little recognition and attention are paid to the fact of men's secret dread of woman?

Thanks to *Deadwood* and Swearengen's drunken blowjob, I can assure Karen Horney that she need worry no longer. It may have been remarkable "that women themselves have so long been able to overlook it" (136) but with such a clear example of the blaming of the mother for the sins of the son, for the overt sexualization of that relationship and for expressing such utter contempt for the poor woman performing fellatio on him, I thank the misogyny and brutality of Al Swearengen. This scene may leave us with a nasty taste in our mouths, but at least Swearengen redeems himself by telling the whore, "OK, go ahead and spit it out. You don't need to swallow." What a gent, what a relief, and long may he reign at the heart of *Deadwood*.

CHAPTER 3

SIX SHOOTERS AND THE FOURTH ESTATE

A. W. MERRICK AND DEADWOOD'S INFORMATION SOCIETY

SHAWN MCINTOSH

I love reading the *Black Hills Pioneer*, you know. ... I could read that all day.

David Milch

It is information—not gold—that is the most valuable commodity in Deadwood in 1876. Although gold is obviously the impetus that created Deadwood, by July 1876, when the series picks up the story of the mining boomtown, information already plays a far more important role in determining wealth and power in the "camp" than actual mining rights. In fact, one of the main storylines of the first season revolved entirely around the issue of information and its use or misuse, and this theme continued at a much larger scale in the second season. In the first season, Al Swearengen's scam with E. B. Farnum to dupe Brom Garrett to buy a supposedly spent claim ironically turns against them when they belatedly learn, after killing him, that the claim is actually one of the richest in Deadwood and worth far more than Garrett bought it for. It is one of the few times in the series in which Swearengen lacks crucial information and it costs him dearly. Much of the underlying tension in the first season between the major characters of Seth Bullock, Swearengen, and Brom's widow Alma Garrett involves Swearengen's attempts and plans to redress his "loss." This is but the first example of many showing Swearengen's astute use of disinformation, strategic knowledge sharing, and communication networks that makes him the most powerful man in Deadwood.

From one perspective, Deadwood in 1876 resembles not so much a typical Old West mining boomtown as a twenty-first-century information society, or what Manuel Castells calls a network society. This becomes more obvious as the second season begins and the makeshift tent stores give way to wooden buildings and growing interest from politicians in Yankton who want to bring Deadwood firmly under their political control. From his balcony, Swearengen curses the arrival of a new challenge to his authority—"messages from invisible sources," he mutters—the telegraph. The introduction of a new communication technology disrupting established communication networks and social patterns and changing power relations presages what we see today with digital media, wireless networks, and the Internet. Looking at the series *Deadwood* through the lens of information or communication issues highlights Wright's contention in *Sixguns and Society* (14–15) that Westerns explore contemporary issues in society more than they examine a specific historical period or place.

It would seem that in a socioeconomic environment such as Deadwood, in which information is king, A. W. Merrick, editor of *The Pioneer*, would play a prominent and important role. However, this is not the case for a number of reasons that will be explored in this chapter. I will at first step outside the series and look briefly at the genre itself and the relatively minor place journalists and writers have undeservedly held within Westerns. I say "undeservedly" because the few Westerns that have had journalists as major characters have largely ignored the important and multifaceted role that actual journalists and editors played in the nineteenth-century Old West. *Deadwood* shows a far more nuanced understanding of the role of communication and journalism in the Old West, not only through the character of Merrick, but also through his interactions with the major characters, particularly Swearengen. Like modern journalists, Merrick is tantalizingly close to—yet at the same time dependent on—the powerful as sources of the important information he can sell to the public. Merrick and the *Pioneer* are in a unique symbolic position within the series to showcase series creator David Milch's complexity of thought regarding the confluence and conflict that we see today between information flows, communication networks, political power, and the role new media technologies play in changing power structures and communication strategies in society.

OLD WEST JOURNALISTS

Journalists have not fared well in Westerns, unlike the sometimes flawed but heroic roles they played, exposing corruption or catching criminals, popular in the newspaper films of the early part of the twentieth century (Good 8). Only a handful of Westerns have had notable journalist characters, and even these are usually differentiated by physical or behavioral traits marking them as Others in the Western milieu. The Western journalist usually requires the help of the hero's gun (Lusted 42) or, just as likely, is on the wrong side of the gun and killed for what he does, as are newspaper editor Dutton Peabody (Edmond O'Brien) in *The Man Who Shot Liberty Valance* (1962) or Frank McHugh (Joe Clemens) in *Dodge City* (1939). In a rare conflation of gunfighter and editor, Ned Britt (Randolph Scott) drops his composing stick and picks up a gun to clean up the town in *Fort Worth* (1951). Even so, his actions compound an underlying Western theme: that when the printing press brings civilization to the frontier, the Old West somehow loses a special part of itself (Barris 91).

Lusted differentiates between how journalists or editors have been portrayed in Westerns and how writers have been portrayed—what he calls the difference between "fiction and faction" (41–2). Writers—Moultrie (Hurd Hatfield) in *The Left Handed Gun* (1958) or Beauchamp (Saul Rubinek) in *Unforgiven* (1992), for example—are the ones penning myth-making dime novels for audiences back East. The journalist or editor, on the other hand, generally stands for an abstract idea of truth or the conscience of a community. The writer's audience, enthusiastically reading largely fictional tales of exaggerated heroics as the myths of the Old West are made, is somewhere else, while the journalist's audience is largely local and part of the community.

The portrayal of the nineteenth-century editor bravely standing up for an abstract conception of truth and a free press is itself largely a twentieth-century myth transplanted into Westerns that portrays journalism as a profession which strives for objectivity and balance. In fact, nineteenth century journalists and editors had no such conceptions, and newspapers of the time were mixtures of gossip, rumors, official government announcements, plagiarized articles from other papers, editorialized news and unabashed civic boosterism that today we would likely categorize as a combination of tabloid, government press release, blog, and advertising shopper (Dary 63–79). Editors in towns in the Old West played just as much a role in Old West myth-making as dime novelists.

Newspapers in frontier towns did play a vital role in keeping citizens informed about the wider world—a far cry from the movie portrayals that represent editors as conduits for encroaching East Coast sensibilities and the imposition of rules upon a freewheeling and free-spirited Wild West. Not only did newspapers keep citizens informed of broader news, a paper's local coverage promoted and legitimized the citizens, businesses, and events of the town or camp the paper wrote about to the distant public—including influential politicians and other leaders who would be playing a role in likely territorial and eventually statehood proposals. Given the common practice among newspapers in the nineteenth century to simply copy stories from other papers (usually without attribution), a "local" story could eventually work its way through newspapers across the country. The real Deadwood benefited from early media hype, as the *Black Hills Pioneer* published stories detailing the exact amounts of gold found in the mines surrounding the camp, even referring to "skeptical newspapers of the East" in its July 1, 1876 issue that were supposedly changing their earlier assessments that there was no gold in the Black Hills (Dary 95).

The real A. W. Merrick clearly had a sense his paper could help establish a spirit of community and civic pride, publishing a story in the July 22, 1876 issue of the *Black Hills Pioneer* about the completion of a theater and a performance that would be the "first dramatic rendition ever witnessed in Western Dakota" (Dary 95–6). In addition to such attempts at elevating the culture of Deadwood, news of violence and death was also prevalent, including a special edition about Custer's massacre and only a few weeks later a story about the killing of Wild Bill Hickok by Jack McCall. In the HBO series, Merrick stops his usual lurking and eavesdropping for bits of news to publish and tentatively asks witnesses about the shooting, noting down everything that is said even when it seems clear that events are being embellished and myths are being made. Given that the practice of interviewing was only about ten years old at that time and still not a common journalistic technique (Starr 148), the scene is interesting in showing Merrick's vulnerabilities and tentative steps toward establishing some sense of what we would recognize today as professional journalism.

Several episodes in both seasons have shown Merrick's willingness to use the *Pioneer* as a propaganda tool for boostering Deadwood. In the first season, Swearengen himself participates in crafting an editorial that downplays the severity of the smallpox epidemic that hits Deadwood so as not to scare away residents. Some light moments in the series come from exchanges between Swearengen and Merrick, as the proprietor of the Gem gets involved with editorial suggestions and even attempts to plant a story. His otherwise excellent plan backfires to some extent when Merrick further exaggerates the story, thus making it less believable to its intended audience: politicians in Yankton. It is unclear whether Merrick uses the only means at his disposal to resist an attempt at media manipulation, or if Swearengen actually demonstrates a more complex understanding of the power of the media.

Merrick, acutely aware of his delicate position in the camp and the potential power the *Pioneer* has, is usually alert enough to know when someone is trying to manipulate the news to his own ends, even if he goes along reluctantly. He refuses ("Complications," 2.5) to compromise the paper's reputation and print the new county commissioner Hugo Jarry's "official notice", which seems to insinuate current claims may or may not be honored and is designed to spread panic in Deadwood; this results in Merrick's shop getting vandalized by Tolliver's henchmen ("Something Very Expensive," 2.6).

The vandalism not only highlights Merrick's vulnerabilities as a newspaper editor in a rough and tumble frontier town; it also reflects what often happened to editors in the Old West who printed articles the locals did not like. It was not unusual throughout much of the nineteenth century for editorial disputes to be settled with guns, violence, or destruction of presses. As Myers points out in numerous anecdotes in *Print in a Wild Land*, editors were as quick to use guns as disgruntled readers. Unlike in the movies, the editor could not count on a hero rescuing him. In 1870, Joseph Pulitzer got in a heated dispute with a lobbyist and contractor and shot him in the leg during a scuffle, and in 1882 John Cockerill, the managing editor of Pulitzer's *Post-Dispatch*, shot and killed an irate reader who came to the newspaper office to confront him (Brian 16-20, 59). Although both events were newsworthy and, in Cockerill's case, had dire repercussions for his career and almost ruined the paper, it shows that the violence seen in frontier towns was not all that unusual even compared to larger, more settled cities such as St. Louis.

BACK CHANNELS, COMMUNICATION NETWORKS,
AND NEW TECHNOLOGIES

The vandalism incident in the series opens a door to show literally a "back channel" connection between Swearengen and Merrick, once again revealing the importance of communication networks in Al's Deadwood empire. In "E. B. Was Left Out" (2.7), Merrick sits dejectedly in his darkened office, convinced he cannot print anymore.[1] Swearengen enters from an upstairs hallway, unaware that their buildings were connected by a hallway, and gives the closest thing to a tender pep talk that he will ever likely give, culminating with a slap in the face to Merrick and the advice "stand it like a man and give some back."

That this literal "back channel" thereafter links Swearengen directly to Merrick (i.e. the mass media) becomes important in the second season as Swearengen's largely interpersonal communication network supplemented by a largely compliant press is threatened by the arrival of the telegraph bringing new sources of information. In contrast with Swearengen's lack of enthusiasm for the telegraph, most frontier communities welcomed the newfound link to "invisible sources." In September 1860, the Wood River *Huntsman's Echo* celebrated the stringing of the telegraph with the following:

> Whoop! Hurrah! The poles—the wire—the telegraph—the lightning! The first are up, the second stretched, the third playing upon the line between St. Jo. and Omaha; and the people of Omaha are exulting in the enjoyment of direct communication with the balance of the earth and the rest of mankind. ... "Thoughts that breathe and words that burn' will glide along the wires with lightning rapidity."
>
> (Myers 31)

Although people in the nineteenth century did not call it such, the passage above is one example that shows they fully understood what modern social theorists such as Giddens or Beck call "time-space distanciation," or "time-space compression": in other words, the changes that electronic communication brought in collapsing temporal and geographic boundaries and patterns of communication. Today these are an integral part of our world, and for some scholars such as Castells or Daniel Bell are harbingers of a new information age or information society. For others, such as Frank Webster or Herbert Schiller, less enthused about the potential for new technology to bring change, new technologies either reinforce existing societal power relations and inequalities or are simply speeded-up continuations of existing patterns from the industrial age. However, even those scholars who discount the information society and disagree with globalization theories accept that there have been some major changes in the media and information environments.

In the nineteenth century, for the most part, such developments were welcomed as a sign of progress—as a way to connect to the world almost instantly even in relatively remote towns. They did not and could not see the problems and issues that would arise from an information-rich networked environment connecting the entire globe, issues that *Deadwood* is able to deal with in an underlying way as more traditional narratives and human dramas take place over each season.

The democratization of information-sharing that electronic technologies like the telegraph began, combined with time-space compression, threaten the kind of stranglehold on information Swearengen maintains in Deadwood through a complex web of interpersonal relations greased by favors, agreements, whiskey, gold, and violence. Swearengen fully realizes that, with the arrival of the telegraph in Deadwood, he loses one of his most precious commodities in maneuvering events to his advantage—time. No longer can he rely on days or weeks for word to arrive or get back to Yankton, or for "accidents" to befall agents on the way to or from Deadwood; now communication takes place in hours, if not minutes. While remoteness and ruggedness of landscape and hostile Indians could maintain Deadwood as a largely self-contained enclave within local control, technology promises to bring the unseen Other into the town's midst. It is no wonder that Swearengen tries to diplomatically bribe the newly arrived telegraph operator—quite literally an Other even among the varied characters of Deadwood in the form of Blazanov, a Russian immigrant with a heavy accent.

It is no coincidence that the telegraph office is located behind Merrick's *Pioneer* office, rather than being located in the freight office of Charlie Utter or the Grand Central Hotel—one a hub of commercial traffic and the other a hub of human traffic, since both also serve as informational hubs from the outside. The placement alongside the *Pioneer* hints at the importance of communication and information over commerce as a source of power over Deadwood's future.

Like the mainstream media today, the *Pioneer* and Merrick are poised tantalizingly close to the people in power even as he positions himself alongside new communication technologies that could threaten his role in the larger information environment—or at least threaten established ways of doing business. However, at the same time, Merrick faces often difficult hurdles in collecting information that will be of use to the readers and serve the larger civic community. Other Deadwood residents seem to mistrust him or avoid him as his very existence threatens the value of that most precious of Deadwood commodities—information. Once a story appears in the *Pioneer*, its worth as an information commodity greatly decreases as that information is shared. In most cases by the time Merrick gets the information to print it has already been utilized by the powers-that-be and as such is already devalued, somewhat like stock tips that get sent to large-scale institutional investors before being leaked to the business press.

This dynamic also partly explains why Merrick is not threatened by the arrival of the telegraph: the *Pioneer* was only breaking news to the outside world, not to the residents of the camp who in all likelihood had heard through rumors and gossip several days earlier what they read in the *Pioneer*. Because the telegraph is not a mass medium in the same way as print (they would have to wait until the early 1920s for the wireless telegraph—the mass medium of radio—to truly threaten print), it does not present a threat to the newspaper. On the contrary, Merrick's ready access to wire service news in a timely manner actually can make the *Pioneer* a more valuable commodity since it brings more timely news of the outside world to Deadwood. This gives Merrick the potential to become more powerful than he was prior to the telegraph because he does not need to rely as heavily on information from local, interpersonal communication networks such as Swearengen's or Tolliver's.

But Merrick must constantly wrestle with the difficult and often-conflicting ethical dilemmas faced by journalists today because of his unique position and power as a media producer. He fully realizes the important role as symbol the *Pioneer* plays in changing Deadwood from "camp" to "town." Merrick also seems to be aware of how various parties try to manipulate the mass media to their own ends—sometimes to the detriment of the camp and sometimes to its benefit. Merrick's desire to fulfill the role of the press as watchdog of the powerful and properly informing its citizens often conflicts with his interests in best serving Deadwood as a civic body whose interests as a community may conflict with outsiders who have their own motives.

The tension between the business of sharing information, its timeliness, and the money to be made from hoarding information or selectively sharing it is in part responsible for moving journalists from their self-perceived roles as the Fourth Estate to that of colluding with the very powers they are supposed to be watching in order to have access to even a portion of the information they feel they need. The need of journalists for proximity to power elites as authoritative sources leaves them susceptible to being manipulated by those who wish to influence public opinion. In *Deadwood*, Swearengen shows himself to be an astute observer of public opinion and, for his time, a master at manipulating the media. His cultivating a professional yet friendly relationship with Merrick, his news leaks, and his attempt at writing a press release presage the kinds of tactics used with journalists by today's PR and marketing firms and governments. Today, just as in nineteenth-century boomtowns and mining camps, accurate information—that resource even more elusive and precious than gold—has far more weight in terms of influencing the market economy than any shiny metal lying in a creek bed.

CHAPTER 4

WHY WILD BILL HICKOK HAD TO DIE

Douglas L. Howard

For all of the card games that he played and the gambles he took, the stakes were probably never higher for James "Wild Bill" Hickok than on August 2, 1876 in Nuttall & Mann's No. 10 Saloon. On that afternoon, as he sat, atypically, with his back to the door, looking down at his poker hand of aces and eights—thereafter immortalized as "the Deadman's Hand"—and considering his next play, the drifter Jack McCall came up behind him, drew his revolver, and fired, killing the man, the myth, and the legend of Wild Bill instantly with a single shot. "His poker hand spilling from his fingers" (Rosa 193), Hickok fell to the floor, looking more like a broken man who had lost his family fortune than an aging gunfighter who had just lost his life. Historian Joseph G. Rosa has said that his death "was one of the most poignant and romantic demises in Western history" (xv); it was also one of the most senseless. *Deadwood* creator David Milch resurrects Wild Bill, both the man and the legend, for his HBO drama, however, and weaves fact and fiction together seamlessly, like the pinstripes on Al Swearengen's suit, to bring meaning to what may have been a mindless act of violence. Within the context of the show, the moment is elevated to almost mythic proportions and takes on a more profound significance, as it puts forces in motion that may well tip the scales in that larger moral gamble that plays out on the town's muddy streets and in its seedy backrooms.

As Clell Watson wistfully tells Bullock from his jail cell at the beginning of Episode 1, the most attractive thing about Deadwood is that "there is no law at all" there,[1] and, without this restriction, prospectors can "scoop [the gold] from the streams with [their] bare hands" ("Deadwood," 1.1), businessmen can scheme and swindle, dope fiends can let their problems fade into narcotic visions, and local pioneers can indulge their most depraved sexual desires. Deadwood is a paradise for all human vices. Even Bullock and Wild Bill, former marshals dedicated to upholding the law, have been tempted by the fantasy of wealth and riches that the town appears to hold and left their other jobs for a chance to stake their claims and make their fortunes. Bullock and Sol Star plan on opening a hardware store and the newly married Hickok, purportedly, wants to establish himself prospecting before calling for his wife. Their attachment to the law, though, is not something that either one of them can so quickly dismiss. As Bullock tells Byron Samson, the law cannot be so easily "called off" ("Deadwood"), neither by those who need it nor by those who carry it out. Bullock, in fact, is so determined to uphold it that, in his last official act as marshal in Montana, he hangs Clell Watson in front of the jailhouse rather than give him over to Samson's angry mob. Immediately perceiving the holes in Ned Mason's story, he is quick to investigate the Indian massacre of the Metz family and to hold Ned accountable for his part in the crime. And, in Episode 11, he bristles at Con Stapleton's appointment as sheriff because he is, in Bullock's words, "a shitheel" ("Jewel's Boot Is Made for Walking") who has no respect for the office and whose loyalty can be bought and sold.

Similarly, for all of Bill's "business plans," the only thing that he really takes any interest in at all in Deadwood, aside from poker, is seeing justice served. During his first night in town, he deliberately abandons his card game with the obnoxious Jack McCall because he, like Bullock, is suspicious of the truth behind Ned's tale. For Hickok, the potential safety of the remaining child is enough to make him ride out into the night and risk the possibility of an Indian attack. (Bill's concern for the child later leads him to give up his room at the Grand Central, in spite of Farnum's objections, so Calamity Jane can protect her and nurse her back to health.) When Bullock finally confronts Ned, after he and Hickok and the rest of their party have rescued the traumatized Sofia, Bill is the only one who stands with him and who supports Bullock's accusations against the nervous drifter because he, too, agrees that Ned must be brought to justice for his part in the crime. To this end, Bill draws with Bullock when the cornered Ned goes for his guns, and, if Bullock is right, his bullet is the one that drops both Ned and his horse out in the street.

Following the brutal death of her husband Brom at the hands of Dan Dority, Bill also agrees to help the widow Alma Garret negotiate her claim and look into Farnum's questionable interest in it. When he confronts Al Swearengen about his role in the sale, he shrewdly sees through the saloon owner's feigned innocence in the matter, and he makes Swearengen pay him to present his side of the story "in a favorable light" ("Here Was a Man," 1.4) to the widow, knowing full well that he will only tell her the truth in the end anyway. Admittedly aware of his reputation and his own limitations in this area, Hickok also puts Alma in touch with Bullock (and brings them together) because he knows Bullock will protect her interests and see to it that her claim is fairly judged.

Moreover, in spite of his reasons for coming and in spite of the fact he never talks about having, as Farnum puts it, "lawman's ambitions" ("Deadwood"), the people in camp continue to see Bill as a source of justice, particularly since they have nowhere else to turn for it. Not only do Brom and Alma immediately come to him for help when they fear they are being cheated, but Swearengen consistently (and mistakenly) believes Hickok is after him and that both Sol and Bullock's bid on their lot and his problems with the Garret claim somehow stem from "the A number one man-killer in the West" ("Deep Water," 1.2). Swearengen orchestrates the failed attempt on Hickok's life in Episode 2 and, as his frustrations toward the widow Garret begin to boil over, he finally charges, in Episode 4, that "Hickok has to die, even if [he] has to kill him [himself]" ("Here Was a Man").[2]

Ironically, though, for all of their actions in the service of this moral order, neither Hickok nor Bullock initially wants anything to do with the roles they are clearly meant to play and, in many ways, already are playing, just as they have difficulty adapting to the roles they would assume in Deadwood. After comparing their careers as lawmen, Hickok jokingly wonders if Bullock has now "come to [his] senses" ("Deadwood") in Deadwood, as if upholding the law is indeed a foolish and futile pursuit, and Bullock affirms that he has. (In spite of his disgust at the appointment of Con Stapleton, Bullock bluntly tells Swearengen he does not want the job when Al mentions it to him in Episode 11.) Yet, while the promise of wealth is what brings them to the Black Hills, neither one seems to take an active interest in making money. Hickok consistently rejects any attempt to increase his income, aside from poker, which he admittedly plays badly. Although Charlie Utter does his best to find a way for his friend to make money in camp and even suggests that Bill could be paid "appearance money" to attract gamblers to Tom Nuttall's saloon, Bill proudly refuses to "shill for the house" ("Deep Water"). In Episode 4, he also dismisses Bullock's offer of prospecting tools because he knows he would only lose any gold he might find to "cocksuckers" at the gaming table. When Alma Garret hires Bill to investigate Farnum's interest in her claim, she gives Bill the option of setting the price for his services, but he instead leaves the decision to her and then gives the money to Bullock, along with Swearengen's bribe, as payment for his assessment of her claim, taking no profit for his part in the matter. As he tells Charlie Utter, he is determined to "go to hell the way [he wants] to" ("Here Was a Man")[3] and to ruin himself on his own terms.[4]

While Milch has said he was intrigued by his research on Bullock because he "was a guy who was a brilliant businessman and cursed with a conscience" (Grego), the show has focused more on Bullock's conscience and how that has superseded his business interests. Not only does he chase a grifter away from his tent in Episode 1, he throws Jack McCall into the mud in Episode 3 and bans him from the store for speaking badly about Bill, an act that leads Sol Star to wonder about "how much future he's got" in retail ("Reconnoitering the Rim," 1.3). And though the future of their business depends on the purchase of Swearengen's lot in Episode 2, Bullock has difficulty restraining his resentment toward him or his insinuation that Bill is their silent partner, to the point where their second negotiation ends with Swearengen telling a seething Seth to "go fuck himself" ("Deep Water").

In the end, then, Hickok and Bullock, as they are portrayed in Deadwood, are both of a type: reluctant lawmen who idealistically believe that justice is possible and are perhaps too stubborn to accept what they really are.[5] (As Milch notes, one of the things that drew him to these characters from the beginning was that they were "men who were absolute mysteries to themselves" [Singer].) What separates them, as Charlie Utter tells Bullock in Episode 2, is that Bullock, for all of the qualities he does share with Bill, knows how to "get along with people, turn a dollar, [and] look out for [himself]" ("Deep Water"), qualities required for the law and by the law in a changing, more complex society. Where Wild Bill was born into the age (and the myth) of the Western gunfighter, a time in which peace could be purchased through a street duel and the law was delivered for people as much by a six-shooter as by a judge's sentence,[6] Bullock is, as John Ames describes him, "the harbinger of the modern, professional lawman" (60), someone who can enforce the law as ably with his words as with his revolver and deal with the kindly as well as the corrupt, with Alma and Charlie as well as Swearengen, Tolliver, and Commissioner Jarry. Bill certainly paves the way for him—he is, if you will, the Obi-Wan Kenobi to Bullock's Luke Skywalker (with Anakin's temper thrown in for good measure)—and, in many ways, the show's first four episodes and Bill's death work as a kind of changing of the guard, from Bill's frontier justice to the shifting loyalties and moral dilemmas of Bullock's Deadwood.

This change is perhaps best illustrated at the beginning of Episode 4 (the episode in which Bill gets killed), as Bill and Bullock consider the future of the camp from the second storey of Bullock and Star's still-under-construction hardware store.[7] Hickok has just cleaned Jack McCall out in their poker game at the Bella Union and is on his way back to his room when he sees Bullock working away on the store at night because it is "cooler" and "quieter." Looking out at the town, Bill concedes it "looks like a good bet" and that laws will soon be established, aspects of civilized society particularly notable by their absence to the former marshal. When Seth responds he would "settle for property rights," Bill questions it, as if he knows that the determined, righteous Bullock, who has already helped kill Ned Mason through a sense of moral obligation, certainly will not be satisfied until law does come to Deadwood. Following Bullock's offer of a sifting cradle and Bill's rejection of it, he finally confesses, "I'm flat-out tired." For Bill, this "fatigue" refers as much to the late hour as it does to his inability to conform to the role that Charlie Utter would have him assume and be something he simply cannot be (an inability that Bill admits to Charlie in the subsequent scene), and to his general feelings toward life and the law he has upheld. Bullock encourages him to "turn in," and, looking out upon the camp himself, he reassures Bill, "I got 'er covered" ("Here Was a Man"). Through this one exchange, the symbolic transfer is made clear. From his storied career, the aging gunfighter Hickok, who has, as Keith Carradine[8] explains, "outlive[ed] his own usefulness" (Holland), steps down as protector and guardian of the people (and ultimately goes off to die) and turns his watch over to his younger successor, the more resourceful lawman Bullock.[9] In agreeing to keep the camp covered, Bullock is assuming responsibility for the town's safety and for the residents he watches over. All that remains is the death that will make this transfer complete and force Bullock to carry out the promise he has made.

That Hickok will die and must die is a given, not only because history says so, but also because all the signs and symbols in *Deadwood* point in that direction. When we first meet Bill in Episode 1, recovering from a hangover in his covered wagon with his eyes closed and his hands across his chest, he is deliberately presented, as Milch explains in his commentary, as if he is "lying in state," a symbolic reminder to viewers of what is to come. Merrick is surprised by his appearance in camp because he "never thought [Hickok]'d live long enough for [him] to meet him" ("Deadwood") and, in Episode 3, we again see Bill, "laid out" sleeping in the hallway of the Grand Central so Jane and Sofia can sleep in his room, and looking like he will when people come to pay their respects to him in Episode 5.

Commenting (in "Reconnoitering the Rim") on Bill's poor performance onstage with Buffalo Bill Cody in Hartford,[10] Nathan Gordon conceives, "I'd a bet U.S. currency that you'd been strangled and killed; you just didn't know you was dead yet." After chasing Gordon away, a coarser drifter tries to gain Bill's favor by graphically describing his violent attempts to defend him in the past, only to have an impatient Hickok summarily dismiss him. Wounded by Bill's disgust, he curses, "I hope you get what's coming to you and I hope it's sooner rather than later. I hope they sort *you* out! And I get to see it! I hope you're gut shot and die slow! And I hope they get ya in this camp!" ("Reconnoitering the Rim"). Following the drifter's tirade, Hickok is noticeably silent and affected, as if he realizes the drifter has spoken some kind of truth and pronounced his fate. Although he is not "gut shot" and does not "die slow," the drifter's wish (and Swearengen's, who also believes that "Hickok has to die") does come true to the extent that Bill is "sorted out" in "this camp" shortly thereafter.

And even Hickok seems to encourage and embrace the end that awaits him.[11] Though he goes to Deadwood on the pretense of planning for his future, he clearly does not want one. His lack of initiative in pursuing any worthwhile career, his destructive poker habit, his "flat-out" fatigue with life, and his expressed desire to "go to hell" all point to the fact he is biding his time and just waiting to die. In his commentary on the first episode, Milch agrees that "he kinda went out there to die." Bill's parting advice to Alma

Garret, to "listen to the thunder," and his attempt to leave her in Bullock's hands also have a strange sense of finality to them, as if he is setting his affairs in order before the end. He sits down to write his wife one last time,[12] and, though Jane stops in to show him that Sofia's fever has broken, her interruption provides them with what Carradine, in his commentary, calls "a moment of good-bye" and a parting that sounds more permanent. Finishing his letter, Bill puts on his red sash, dressing for the bloodshed that is to follow, "dressing," as Carradine suggests, "for his own death."

The scene in which Tom Mason attempts to take revenge on his brother's death in Episode 2, moreover, eerily foreshadows Bill's death and also reinforces the notion that Bill virtually wills it. Manipulated and spurred on by Swearengen, Tom and Persimmon Phil plan their attack on Bill as he plays cards in Nuttall and Mann's. While Mason does little, if anything, to convey his intentions to Hickok—a perplexed Phil later tells Al, "Hickok must've just smelled him"—Bill presciently tells Bullock at the bar, "Fella in the far corner to your right intends me harm" ("Deep Water"), and asks him to "keep an eye" on Persimmon Phil in case they both make a move toward him. Returning to the card game, Bill sits with his back to the wall, in full view of the scene unfolding before him, and stares intently at his cards until Mason begins to walk toward him. Only then does he turn and fire, dropping Tom to the floor. As Tom writhes in agony, Con Stapleton argues that Hickok had no reason to shoot him, since his "gun never left his holster," but a dying Mason confesses his intentions, charging that Hickok killed his brother, and, in the process, justifying the gunfighter's actions.

These circumstances are essentially repeated in Episode 4, although the outcome is dramatically different. Again, Bill is playing cards in Nuttall and Mann's, and, again, someone comes into the saloon "meaning to do him harm." The earlier attack establishes that Bill, either through experience or some kind of psychic awareness, generally realizes when he is in danger; in Episode 4, however, though Bill may be aware trouble is coming, he does nothing to stop it. In fact, he tempts fate by avoiding his usual precautions. He takes a seat that puts his back to the door, even though it makes him vulnerable to an attack from behind, and looks at the chair knowingly before he sits down. Rosa states that, in real life, Hickok accepted this seat begrudgingly, because the player in the "wall seat" simply "refused to give it up" (194), but the writers here, following this notion of a "deliberate death,"

have him take it complacently, without an argument. When McCall enters
Nuttall and Mann's and walks up behind him, the camera shows Bill look
up from his cards, aware,[13] hearing his assailant move toward him, knowing
and inviting the end being prepared for him, allowing McCall to pull the
trigger and kill him.

Others have died before and after Hickok in the series, but the writers and
producers of *Deadwood* make a point not just of building toward Bill's death,
but also of emphasizing its significance when it happens. In fact, for all of the
drifters and prostitutes callously, haphazardly murdered in camp with barely
a tear, his death resonates through the end of Episode 4 and continues to
reverberate into the episodes that follow. From the crack of McCall's pistol,
Bill slumps forward onto the table, and McCall runs out of the back of
the saloon; everyone in town is affected, as the real drama of the moment
builds to a chaotic crescendo. Gustavo Santaolalla's haunting instrumental,
"Iguazo," plays in the background. A crowd forms around the captured
McCall, and the street fills with commotion. Wracked with smallpox, Andy
Cramed stares out from his bed at the Bella Union in horror. Bullock and
Sol Star turn away from their work on the hardware store. Alma and Jane
stare out into the street, and an apprehensive Jane leaves Sofia with Alma (for
good as it turns out) to investigate. Swearengen curiously goes to his window.
Farnum watches from the front of the Grand Central. And, astonished,
Con Stapleton gives Jane the awful news: "He shot Wild Bill Hickok." A
Mexican drifter rides into camp proudly brandishing the severed head of an
Indian, the first to collect on the bounty Swearengen sets on the "godless
heathen cocksuckers" after rumors of an Indian massacre break in Episode
1.[14] Bullock removes his hat politely as he walks into Nuttall and Mann's just
as Hickok's body, with its back still to the door, falls from its seat onto the
floor. Humbled by the moment, Bullock falls to his knees. Overwhelmed,
Jane swigs deeply from a whiskey bottle, as a teary-eyed Bullock grieves for
the death of his friend, for the death of a legend, for this world that has, as
the closing music suggests, "fallen from grace."[15]

Carradine has said Bill's death amounts to "a cosmic shift in the
universe," and, while this seems like a rather strong epitaph for an over-the-
hill, out-of-work lawman with a gambling problem, he is, within the context
of the show, that important. The camp, in fact, never seems to get over his
death and is still dealing with the effects of that day a season later. Bill's

letter becomes a minor plot device in Season Two, as Farnum, after getting it from one of his workers in Season One ("No Other Sons or Daughters," 1.9), sells it to Wolcott, who, in turn, gives it to Charlie Utter, who goes on to deliver it to Bill's widow. Charlie has "conversations" with Bill at his grave, and, as he tells "Bill," since his death, Calamity Jane has become "a drunken fuckin' mess" ("Childish Things," 2.8). Jane is fiercely protective of Bill's robe and refuses to let Jarry use it as a bedroll, even for money. Swearengen continues to have "Shakespearean asides" about the meaning of life with the severed head that the Mexican brings in for the bounty. In addition, Alma's "adoption" of Sofia is largely the result of Bill's death, since Jane leaves her with Alma when Bill dies, and Bullock's relationship with Alma (and all that comes of it, from the assessment of her gold "bonanza" to her pregnancy and even her marriage to Ellsworth) is primarily a by-product of the contract Bill establishes between them and Bullock feels at least partially obliged to fulfill out of respect. To the extent they have both suffered personal losses through murder—Alma has lost her husband Brom and Bullock has lost his friend—and to the extent these losses have forced them to take more assertive roles in camp—both admit that they are "changed" somehow when Bullock returns ("Bullock Returns to the Camp," 1.7)—Bill's death is that final traumatic event that psychologically as well as physically makes them compatible and unites them.

But more than any of these effects or consequences, Bill's death is that important because it marks the end of an era. If they ever did exist in the first place and if there ever was anything so simple or idyllic about them, the days of frontier justice and street duels and lawmen maintaining order largely with their guns are over. And if Deadwood is any kind of metaphor for the social, political, and economic (not to mention moral) direction of a nation, then Hickok's death also refers to that nation's need for men like Bullock, as opposed to Hickok, to protect its people, to carry out its laws, and to preserve its order. For all of the affairs he puts in order before his death, he essentially leaves Deadwood (and through it, perhaps, the future of America) to Bullock. Realizing he has "outlived his usefulness," Bill allows himself to be killed, an almost Christ-like sacrifice,[16] so that Bullock, in spite of his reluctance, can take over for him. (Again, I am reminded of Obi-Wan Kenobi, the old Jedi, allowing Darth Vader to kill him so Luke, the apprentice, can escape the Death Star and go on to save the galaxy.)

Following Bill's death and McCall's ludicrous release, Bullock goes after Bill's murderer to see to it that justice is served. As Bullock tells McCall when he and Charlie Utter finally confront him, "If you got your head blown off, sitting here with your back turned, that'd be as fair a play as you gave him" ("Bullock Returns to the Camp," 1.7). Bullock, however, does not avenge Bill's death in this way, and, instead, takes McCall off to Yankton to stand trial for his crime. Later, at Bill's graveside, Jane irately wonders why Bullock and Charlie did not kill McCall on the spot, but she fails to appreciate Bullock's more advanced sense of justice. While this "eye for an eye" mentality may well have been acceptable in Bill's day, Bullock idealistically believes in the law and in the civil workings of the system, so much so that he restrains himself and lets the system set the terms of McCall's punishment. As opposed to that attitude that allowed tempers and six-shooters to settle scores, Bullock demonstrates faith in the system that the growing nation needs to endure and survive.

When Bullock comes to complain about Stapleton's appointment in Episode 11, even Swearengen realizes Bullock is, legitimately, the right (and the only) man for the job in camp. If Bill were still alive, he, given his background and experience, might well have been the town's first choice for sheriff, and Bullock, in all likelihood, would gladly have stepped aside for him. But Hickok clearly is not what Deadwood needs; it needs Bullock, and, in spite of all their antagonism, even Swearengen can see that.[17] Though his idealism is at odds with Swearengen's more jaded view of the world and his general faith in the immorality of the populace, he admittedly admires Bullock because he is "not a fuckin' whore" and encourages him to take the job because he is "one of those pains in the balls who thinks that the law can be honest" ("Jewel's Boot Is Made for Walking"). Accepting the position as much to protect Alma and himself from Otis Russell's revenge[18] as to rescue it from the degradation that Stapleton and others like him would bring to it, Bullock is also shrewd enough to know that justice is not always served with a gun—he barely draws it in Season Two—and that he must often work with his enemies for the greater good. While they beat each other into bloody messes in their epic fight at the start of Season Two, Bullock and Swearengen actually work together to deal with Commissioner Jarry and negotiate the agreement with Yankton that officially brings Deadwood into the county. Bullock takes Al's advice "to fuckin' look out" for Jarry when a mob goes after him in Episode 17, and, when they later meet to discuss who might be backing the commissioner's play in town, they even drink from the same bottle. As Swearengen, recuperating from a kidney stone and a minor stroke, promises to "carry [his] share of the water" if he gets well, an encouraging Bullock affirms that his "money's on [Swearengen]" ("Complications," 2.5), both to recover and to do his part in dealing with the political intrigue in camp. Clearly, these are men who respect one another. And though Bullock may not necessarily like Swearengen, he still must give him his due because Swearengen is a force of order in Deadwood. Even as he deals with William's tragic death, Bullock still allows Swearengen to speak on his behalf in his conversations with Jarry because, ultimately, he believes Swearengen has the camp's best interests (as well as, of course, his own) at heart. From the tension and animosity that characterized their earlier meetings, Bullock and Swearengen develop a degree of trust, and that trust is, to a large extent, what makes the Yankton agreement possible. If the West was won with Hickok's bullets, it was tamed, as *Deadwood* suggests, with Bullock's political savvy.

David Bianculli, the television critic for the *New York Daily News*, has said that Hickok was "the most compelling and magnetic central character" ("*Deadwood* comes alive"), and that his death in *Deadwood* is "stunning in its suddenness ... the six-gun equivalent of Janet Leigh being stabbed in the shower in *Psycho*" ("There's no deadwood in this cast"). It is also that moment when the show changes from a seemingly formulaic Western to a complex character drama with subtler moral shades. Initially, Milch and his writers appear to use Deadwood as the stage for that age-old conflict of good versus evil, with the virtuous Hickok and Bullock facing off against Al Swearengen, the devilish saloon owner. From his dark suit to the downward turn of his dark moustache to the snarl in his voice, Swearengen even looks the part of the devil, and the Hickok episodes certainly reinforce that sense of his character. He is agitated by the Metz massacre largely because of its effect on business and because he never received his share of the take; as coarse and as confrontational as she is, he reduces Calamity Jane to tears with little more than a look in "Deep Water" and considers having the orphaned Sofia killed to avoid the complications that her story might cause in camp. As these episodes portray him, Swearengen seems to be the most sinister villain that the West has ever seen, and men, women, and children have meaning for him, primarily, insomuch as they figure into his profit margin. Just as we are fascinated by him (and just as Ian McShane captures the screen like James Gandolfini in *The Sopranos*), we must also wonder how Milch's heroes, Hickok and Bullock, will ever bring him down and bring law and order to Deadwood.

But with Hickok's death, a death that Swearengen has nothing to do with, the scope of the show itself begins to change. The line between good and evil, between hero and villain becomes a little more blurred as the moral terms that separate them become more ambiguous. Swearengen, the unrepentant devil, as we learn in Episode 23 ("The Whores Can Come," 2.11), did not simply appear in Deadwood to sell liquor and run prostitutes, but rather developed through a tragic childhood that included an abusive father and the harsh realities of Mrs. Anderson's orphanage. And though he turns the epileptic Reverend Smith out of the Gem because he is bad for business, he understands the reverend's condition from his brother's "fits" and is the one who mercifully puts him out of his misery, an emotional moment that moves him to tears.[19] (Swearengen is also significantly "humanized" during the kidney stone episodes in Season Two, as he suffers through Doc Cochran's makeshift "penis probes.")

Bullock, on the other hand, has a temper to rival Swearengen's—consider the savage beating he gives Otis Russell at the Bella Union—and has difficulty negotiating his passion for Alma Garret with his responsibility to his wife because the "right way" is not so clear-cut. While his marriage is by no means a love match—he married his deceased brother's wife and is helping her raise his brother's son—he ultimately upholds his obligation to her when she arrives, even though his heart is elsewhere. At the end of Season Two, as a pregnant Alma marries Ellsworth to keep up appearances, Swearengen himself must remind Bullock where his home is, but, for Bullock and Alma, this moral conflict clearly is not over. As William Blake says in *The Marriage of Heaven and Hell*, "Without Contraries is no progression"; inasmuch as *Deadwood* chronicles the birth of modern America, from Hickok's death, the show demonstrates exactly how characters who were capable of being, at times, both good and bad (or at least, capable of redefining what those terms were), of killing and bribing as well as loving, were necessary in making that progression possible.

Finally, within the framework of the Western, Hickok's death, like the show itself, marks a dramatic change in the genre and sets a new standard for its portrayal on television.[20] In discussing the conventions of the Western, Jane Tompkins notes that "[o]ften, death makes a sudden, momentary appearance early in the story, as if to put us on notice that life is what is at stake here, and nothing less" (24). As the adult Western has developed on television, writers and directors have increasingly tried to find creative ways of reminding viewers of these stakes from early on and to use the ever-present possibility of death to create suspense in between the commercial breaks. Matt Dillon actually lost his first gunfight on *Gunsmoke* (but made a full recovery and avenged this defeat),[21] and he typically began each episode philosophizing about his responsibilities amidst the graves out on Boot Hill. Brett Maverick's life was threatened on a weekly basis by corrupt politicians and callous card sharks, and mountain men, ranch hands, and distraught love interests frequently lost their lives before the final act as the Cartwrights defended their land from scheming businessmen and rival landowners on *Bonanza*. Through the hanging of Clell Watson, the massacre of the Metz family, and the death of Ned Mason in Episode 1, *Deadwood* follows in this tradition and immediately establishes that life is on the line out in the Black Hills of South Dakota. With Bill's death, however, the series goes on to up this ante. Rarely, if ever, has a *central character* died so quickly and so brutally, particularly in a television Western, and this "sudden, momentary appearance" of death (along, of course, with the show's colorful language) lets viewers know that this is not their parents' Ponderosa or Marshall Dillon's Dodge City, and that, in Deadwood (as in the history that inspires it), regardless of whether they are nameless and have Ennio Morricone music behind them or not, pretty much anyone (within certain historical parameters) is fair game. Would Hoss and Little Joe last five minutes in the Gem Saloon?

Hickok's death, though, also suggests that more than life (or, at least, more than an individual life) hangs in the balance here. While it is tragic, it further illustrates, within the chaos that is Deadwood, the dangers of living in a society "with no law at all." History and the future of America itself are at stake at that table in Nuttall and Mann's (and throughout the muddy camp itself), and Milch, his writers, and his cast and crew make that history matter by daring not to sugarcoat the pill, by daring to show our ancestors, in all of their vicious glory, as they recognize the need for civilized institutions. Inasmuch as the dead help them to learn that lesson (and us to appreciate it), they become necessary sacrifices now laden with historical meaning. For all of the mindlessness behind his death, if the bullet that went through Hickok's head and landed in Captain William Massie's wrist on that fateful day in August is also the bullet that puts that star on Bullock's chest and brings Deadwood under government control, then it is a bullet, in that larger sense, that needs to be fired. Jack McCall may have killed him needlessly that day, but, as the series now recasts his death and reconsiders its consequences, for justice to be born in Deadwood, Wild Bill must die.

PART 2
THE WOMEN OF DEADWOOD

CHAPTER 5

MYTH MAKETH THE WOMAN

CALAMITY JANE, FRONTIER MYTHOLOGY AND CREATING AMERICAN (MEDIA) HISTORICAL IMAGININGS

JANET MCCABE

[Calamity Jane] became the heroine of many a tale that found ready sale during the 1920s and 1930s. If facts were not known, they were invented. No one could prove them false.

Roberta Beed Sollid

This is the West, sir. When the legend becomes fact, print the legend.

Maxwell Scott, from The Man Who Shot Liberty Valance
(John Ford, 1962)

Nothing about Calamity Jane (or Martha [Jane] Can[n]ary) is straightforward. Hardly anything is known about her. Few reliable sources survive, those writing letters or who kept journals did not care to write about such a woman, and documentation is scarce (apart from her death certificate). In her lifetime she gained notoriety as a hard-drinking, profane dissolute woman, almost entirely forgotten by contemporaries after her death on August 2, 1903. Beyond polite society, falling outside dominant discourse, relegated to the margins of history, she remains an intangible figure—or as Roberta Beed Sollid put it "no career is so elusive to the historian as that of a loose woman" (xvii).

But her legend lives on.

Reclaimed by popular culture in dime novels, Hollywood movies—and now the HBO original series *Deadwood*—the real Martha (Jane) Can(n)ary

fuses with the fictional heroine in the popular mind to become the legendary
figure known as Calamity Jane. Celebrated less for what she did than for what
she was imagined to have done, she immortalizes the Wild West of popular
imagination along with other quintessential frontiersmen like General
George Custer, Buffalo Bill Cody, and Wild Bill Hickok. Professional
historians may have long lost interest in the frontier these figures represent,
and mercurial characters like Custer now conjure up hubristic ambition,
imperialist conquest, and ethnic genocide, but the familiar frontier image of
an unspoiled wilderness peopled by epic men and women continues to exact
a powerful hold over our collective imagination.

We grew up with these stories. But then the West is largely built on
storytelling and "the pleasures of good stories" (Fabian 224)—gripping tall-
tales and epic myths. Calamity Jane herself added much to the hearsay and
speculation surrounding her life—and to her legend-in-the-making. Her
pamphlet entitled *Life and Adventures of Calamity Jane by Herself*, written
with the help of an anonymous collaborator in 1896, was designed more
to enhance her reputation as a frontier heroine rather than to record fact.
Her claims of scouting for Custer, single-handedly rescuing the ambushed
Cheyenne-to-Deadwood stage after its driver was fatally shot by Indians,
apprehending Jack McCall, Hickok's assassin, with a cleaver, and her
escapades as a pony express rider created the basis for her status as something
of a legend in her own lifetime. In the same year, exhibited as a featured
attraction, she embarked on a dime museum tour of large Midwest cities,
displaying her Wild West skills and telling stirring tales to a curious paying
public. And then, of course, there was her bragging, normally fuelled by hard
liquor, where she entertained those around her with ripping yarns of her
participation in the Old West. Say it would be so. But sadly no. "The great
majority of the stories are rejected as obviously fictional, with most of the
remainder labeled at least partly false or else doubtful" (Riegel 64).

Numerous writers and later filmmakers picked up on these erroneous
tales and improbable memoirs, embellishing them even further and crafting
her into a truly compelling character of the Wild West. Sensationalist writer
Edward Lytton (Ned) Wheeler featured Calamity Jane as his heroine. Selling
stories like *Deadwood Dick on Deck; or, Calamity Jane, The Heroine of Whoop-
Up* (1878) and *Deadwood Dick's Doom; or, Calamity Jane's Last Adventure*
(1899?), to the New York-based publishing team of Beadle and Adams, which

specialized in what popularly became known as dime novels, he told thrilling tales of derring-do brimming with courageous last-minute rescues, daredevil deeds and gallant acts of fearless bravery. Other stories like "Calamity Jane as a Lady Robin Hood" (Ward 46-7) and biographies such as *Calamity Jane and the Lady Wildcats* (Aikman) or Ethel Hueston's 1937 *Calamity Jane of Deadwood Gulch*, further turned her into an enthralling and highly attractive protagonist of the frontier. Such romanticized fare interested Hollywood, and Calamity Jane softened into a pretty but vivacious young woman in *The Plainsman* (Cecil B. DeMille, 1936), and later a spirited feminine tomboy clad in form-fitting buckskins in the musical comedy *Calamity Jane* (David Butler, 1953).

Weaving fictional stories with the historical archive has long been central to building the idea of the West; and, in its use of language and highly elaborate storytelling forms, *Deadwood* continues in that hybrid tradition. What *Deadwood* does is take incidents that may very well have partial basis in fact—the shooting of Wild Bill Hickok in the Saloon Number 10 by Jack McCall in 1876, the smallpox epidemic that came to Deadwood in 1878—and turn them into compelling drama, into a new mythology and a modern historiography. *Deadwood*'s appropriation of the past makes visible the competing ways in which versions of America's Western history have become known, where "the scholarly and the popular, the factual and the legendary are so thoroughly entwined that they cannot be separated" (Fabian 226). This latest purveyor of frontier mythology understands only too well the crucial role played by popular culture and the mass media in perpetuating an idea of the historical Western frontier as well as recognizing the complexities involved in turning contested history into enduring myth and popular mythology into historical fact. Bearing in mind the specific existence of popular cultural forms and historical artifacts, I contend that the most recent incarnation of Calamity Jane played by Robin Weigert operates as a formal nexus point in *Deadwood*. She negotiates the tensions between the formal layers, between historical fact and popular fiction, between orthodox histories and modern historiographies, between traditional storytelling and the mass media, between the oral and the visual, and between different speech patterns and language forms used to convey these stories.

"HER GUTTER MOUTH ... CONVERSATION FOR THE AGES": ORAL TRADITIONS AND THE FRONTIER MYTH

Deadwood first finds Calamity Jane traveling with Wild Bill Hickok, legendary gunfighter and celebrated frontier marshal, as part of a wagon train descending into Deadwood for the last American gold rush in 1876 ("Deadwood," 1.1). In her autobiography she claims: "I started for Fort Laramie where I met Wm. Hickok, better known as Wild Bill, and we started for Deadwood, where we arrived about June" (reprinted in Sollid 127). John McClintock (1939), Deadwood resident turned pioneer historian, corroborates her story, recalling how he saw them ride into town probably sometime in June. Rumor has it that she was placed on the wagon train as a means of getting her out of Laramie after a drunken night carousing with soldiers. Whether true or not, it is the iconic pairing of Calamity Jane with Wild Bill Hickok on the road to Deadwood as a metaphoric evocation of a frontier past that persists.

It is an enduring image nurtured by dime novelists, filmmakers, and other purveyors of popular culture, including the HBO original series. From the briefest of acquaintances, which may or may not have occurred, and based on the flimsiest of historical evidence, the alleged meeting spawned a mythic tale that has enormous appeal. Retelling the story is in part about a nostalgic yearning, embedded right into the *Deadwood* text, for what will soon be lost—as the history books tell us, Hickok does not have long to live, shot only months after his arrival. But it is also about indulging in an elegiac longing for the fading splendor of the old pioneer days that Calamity Jane and Hickok have come to represent.

Quite literally caught between the wilderness and the lawless boomtown, at a historical moment when the frontier is fast closing, at a time of the last gold rush in the Black Hills territory of South Dakota, the poignancy of a weary Hickok and the rugged foul-mouthed Calamity Jane simply turning up to take part in this transitional moment of frontier history makes visible how the series uses myth at an ideological level to document a vanishing world, authenticate a real historical moment—but, and possibly more importantly, offer new fantasies of the frontier and the nation's traumatic past. For, rather than unmasking what these mythic tales might conceal, the narrative instead explores the potency of myths about Western adventures and the strength of its mythic appeal for the popular imagination.

The visual appearance of Calamity Jane in her buckskin trousers and jacket, unwashed and swaggering around spitting out expletives, is a far cry from Doris Day as the perky tomboy, but nonetheless plunders a rich familiar legacy of Western iconography. This post-9/11 Calamity Jane has more in common with the revisionist Westerns of the 1960s and 1970s, in which the new historiographies stressed social schism, ethnic persecution and racism, environmental issues and gender inequalities, as well as modern novels like Peter Dexter's *Deadwood* (1986) and Larry McMurtry's *Buffalo Girls* (1990) that describe her as "not much cleaner than the filthy tents and lean-tos into which she flops" and as somehow "increasingly out of step with change, and unable to find new moorings" (Etulain 160, 161). Weigert's performance is dark, dangerous, raw and gritty, full of repressed anger, emotional uncertainty, and undercut with sudden bursts of violence, that speak volumes about HBO's vision of the frontier. The hideously beautiful (not unlike Calamity Jane) visual referencing combines a nostalgic haze with a coarse realism in its sepia tones and gritty *mise-en-scène*, replicating the verisimilitude of nineteenth-century photography as well as modern interpretations of the genre—not too surprising given that Walter Hill, director of *The Long Riders* (1980), took the helm for the pilot.

But what really marks out this modern-day Calamity Jane is her striking use of foul language. What first comes out of her mouth is truly astounding. "Ignorant fucking cunts," she curses ("Deadwood"). Shocking because it is a woman (even as coarse a one as Calamity Jane was suppose to be), but also because of the vehemence with which these words are uttered. With such obscenities, Calamity Jane formally announces what the series is about with its concentration on language—verbose, ornate, rhythmic, profane—and here she puts her stamp on the series at an oral level, which she will maintain throughout. Revising the Western places formal emphasis on the oral alongside the visual as never before. It ushers in a new media vocabulary for how the West will be imagined—made possible by HBO. Series creator David Milch maintains that "the incessant cursing has a historical rationale." He contests "that, in the original Deadwood, extreme talk served as a kind of preemptive guard against violence, signaling that the speaker would resort to any means necessary to protect himself" (Martel 34). And Calamity Jane certainly uses profanity with anarchic disdain and as her defensive armor, here to protect Hickok—but possibly against her own feelings, since she is clearly smitten by him. Maybe it is a much closer historical approximation to the speech patterns heard out West but such verbal vulgarity is unprecedented on television. Only on HBO can a series get away with being so rude and crude. With no advertisers to placate, no FCC to answer to, and an institutional policy that grants writers more freedom to tell stories differently, the premium cable channel stakes its reputation on saying what the networks cannot. License granted by HBO—itself, like the town, beyond the normal restrictions governing network television—enables *Deadwood* to provide "a television answer—or, perhaps more accurately, a series of questions—to the cinematic Western" (Lawson 17), but also the latest popular culture dialogue with Western historiographies and the mythologizing of the West.

Entangling myth with history, iconography with language, is further complicated when Calamity Jane first spies Deadwood. It is through her eyes that we first glimpse the town. The camera charts the trajectory of her gaze, following the steep trail, across the mountainous slopes thickly covered with Ponderosa Pines, until settling on the town nestled in a narrow canyon some way in the distance. The romance of this bucolic scene is given further nostalgic texture through the soulful and haunting sounds of a fiddle and strummed guitar overlaid on the soundtrack. Seen through the eyes of Calamity Jane, and given added poignancy through the melancholic use of music, Deadwood seems a remote place lost in time—part of a familiar epic landscape that holds the promise of possibility common to frontier mythology. But it is through Seth Bullock's eyes that we see the actual settlement—a barbarous place with its muck and grimy tents, full of raucous trading, drunken rowdiness and coarse (male) prospectors thronging the streets. No elegiac themes here. Just the diegetic sounds of commerce and traffic. This earthly world of perdition sharply contrasts with the mystical and mythical quality of the pristine one previously shown. Editing between these two point-of-view sequences stakes a claim to competing versions of the Western past that prove every bit as compelling as each other.

If Calamity Jane (with Hickok) offers us melancholic symbols of frontier virtues about to disappear, then Bullock represents the Westward expansion through capitalism, arriving with Sol Star not to prospect for gold but to set up a hardware store. It visually codes the difference between the different versions peddled in Buffalo Bill Cody's Wild West Show and in Frederick Jackson Turner's academic 1893 paper on "The Significance of the Frontier in

American History"—between sensationalist tales of daring frontier adventure and a progressive thesis based on the economic and social colonization of the West. Although the series problematizes mythical formations and the ideological assumptions that these two sequences described above evoke, and will come to acknowledge a multiplicity of histories colliding and competing for prominence as the town evolves, these opening moments keep the beguiling romance of the founding stories vividly alive in the very forms it chooses to convey the legendary past. It visualizes through sound and image the entangled preferred and approved old stories of what the frontier means to American culture, while at the same time making them appear sufficiently unfamiliar—for this is the first time either character has looked on these scenes—hinting at the possibility of alternative ideas of what constitutes history and legend.

But the formal shift and literal border crossing have gender implications. Back in July 1876, the *Black Hills Pioneer* announced to its readers, "Calamity Jane has arrived" (quoted in Sollid 41). Historical evidence thus points to the fact that Calamity Jane was as much a nationally recognized figure as Hickok at the time (McClintock 117; Sollid 41–3). But in *Deadwood* her arrival goes unnoticed. Hickok is greeted as a celebrity, subject to gossip and rumor, with his every movement watched by A. W. Merrick, editor and proprietor of the *Deadwood Pioneer*, sensing a good story; Calamity Jane in contrast does not warrant mention. Only referred to by others (but not the press) as "the woman with Hickok," she remains instead on the outside, prowling on the social margins, hanging outside bars, loitering in doorways—and on the fringes of the narrative. What I draw from this surprising excising—and after all even we know who she is—is how the erasure becomes symbolic of her nexus position within the text. It in part references her ambiguous position amongst the women. One only need think of when Deadwood's new schoolmistress comes to town, and how Merrick fawns over the new arrival seeing her as worthy of press attention ("Something Very Expensive," 2.6). It hints at the fact that Merrick may have refused to give her the public recognition she deserved because of who she was. He more than anyone knows how Deadwood thrives on particular versions of the West, and how the present prosperity only makes sense through stories about old-fashioned rugged individualism (Hickok), commercial venture (adverts for business openings), civic enterprise (town meetings), and the coming of Victorian respectability (the arrival of a new schoolteacher). Calamity Jane troubles the legendary past but also the "progressive" story of municipal endeavor and bourgeois gentility.

Maybe. But does it not also say something about America's "tangled" memories of its mythic past (Sturken): about recording official histories and those events remembered only in memory; about what can and cannot be said about bygone days; about what gets remembered and what is forgotten in the historiographies; and about "the choice of a good story over the hard facts" (Fabian 227). *Deadwood* labors to dissect the history-making process and to demystify past representations while becoming entangled in those very representational practices it seeks to interpret. The series as a piece of popular culture turns history into popular legend and compelling myth into historical verisimilitude. Whereas Merrick sells the myth to his readers, and HBO circulates its version of the West to its viewers, Calamity Jane rips through the fabric of that myth-making process to reveal trauma, where history, myth and legend are reconsidered as well as a new media vocabulary for re-imagining the Western past. In the act of telling her stories, often using an ornate arcane language littered with expletives, she makes visible how myths get made and circulated as a referent within culture to mask historical trauma—and thus provides a space where that trauma can be reconsidered and reinterpreted.

THE BLACK HILLS FLORENCE NIGHTINGALE: TALES OF VIRTUE AND GENERIC TRAUMA

> Calamity Jane laid aside her guns and became a nurse, an awkward one, but endlessly gentle and patient.
>
> *William Elsey Connelley*

> I am talking about nurse of the plague, fucking tent operation. Caring of the sick in the fuckin' tent!
>
> *Calamity Jane ("No Other Sons or Daughters," 1.9)*

Much has been made in the historical recollections of Calamity Jane's service to the Deadwood community during the smallpox epidemic of 1878. After her death in 1903, the *Pioneer-Times* reprinted the funeral eulogy. Written in poetic cadences, the sermon transformed her from social pariah into beatific savior when recalling her attending to the sick during that time: "When the romance is written whoever may be the heroes, [Calamity Jane] will in all the deeds which kindness and charity dictated in those days be the heroine" (reprinted in Sollid 62). Others like Jessie Brown and A. M. Willard (415) and William Elsey Connelley (188–9) were not slow in praising her efforts in similarly lyrical tones. One of the most comprehensive accounts of her nursing can be found in Estelline Bennett's 1935 reminiscences of what life was like in Deadwood:

> And everyone of them was remembering those days in '78 when Calamity Jane alone took care of the smallpox patients in a crude log cabin pest house up in Spruce Gulch around behind White Rocks.
>
> ... She came unscathed through the long smallpox siege and most of her patients lived. Dr Babcock believed that without her care not one of them could have pulled through.
>
> She never left the pest cabin during those hard weeks except to make hurried trips down to Deadwood for supplies that the grocers gave her.
>
> (223)

No other single event in the real Calamity Jane's life seems to have generated so much interest or received so much applause as her nursing charity. (Although it must be said that Calamity Jane made absolutely no mention of her time ministering to the sick in her autobiography—possibly because it did not suit her own legend-in-the-making.)

Why commentators from the time unanimously recognized her service says much about late-Victorian ideals of feminine virtue and the culturally prescribed rules governing female propriety and behavior. Looking closely at the language used to describe her caring for the sick, I am struck by how Calamity Jane is time and again spoken about in terms similar to those ideals labeled by the historian of American women, Barbara Welter, as "The Cult of True Womanhood" (151–74). Writings by those remembering times past assimilate the rhetoric of the Victorian prescriptive literature, projecting an image of Calamity Jane that reflects "the cardinal virtues of 'true womanhood': piety, purity, domesticity and submissiveness of the male" (Jameson 146). "It was here that this outcast woman, true to the better instincts of her sex, ministered day and night among the sick and dying, with no thought of reward or of what the consequences might be to herself," wrote Lewis Crawford, historian of the Old West, in 1926 (274). Edwin Legrand Sabin waxes lyrical about her efforts adopting a similar tone to Crawford:

> But she it was who, while the smallpox ravaged Deadwood in 1878, like a Florence Nightingale of the battlefield week after week nursed from bed to bed and bunk to bunk throughout the gulch, took risks that no one else would take, and asked nothing in return ... The woman in her was bound to come out in one way or another.
>
> (339)

With such words, Calamity Jane is redeemed for the historical archive, reclaimed as someone worth remembering for her selfless conduct and stoic endurance. Achieving respectability, and finding her true feminine self along the way, Nurse Calamity fits one of the pervasive descriptions of frontier womanhood circulating in newspapers, popular histories, and magazines at the time—that of the strong and uncomplaining helpmate. But such vocabulary turns her from a distinctive individual heroine who violates the tenets of Victorian "womanliness" into an allegory, a generic symbol of womanhood. Her reputation as a nurse may or may not justified, and/or it may be rooted in some partial truth, but its foregrounding in the historical archive illustrates a familiar tale of how women continued to be defined in relation to morality and selfless virtue.

The way in which *Deadwood* reinterprets these older tales of Calamity Jane ministering to the sick gives rise to tensions involved in contested debates over what is remembered and forgotten in the tangled memories of frontier history and legend. Calamity Jane's nursing skills are first put to the test when she comes across Andy Cramed out in the woods ("The Trail of Jack McCall," 1.5). The first in Deadwood to succumb to smallpox, he has been left to die on the orders of Cy Tolliver. Nothing must come in the way of business. Cramed's diseased body is literally ejected from the community, abandoned in the wilderness to decay and be forgotten. Along comes Calamity Jane. Distraught over the death of Hickok and drunk out of her mind, her attempts to help are clumsy, if not slightly brutal. Returning to his body after collecting water from the creek, she nearly chokes him as she pours it down his throat. Cramed splutters. "Ah! There you are. Chokin' and coughin' just like the rest of us," she responds. Her act of retrieval, her bringing of Cramed back from the brink, reveals her nursing as less about moral feminine virtue than about rescuing the marginalized, those the camp has rejected and abandoned to its outskirts. (Cramed will become a kind of nemesis for Tolliver, a constant and uncomfortable reminder of what he did—of what cannot be forgotten.) Later Calamity Jane tells Doc Cochran of what she saw out in the woods ("Plague," 1.6). In so doing she keeps alive events others would wish to forget.

These encounters with the sick, however, allow Calamity Jane to enact a process of historical revision based on subjective experience, memory and trauma. Cathy Caruth reminds us that overcoming trauma involves the ability to tell a story. On the one hand it is about perception and remembering overofficial histories, and on the other it is about a narrative challenging ideas of what we mean by subjectivity, memory, and history. It is here that Calamity Jane's speech patterns and bad language play an important role. Slumped besides Cramed's body, she tells him of what she has just seen— "the widow's husband in the creek ... tethered, wrapped up, and floating like a lure for some huge fuckin' fish ... and I saw as they laid my poor fuckin' Bill to rest." She starts to sob. Talking about what has been lost to Alma Garrett (her husband) and to herself (Hickok and Sofia), her testimony is about coming to terms with the past, about mourning personal losses. Yet the violence of her language when recalling what she has just seen reveals the act of remembering as a form of trauma. Her florid storytelling style, using an anachronistic language associated with the Old West, is spoken in a pared-down almost inarticulate form associated with the laconic Hollywood cowboy made reticent by the Production Code. What emerges here is not so much about uncovering some hidden truth about the past as about how bearing witness to an event is in some sense a performance enacted in the now.

Her memory as a media narrative retrieves past events for the audience, offering us a textual reminder of what has previous happened on *Deadwood*, like the murder of Brom Garrett, the fate of Norwegian foundling Sofia, and the burial of Hickok. Her memory as personal narrative does not simply replicate those events (some of which we have already seen); it acts instead as "a form of interpretation" (Sturken 7). Her stream of consciousness, as one narrative gets laid over another, is about the telling of a number of fragmented and incomplete stories colliding and struggling for attention in a television series busy remembering the past for contemporary popular culture. In her performative act of storytelling, historical knowledge and cultural memories—what is said and how it gets told—are given shape. It is about what a culture chooses to forget—what we hear about but is never seen (the fate of Brom)—and what it wants, possibly needs, to remember—what we ourselves witness (the burial of a frontier legend). In the telling she keeps both stories vividly alive, making visible how every story told is steeped in this entanglement of history and memory, of forgetting and remembering, of historical events and media reconstruction, of screen memories and memories re-presented on screen.

Lapsing into the profane—spoken as guttural muttering where less is more—Calamity Jane often uses language to transgress codes that normally describe the mythic male hero. "You're one sick fuckin' customer," she says when she first comes across Cramed. Soon recruited by Doc Cochran to help out, "bein' [that she has] a gift for it," she is nursing those with the smallpox ("Plague"). (Rumor had it that the alcohol in the system of the real Calamity Jane gave her immunity from the disease.) Re-presenting an authentic historical event (although dating the epidemic much earlier), *Deadwood* reclaims a past trauma to interrogate our continuing investment in generic archetypes as well as the trauma pervasive in rejecting the grand narratives of popular legend. Maybe because she is still grieving the loss of Hickok, her language to describe her patients—"you're one pitiful specimen" ("Suffer the Little Children," 1.8)—is far from benevolent. Telling it as it is, she says what is normally kept hidden in the mythology of the Western cowboy. Far from being robust and vigorous, rugged and hard, the vulnerable male body lying out of sight behind frayed muslin curtains and the grubby tarpaulin is diseased and decaying—and it is to these physical frailties that she bears profane testimony.

Nowhere is this more evident than with Reverend Smith, whose incurable brain tumor means he is suffering memory loss. Even through a haze of alcohol, Calamity Jane sees what the forgetful Reverend can no longer comprehend: "I see you skulkin' around when the Doc comes in. You're tryin' to hide your fuckin' eyes, tryin' to hide your fuckin' arm. You're a fuckin' mess," she rants at the man who now imagines he can smell his own body putrefying ("No Other Sons or Daughters"). Bad language once again is used to break the rules, her rudeness here contravening what the traditional Western must never reveal. Convention dictates that the male hero must somehow transcend the corporeal to become the legend—a monolithic "totality" that the generic rules work hard to protect. While Al Swearengen literally puts the Reverend out of his misery, smothering the putrid body that unsettles generic sensibilities ("Sold Under Sin"), Calamity Jane enacts violence against that same frail mortal body with her foul language. She may serve a narrative function to heal and redeem broken male bodies for the generic order but her fierce language—that of a rugged, individualistic masculinity embodied by Hickok—is unforgiving against those violating convention. Her standards are high. But the violence of her language betrays generic trauma, making visible the impact revisionist histories have had upon the legendary versions of the Western past Americans have most often favored as well as the value particular (male) bodies have to those (generic) memories.

THE BLACK HILLS AND ITS INCREDIBLE CHARACTERS: RECLAIMING STORIES AND MEMORY WORK

The memory work performed by Calamity Jane extends to how she has been imagined in popular culture and what her legendary reputation means to us. Nowhere is this more evident than with her alleged relationship to Hickok. Legend has it that the two were lovers. Speculation first grew with her dying request to be buried alongside him in Mt. Moriah Cemetery, and around the strange coincidence that she passed away on the anniversary of his death. Ned Buntline wrote of the supposed affair in his 1912 dime novel, but the story took on new momentum in 1941 when Mrs. Jane Hickok McCormick came forward declaring to be their daughter. She produced a diary and various papers (including a marriage certificate) to verify her claim, but historians have long since proved her allegations false.

Yet the myth persists, fueled by dime novels and perpetuated by Hollywood. Romance blossoms between Calamity Jane (Jean Arthur) and

Hickok played by Gary Cooper while she helps him quell an Indian uprising in *The Plainsman*; and Doris Day eventually finds true love with Hickok (Howard Keel) in the musical comedy *Calamity Jane*. In both cases, the love of a good man re-educates the feisty Calamity Jane, whose identity is somehow out of line with accepted ideals of femininity. Nowhere is the makeover more dramatic than in the Doris Day version, where her transformation from spirited adolescent to glamorous adult female—superficially aided by Max Factor cosmetics, corsets and fine gowns—is only made possible through the promise of heterosexual romance. Proper femininity is restored and female normalcy assured. (Ironically Joanie Stubbs fails in her endeavor to effect a similar transformation in our modern-day heroine, in "The Whores Can Come," 2.11.) If these cinematic representations have come to imprison the mythology of Calamity Jane in a quixotic haze of heterosexual politics and feminine glamour, then what are we to make of *Deadwood*'s attempt to liberate her image from its glitzy Hollywood-ization?

In *Deadwood*, amorous intentions seem a little one-sided. Calamity Jane may have special affection for Hickok, but she does not seem that eager to act on those feelings. Instead she seems more than happy to act as his helpmate, taking care of Sofia, who Hickok had a hand in rescuing ("Deadwood") or chaperoning his meetings with Alma ("Here Was a Man," 1.4). The only moment indicating that there could be more to the relationship than unrequited spinsterly yearnings comes during their final encounter. Carrying the child in her arms, she enters his room on the pretext of telling Hickok about Sofia's improved health. A stilted conversation ensues as she conveys news about the little one and enquires about his handling of Alma's affairs. Silence. Eyes down. Hickok tickles the child. She giggles. Sad glances are exchanged. Warm smiles traded. Calamity Jane says that they should leave him in peace. "I'm writing my wife," he says. "Why didn't you say somethin', damn you?" Did she know about his wife back in Cincinnati and feel guilty for imposing, or is something else going on? We never find out. It is the last time the couple will ever meet.

Hickok's murder signals the end of Calamity Jane's attempt to participate in the community. She can no longer live in a town in the process of becoming modern and descends further into alcoholism. On first coming across Cramed, she drunkenly tells him: "My best friend died. The man I had my best friend feelin' about in the world. Took as he found you, thought

the best a you. Sweet to me!" ("The Trial of Jack McCall," 1.5). Given that
the real Calamity Jane was supposedly quite promiscuous and had allegedly
worked as a prostitute (the truth cannot be verified but it was common to
label women defying convention as loose), this modern-day version seems
remarkably chaste. High regard, deep loyalty, and devotional respect guide
her feelings; and her fondness for Hickok is based less on a lustful reality
than on a romantic ideal for what he represents. She becomes a woman
increasingly haunted by his glamorous legend, literally and metaphorically
preserving his reputation as a male heroic archetype of the Old West,
someone who embodies the special character of the American people.
Observing a tradesman leaving Hickok's old room at the Grand Central
Hotel, she challenges him: "Mr. Millenary sample suitcase cocksucker, you're
staying in the former room of someone you ain't fit to lick the boots of!" No
need for the lesson. The millenary already knows: "Wild Bill Hickok. I paid
two dollars a day extra. Had you any connection to Wild Bill?" She remains
silent ("Plague").

Giving up Sofia into the custody of Alma (and Trixie) is a pivotal moment
for Calamity Jane ("Plague"). Without Hickok, her caring for the child no
longer makes sense. Practically, she realizes she is incapable of doing the
job, but there is another metaphoric reason. If he had lived, she might have
continued with the progress narrative, becoming integrated into the modern
community, possibly even contributing to its progress. But with him gone
she must now perform another function—that of storyteller and protector of
the Hickok myth. She more than understands what he means to American
frontier history, a narrative about heroic deeds and last stands that no longer
has a reality but nonetheless is endlessly repeated and re-presented in pastiche
forms in the present.

After three episodes spent in the pest tent attending to the smallpox
victims, she is drunk—again ("No Other Sons or Daughters"). Truth be told,
the sheer grind of caring for the sick took its toll on the real Calamity Jane,
who was renowned for her binge drinking once her patients had sufficiently
recovered. No difference here then. Charlie Utter eventually finds her
about to leave town. "I will not be a drunk where he's buried and I cannot
stay fuckin' sober," she tells him. There is nothing left for her. Getting up,
she picks up her saddle bag, bed roll and rope—kitted out with Wild West
accoutrements—and declares: "If the subject comes up, explain to Bill."

That she and Utter are known to regularly visit Hickok's grave explains her seeming lapse. But the weariness of her words implies that she, like Hickok, has outlived her usefulness to the camp. The visual of her sloping off into the night mirrors a similar image from earlier when, after a bruising encounter with a "fan," Hickok heads off to the saloon to drown his sorrows and gamble ("Reconnoitering the Rim," 1.3). He has been helping Bullock and Sol build their hardware store. Turning his back on the construction site—a symbol of the modern town—he literally carries the weight of his legacy in his gait. Calamity Jane takes this burden on in her deportment. Physically walking against the traffic, and into the dark night, she now bears the heavy responsibility for a mythical past that is already fading fast. Without turning back, she wearily waves to Utter—an elegiac moment of poignancy signaling that she no longer belongs to the modern but embodies a nostalgic longing for a mythical past.

When Calamity Jane returns to Deadwood in the second season, her position becomes far more metaphoric than in the first. She serves as an important nexus point around which history, legend and genre memory become more deeply entangled, and forgotten histories and popular myths are further interrogated. This working on the border is narratively rationalized by her social position, which is more marginal than before. She has come back to Deadwood to die, or so she tells the Doc ("A Lie Agreed Upon," Part 2, 2.2). Alcoholism is taking its toll—"your liver runs from your chin to your genitals," explains the Doc—and she increasingly becomes a ghostly presence around town haunted by the past and burdened with that knowledge in the present.

One of her first acts is to accompany Bullock when he goes to retrieve his badge and weapon from Swearengen. The visual of the trio arriving at the Gem, with Bullock flanked on either side by Calamity Jane and Utter, is striking, especially in how it symbolizes the complicated authority held by Bullock as town sheriff but also in the narrative. If Utter, the businessman and freight company owner, represents modernity, then Calamity Jane stands for an older-style frontier justice previously embodied by Hickok (a template for Bullock, someone he desires to emulate). That said, one cannot imagine Hickok calling out: "Be aware Bullock, some fungus-faced fuck has a rifle on you from this shit-box's version of a kitchen." But then the old generic rules no longer apply.

As she prowls around the town, usually guzzling from a whiskey bottle, encounters with others explore the fissures and lapses in the official stories. What gets uncovered are multiple and contested memories that relate to a complex and often traumatic experience in the narrative reshaping of modern frontier historiographies. On one occasion she meets an African-American named Samuel Fields. Better known as "Nigger General," he has recently returned to Deadwood to pay for a horse he rented earlier from livery stable owner Hostetler. Coming across Calamity Jane, who as usual is drunk, he asks if she would consider selling him the bottle ("Complications," 2.5). "Is that some dilapidated-type fucking uniform? I scouted for fucking Custer," she barks. Fields replies that he was "a great man." "He was no great fucking man!" comes back the reply. "He was a long-haired cocksucker that could have saved many lives by more drinking and stop being so fucking ambitious, and many still above ground and not scalped by the fucking heathens and their guts spread over the plains." Ironically her response contests her own glorious version of events that appear in the 1896 autobiography when she professed to have scouted for Custer (reprinted in Sollid 126). Revising "her" opinion recalls well-known revisionist histories that interpret Custer as nothing more than a genocidal imperialist. But drinking with an African-American (someone whose experience of the frontier is rarely documented) and exchanging stories that the Deadwood Pioneer would never print points to the continuously unfolding palimpsest history of the frontier that this modern-day Calamity Jane comes to represent through listening to and telling stories. Here I am reminded of Thomas Elsaesser's notion of trauma theory as "not so much a theory of recovered memory as it is about one of recovered referentiality" (201). Suggested is that trauma refers less to a catastrophic event than a revised reassessment of what it signifies to us in the present. In short, why does Deadwood offer these screen memories now? How do these representations help us come to terms with the past?

The 1890s saw the frontier declared closed, and the Wild West subject to obsessive and repetitive re-enactment on stage and later screen. At that very moment, the real Calamity Jane made the first of a series of live appearances, hired by the Kohl & Middleton Company, across the Midwest. The sensationalist 1896 publicity announcing her first appearance in Minneapolis read as follows:

The famous woman scout of the Wild West. Heroine of a thousand
thrilling adventures. The terror of evildoers in the Black Hills! The
comrade of Buffalo Bill and Wild Bill Hickok. See this famous
woman and hear her graphic descriptions of her daring exploits.

(reprinted in Sollid 77)

That Calamity Jane's legend is entangled with a theatrical version of frontier
reality says much about what she has meant to us as a pastiche of the past
almost from the beginning. She enters show business at the very moment
the history she represented was disappearing and the historians were busy
writing it into discourse. Long has she been a symptom of the postmodern
condition, in which a sense of history vanishes, amnesia rules and the past is
raided by the present for images. Only recently did HBO install an exhibition
about the show to join the historical archive, including images of the real
Calamity Jane, at the Adams Museum in Deadwood (Billard F3).

Even the *Deadwood* text seems to take pleasure in plundering other
media scripts from Hollywood movies to dime novels as it plays with our
generic expectations in representing the modern-day Calamity Jane. One
only need think of her relationship with Joanie Stubbs, for example, which
evokes generic memories of the friendship between Calamity Jane and Katie
Brown (Allyn Ann McLerie) in the 1953 musical comedy. Later, our latter-
day heroine is seen wearing a dress at the wedding celebrations for Alma and
Ellsworth ("Boy the Earth Talks To," 2.12). But rather than being flattered by
male attention, and finding romance like Doris Day, she starts to push, shove
and verbally abuse her would-be suitor. More slapstick silent comedy than
romantic Hollywood endings, but the depth of past media referencing that
Deadwood builds into the generic memory further demands that we consider
what her role as a changeable script means to current cultural climate.

Our culture cannot quite stop obsessing about Calamity Jane. She
resurfaces within our cultural imagination every now and then, a recurrent
and repetitive image that never quite goes away and never means the same
thing twice. Her media treatment, as I suggest, says much about her narrative
function for catharsis and healing in the post-9/11 era—a time of perceived
national crisis related to global terrorism, political and religious schism, and a
controversial war involving the latest gold rush—oil. HBO chairman and CEO
Chris Albrecht has said that "in the months after 9/11 ... I had been thinking

about the fact that the country was really starting to feel better about all these American institutions, finding them comforting," and "his early affections for Westerns came back to him" (Carter, "Town," 4–5). Resurrecting a classic American genre taps in part into a seemingly unappeasable desire for Wild West romanticism. Given that Calamity Jane repeatedly re-enacted that Western mythology to an eager paying public during her own lifetime; given that her myth keeps returning to us as a "recovered referentiality" at moments of seeming social and political transition (Elsaesser 201), reveals how she remains an importance storytelling figure for our culture. But in its complex portrayal of Calamity Jane as someone not able to adjust to a closed frontier, as someone intimately entangled with history and (media-produced) legend, *Deadwood* uses her to meditate on the uneasy relation between historical events, myth and cultural fantasy, and screen memories and media re-presentations. What makes this Calamity Jane unique is that she may tell us the familiar stories that we want to hear but how she narrates them often makes for uncomfortable listening.

CHAPTER 6

WHORES, LADIES, AND CALAMITY JANE

GENDER ROLES AND THE WOMEN OF HBO'S DEADWOOD

KATHLEEN E. R. SMITH

WESTERN WOMEN

In 1876, it seemed as if the West might be the perfect place for a woman to express herself—to act on feelings and aspirations that Victorian culture had forced her to suppress. Most of the reports women heard in the East gave the impression of the frontier settlements as informal, cooperative, tolerant, and marvelously free. Westerners were widely and justly celebrated as rugged individualists, which suggested they would not deny any newcomers—even women—the cherished privilege of being left alone and, within reason, doing as they pleased. As a result, the West attracted a legion of nonconforming women: mavericks, recluses, eccentrics, and explorers—women out to explore the boundaries of American society or to push those boundaries to the limit. Two of the female characters in the television series *Deadwood*—Miss Isringhausen and Calamity Jane—represent some of these free spirits who defied the notion of a woman's place and a woman's work.

At the opposite end of the spectrum is the role of woman as helpmate and/or representative of the "Cult of True Womanhood," as enunciated by the characters of Martha Bullock and Alma Garret. The longstanding image of American women as primarily wives and mothers, living as submissive, domestic beings, was still firmly entrenched in society. In the ideology of the last quarter of the nineteenth century, women and men were supposed to inhabit separate spheres: men would run the world of business and politics, while women filled the domestic role and were responsible for maintaining piety and virtue, not only in the home, but in society at large. In the past, historians of the American West generally depicted the Westering woman as the "gentle tamer," a lady of some refinement who, though resigned to her harsh lot of monotonous drudgery, was determined to ensure her children a better life by imposing the Victorian woman's version of civilization on the American wilderness.

There is a third group of women who live on the fringe of society in *Deadwood*, who deviate from the model of American womanhood: the prostitutes and madams, as portrayed by Trixie and Joanie Stubbs. They do not exhibit the qualities associated with domesticity and true womanhood, such as virtue and piety.

Despite the propaganda, the West was no picnic for a woman, whether she was law-abiding or otherwise. Once a frontier community was solidly established, the constricting Victorian social conventions of the East came pouring in. Prime among these was the firm belief among males—and a great many females—that home was the only proper place for a woman and that her only proper work was caring for her husband and children. According to Anne Butler and Ona Siporan, "It is important to note that most women agreed with this belief, and the fact that most of them conformed to it made life harder for those who would not" (161).

Was the West truly a freer place for women? Many women of independent mind, high spirit, and strong ambition found the untamed West less rigid and thus more accepting of change than the East. Any woman who dared to venture out on an uncharted course stood a better chance in the West of reaching her objective—even if she did have to endure what one early comer described as society's reaction to nonconformists: "unkind feelings, even without supposing bitter animosity" (Butler and Siporan 6). Alternatively, she was the antithesis of that stereotype—the backwoods belle, the soiled dove, the female bandit, a woman of unsavory character, although perhaps less one-dimensional than her pure and passive counterpart (Butler and Siporan 7).

In *Deadwood*, the women portrayed are strictly stereotyped. They fall into one of three common images: the refined lady, the helpmate, and the bad woman. The lady—who may be a schoolteacher, a missionary, or a woman with civilized tastes—is defined as being too genteel for the coarse West. She is either uncomfortable, unhappy, or literally driven crazy by the frontier. Ladies understood their prescribed roles and lifestyles. If they were unsure, there was a plethora of prescriptive literature to guide women stressing the need for a woman to marry, to ensure not only her happiness but also her economic welfare. Apparently, in some cases, the only way she can prove her gentility is to become a victim, such as the character Alma Garret, the refined, educated young woman, who marries the wealthy New Yorker Brom Garret, in exchange for money to pay her wastrel father's debts. In the initial episodes, Alma numbs herself to the reality of her life in Deadwood with tincture of laudanum, a drug derived from opium. She is clearly addicted.

On the other hand, the strong and uncomplaining helpmate, such as Martha Bullock, adapts to the West but, in the process, she becomes a work-worn woman, losing all her individuality. The bad woman (typified by Trixie, Joanie Stubbs, Miss Isringhausen, and Calamity Jane) has a perverse type of glamour and power but is in constant danger of losing them, as her life is usually connected to dangerous men (Armitage 10).

In the Western frontier, even in mining camps and towns, women were not passive in community building: they selected community projects (building schools and churches were usually the first priority), lobbied for them, and raised money for them. But when the moment of formal organization came, women stepped back. Men were elected as officials and were often given credit for the entire enterprise (Armitage 13). An exception to this theory is Alma Garret and her active involvement in the formation of the first bank in Deadwood. It is the gold from her mine that provides the largest amount of the money to fund the new bank. Others put in their share, but it is Alma Garret's involvement that makes the bank possible. Despite her great wealth and participation in the founding of the bank, Alma maintains her Victorian sensibilities: when she ventures onto the streets of Deadwood she still has an escort (Ellsworth or Richardson).

The official story and the informal stories of women in Deadwood are not the same. Because newspapers document the official facts, not the informal ones, historians who rely solely on newspapers in their research perpetuate the invisibility of women. In Victorian culture, a woman's name and picture never appeared in newspapers, with the possible exceptions of her marriage and her death. As Elizabeth Jameson shows so clearly in her article, "Through a Woman's Eyes: A New View of the West," oral histories have been a major source of documenting women's informal community activities and to make us examine our assumptions. But think about it: who could seriously imagine a raw, untamed frontier populated by ineffectual, ornamental women? (Armitage 14). Women had to participate in community building as well as seeing to the welfare of their families. Sometimes the line between the two is blurred as women are given more opportunities to have their voices heard in the West. After all, it was the Western state of Wyoming that first gave women the right to vote and first sent a woman to Congress.

In HBO's *Deadwood*, the viewer encounters real women who led real lives. The fact is that even the most heroic people lead ordinary lives ninety-nine per cent of the time. Because some men in Western history achieved heroic status, we may think we need to create female figures in the same mold (Calamity Jane). Ordinary lives are the true story of the West, for men as well as for women.

With the invisibility of most women in Western history, one important group of Western women who definitely fall outside the nineteenth century's "Cult of True Womanhood" are prostitutes. They had left the "private sphere" to become the most public of women and left it for sexual commerce, while "true women" were supposed to be asexual. There is a definite separation between "lewd and dissolute female persons" and "women." Western mythology softened this distinction by creating the "whore with the heart of gold," (Trixie) who had all the virtues of a proper woman, or by calling prostitutes by euphemisms such as "soiled doves." In reality, there were no "whores with hearts of gold," but there were women whose lives were as much affected by economic circumstances and emotional needs as were those of other women (Joanie Stubbs) (Murphy 193). Because mining towns had many more men than women (some sources report women in frontier camps and mining towns were outnumbered by men at the rate of one hundred to one), the male population supported large red-light districts and made "private life" fairly public (Murphy 193). In the world of prostitution, the division between public and private, which was so central to nineteenth-century women's lives, was virtually non-existent.

ALMA GARRETT

At first glance, Alma Garret seems to fit the stereotype of the frail, lonely woman, too gentle for the harshness of the West. We pity her. She has left behind her emotional and familial support. A woman who has lived very much the life that is expected of her, she has done the things that she is supposed to do for her family, for her father, and for this society in which she lives. Her husband is a rich dandy, sent West by his family to seek his fortune (or add to it) in the gold rush of the Black Hills in 1876–1877. He knows nothing of the enterprise on which he has embarked, and Alma keeps herself anesthetized to the harshness of her surroundings by taking laudanum, a tincture of opium that was often prescribed for both men and women, but most often to women for headaches or hysteria—a typical diagnosis for middle- and upper-class women of the nineteenth century. Alma's health is uncertain, and she is desperately lonely. She may have been a reluctant pioneer but, after the death of her husband, her reluctance gives way to adaptation.

Widowed by her husband's murder (carried out at Al Swearengen's behest), Alma goes to Wild Bill Hickok to enlist his help in determining whether the gold claim her late husband purchased for $20,000 is truly a gold strike. She also consents to help Calamity Jane care for Sofia, the orphaned child. Alma confides to Jane that she married Brom Garret for his money, that she "sold" herself to pay her father's debts. After Wild Bill Hickok is murdered, Jane goes on a drunken bender, leaving Alma to care for Sofia alone. Because Al Swearengen wants to keep an eye on the child (his henchmen are responsible for the murder of her family) and also desires the Widow Garret's gold claim, he sends his favorite whore, Trixie, to spy on Alma and also keep her supplied with "dope" ("Here Was a Man," 1.4 and "The Trial of Jack McCall," 1.5).

Realizing her responsibility for Sofia, Alma decides she must overcome her drug habit. With the aid of Trixie, who admits she was once an addict as well, she does exactly that. An unlikely bond is formed between these two women who come from such different worlds. But what they do have in common is they have both sold themselves for money, albeit in different social worlds. Eventually, Alma offers to send Trixie to New York City with the child, an offer Trixie spurns with a stream of profanity aimed at Alma. Trixie evidently has her own sense of morality, and Alma cannot buy her off.

In "Bullock Returns to the Camp" (1.7), Brom Garret is buried and E. B. Farnum, the proprietor of the Grand Central Hotel, offers (at Swearengen's bidding) to buy Alma's gold claim. Now she is convinced the claim is genuine and seems to be a huge strike. A change comes over the Widow Garret as she gathers strength and sets herself on a new path. She is still a lady, but now she is feeling empowered by her newfound wealth and ability to overcome drug addiction. She is also attracted to Seth Bullock, who is tracking her husband's killer and verifying her gold claim, and they become lovers. Her intellect and growing confidence continue to be revealed throughout Seasons One and Two, so that by "Boy the Earth Talks To" (2.12), she has turned her life around and is no longer an adornment but a vibrant, confident woman. After visiting Brom's grave in the Season Two's final episode, Alma Garret talks to herself saying she is afraid, "My life is living me and soon will be over and not a moment of it will have been my own, but now my body tells me it is right and good." She has come to accept her pregnancy (Bullock's child) and her arranged marriage to Ellsworth, but it is obvious to the viewer she will not return to her previous role as a Victorian lady whose purpose is to be an ornament and live only for her husband and children.

MARTHA BULLOCK

Another prevalent type of Western woman was the "gentle tamer." Her very presence on the frontier was enough to make rough and rowdy men think about polite behavior and the establishment of civilized institutions like schools, churches, and libraries. In *Deadwood*, this is Martha Bullock, a widow with a young son, who has married her dead husband's brother in an arrangement of convenience. What is striking about this stereotype is the unbelievable passivity of such women. Martha Bullock feels she must ask permission from her husband, Seth Bullock, to teach the children of Deadwood, since the schoolteacher who was originally hired did not last a day in the rowdy, dangerous camp.

Martha Bullock's behavior is passive in other ways. She speaks in a calm, low voice; her clothing is neat, clean, and very modest. She has no opulent dresses or gowns like Alma Garret, nor does she ever appear less than fully clothed—even in bed with Seth she has on a modest nightgown. It is apparent Martha Bullock is well educated, but it is also clear that her understanding of her role in life is to be a wife and mother and to keep a home that is a refuge from the evils of the world outside her door. She has married her dead husband's brother to provide a father for her son and security for herself. She is subservient to him and attempts to make their home (the first real home built in Deadwood) a haven. She constantly cooks, cleans, and attempts to please Bullock. She is living exactly as the "cult of true womanhood" prescribes.

CALAMITY JANE

Gerda Lerner's definition of women's history says: "The true history of women is the history of their ongoing functioning in [the] male-defined world, on their own terms" (14). If ever there was a woman who fits this description, it is Martha Jane Canary: Calamity Jane. She dresses like a man, drinks to excess, and tosses about curses and obscenities as well as any man on *Deadwood*. She adores Wild Bill Hickok, tolerates Charlie Utter, and eventually develops a relationship with Alma Garret (as a result of Jane's caretaking of the orphaned Sofia).

As portrayed in *Deadwood*, Jane is earthy—she wears buckskins to recall her past as a scout for the US Army and as a bullwhacker. She definitely has a masculine look, not only in dress but also in manner. She walks like a man, is armed (sometimes with an ammunition belt), and wears a male's derby hat (with a jaunty feather that further sets her apart) and layers of leather, patches, and dirt. Having lived her life acting as a male, this is how she has survived. She is a woman bravely making the best of the hand she has been dealt by life. The fact that Jane is a heavy drinker and often disappears from Deadwood for days or weeks at a time is offset by her benevolent role in the rescue of Sofia. In "Deadwood" (1.1), Jane goads the men in camp to ride out in the night when they had planned to wait until daylight to search for the murdered immigrants. Her nursing and protecting of the child and her care of the smallpox victims in camp are also evidence of a compassionate side of Jane's personality that she rarely lets show.

In the second season of *Deadwood*, Calamity Jane's character begins to move away from the more caricatured portrayal of Season One. She forms friendships with Trixie and Joanie Stubbs. Trixie and Jane do not judge one another and, in a wonderful scene in "New Money" (2.3), they share a bottle of whiskey outside the Gem Saloon while discussing the merits of men in general and Al Swearengen in particular. Jane tells how Al tried to have Sofia killed; Trixie responds with the story of how Al rescued Jewel (the crippled cleaning woman) from an orphanage. Jane agrees that it is possible Al has a good side and they part as Jane says, "It's nice to see you." It is a remarkably tender scene—one that might take place in a café. It is easy to picture these two women dressed in middle-class clothing, sharing a cup of tea and having the same discussion, minus the coarse language.

MISS ISRINGHAUSEN

A second character living her life on men's terms, Miss Isringhausen is a minor character, appearing in just a handful of episodes in Season Two. Her purpose is to act as a catalyst and set other characters in motion. Hired by Alma Garret as a tutor for Sofia, Miss Isringhausen seems to be the perfect lady, impeccable in her dress, manner, and speech. She is reserved with her employer and with Sofia, which makes her seem to be exactly the right choice to tutor the adopted child of a wealthy New York woman. In fact, Miss Isringhausen plays her role so well that it is not long before Alma Garret is confiding some of her secrets, including the fact that Seth Bullock has asked Alma to go away with him. (This is after his wife and son have arrived in Deadwood, and the two have also begun the sexual relationship that results in Alma's pregnancy.) Alma uses the tutor as a sounding board without realizing she is really a spy for Brom Garret's family in the employ of the Pinkerton Detective Agency. The Garret family hopes to link Alma directly to their son's death, in which case they will have full access to the goldmine. (Alma is in an enviable position, when it comes to her late husband's estate. Although many states had altered the laws forbidding women to have access to their own property by 1876–1877, one of the exceptions to the prevailing custom was the privilege of a widow to control her estate, especially if there was no male relative to assume the role of her guardian, no matter the woman's age.)

When Al Swearengen discovers Miss Isringhausen's true mission, he does not cow her. In fact, she is one of the few characters on *Deadwood* who does not seem to be afraid of Al. She admits her duplicity, lays out her terms, and seems to be just as smart and devious as he is. When she does depart the camp, it is with money and a bodyguard. She has betrayed her employers for safe passage out of Deadwood. No other characters are able to do this.

When Cy Tolliver catches a couple of young con artists plying their trade at the Bella Union, he shoots the boy and makes Joanie shoot the girl. The same type of swift, frontier justice is doled out by Al Swearengen in the Gem Saloon and by Mr. Wu in Chinatown. If a character crosses them, he or she usually winds up dead and possibly fed to Mr. Wu's pigs.

TRIXIE AND JOANIE STUBBS

One important group of Western women who definitely fall outside the nineteenth century's "Cult of True Womanhood" are *Deadwood*'s prostitutes. In the world of prostitution, the division between public and private, which was so central to nineteenth-century women's lives, was virtually non-existent. Women like Trixie and Joanie Stubbs, while prostitutes, are definitely on a higher level than the other girls and women in the Gem Saloon and the Bella Union.

It is apparent from the first episode that Trixie is a survivor. She kills a customer who beat her, and then she has a brutal confrontation with Al. Despite Al's threats, she continues to carry a gun to protect herself. Trixie's character evolves from the first episode. No ordinary prostitute, she has a special relationship with Al. Her clothes are just a notch above the other girls in the Gem, signified by the tattered red ribbon running through her ragged corset. By the second season, Trixie has graduated to velvet corsets and then ordinary dresses as her relationship with Sol Star, Seth's Bullock's business partner (who is teaching her bookkeeping), advances. Another symbol of Trixie's growing independence is evident in "Amalgamation and Capitol" (2.9), when Trixie reveals several lumps of gold she has saved and asks to be the first depositor in Deadwood's new bank. In a step outside the boundary of polite society, Alma Garret, a founding member of the bank, not only accepts Trixie's deposit, but also insists on being the one to record it. Both women have spurned Victorian custom by crossing into the male sphere and actively taking part in the business world.

Joanie Stubbs, the madam for Cy Tolliver's Bella Union saloon, is set apart from the other prostitutes from her first appearance on screen. She is dressed in fine clothing and wears a hat with a trailing scarf. She sets a high tone for the Bella Union and is thus a threat to Al Swearengen's decidedly lower-class operation. It is not until "Sold Under Sin" (1.12) that Joanie's past is revealed. After her mother's death, Joanie's father began to sexually abuse her and eventually sold her to Cy Tolliver. Now she is a modern businesswoman, trained by the ruthless Tolliver. She is feminine in her dress, although usually with just a touch of inappropriateness, i.e. wearing her bodice too low, but she also takes on the masculine role of business owner as the madam of the Chez Amis, a high-class bordello. Cy Tolliver has encouraged her to go into business on her own and has helped fund it. Even in this, Joanie proves her business intelligence: she has been putting money aside, has equipped her new place with expensive fixtures and opulent furnishings, and has taken on a partner, Maddie, an older, more experienced madam who rides into town with a stagecoach of new prostitutes.

Joanie's new venture is doomed by the arrival in Deadwood of Francis Wolcott, George Randolph Hearst's agent. Joanie's judgment is called into question when Maddie informs her that "Mr. W." is going to make them wealthy, without revealing his methods. In "Something Very Expensive" (2.6), Wolcott murders two of the Chez Amis prostitutes, Maddie forces Joanie from the Chez Amis at gunpoint, and when Maddie attempts to extort Wolcott, he slashes her throat as well. Upon discovering the murders, Joanie runs to Cy, saying, "There's trouble at my place." Tolliver removes the bodies and has the place cleaned while Joanie hires a wagon from Charlie Utter and borrows money from the bartender at the Bella Union to spirit the rest of her girls out of town. Cy asks Joanie to move back to the Bella Union so he can protect her, but she refuses. Joanie Stubbs shows that she is determined to make her business work. She is out of Cy Tolliver's power and she intends to stay that way. She does confide the horror she witnessed to Charlie Utter, marveling that Maddie was the only woman she ever knew "who was not afraid of men." And look what happened to her. Joanie resolves to stay at the Chez Amis, as spending even one night away would be admitting defeat. She is determined to start again.

After severely beating Wolcott in the street (supposedly for stepping on his toe), Charlie Utter comes upon Calamity Jane, who is distraught after passing out on Wild Bill's grave the night before. Charlie suggests she clean up and go to the Chez Amis to comfort "another girl who has lost her friends," and thus begins one of the most interesting friendships among the women of *Deadwood*. In the next few episodes, Joanie and Jane will comfort each other, assist Doc Cochran with surgery, attend William Bullock's funeral, and finally participate in the wedding celebration of Alma Garret and Ellsworth. The latter event is a revelation, as Joanie cajoles Jane into taking a bath, dressing in women's clothing (including undergarments), carrying a bouquet of flowers, and eventually even dancing.

WOMEN'S CHOICES

The closing scene of "Boy the Earth Talks To," Alma and Ellsworth's wedding, is a montage of the tenets the Cult of True Womanhood applied to Victorian women, no matter their class. Through her marriage, Alma Garret allows the men and women of Deadwood to participate in a time-honored ritual. Her adopted daughter, Sofia, the flower girl and Trixie, the bridesmaid, precede the bride down the stairs. And although under normal circumstances, Trixie would not have been a member of the wedding party, her bond of friendship with Alma overrides convention. Trixie, after all, had been the woman Alma turned to for advice on abortion when she discovered she was pregnant, and it was Trixie who also arranged Doc Cochran's prenatal visit with Alma and her marriage to Ellsworth to prevent the stigma of unwed motherhood.

The marriage vows are repeated in a public ceremony, so all present will understand that Alma and Ellsworth have entered into a legal covenant. What should be a most private exchange is accomplished in a very public way. Thus, the concept of domesticity as the true calling of women is reinforced. Even on the frontier there was a widely held belief in the ideology of the Cult of True Womanhood that preached such virtues to all women regardless of their social or economic class. Farmwomen, poor women, and working girls—all began to aspire to true womanhood. Unfortunately, few in their situations ever achieved such glorious domesticity. Some prostitutes did eventually marry and become part of the community. How was this possible? The belief that women should become wives and mothers overrode other considerations, and the concept of a fresh start in life was also paramount in the ideology of the American West. So what one had been in a previous state or part of life could be erased or re-imagined in the West.

Breaking free of stereotypes is difficult in Western history. The story of the West, the frontier myth, and the overwhelming sense of adventure continue to engage us. The Western legend invokes a sense of people challenged by the pioneering experience, made larger and better for it. But the gender bias underlying Western history has led us to believe that stalwart men and incidental, unimportant women built the West. The men are so dominant that the women are all but crowded off the stage (Murphy 7). The women of *Deadwood* operate within an extremely limited set of options, but the series' genius is that it is subtle enough to show an interesting variety of strategies women adopt to maneuver their way through those narrow options, despite the fact the majority of the women are prostitutes, and all they can aspire to is being a madam.

The other woman who manages to make space for herself outside the narrow confines of acceptable Deadwood behavior is Calamity Jane, who does this by co-opting the male lifestyle. Nothing on *Deadwood* makes one more of a man than the ability to cuss with distinction, and Jane has one of the most amazing repertoires of vulgarities and curse words in the camp, which in some odd way makes her the best man in the camp, as well.

The women of *Deadwood* have made a choice to come to a place where there are no rules—Deadwood is, at least in the beginning, completely lawless. In *Deadwood* some of the women, like Alma Garret, Martha Bullock, Calamity Jane, and Joanie Stubbs are given the opportunity to discover who they want to be and choose their own identities. As Trixie tells Alma, "Few choices are ours to make. Others should stay the fuck out of the process" ("The Whores Can Come," 2.11).

PART 3
DEADWOOD
AND GENRE

CHAPTER 7

"THE HORSE DOESN'T GET A CREDIT"

THE FOREGROUNDING OF GENERIC SYNTAX IN DEADWOOD'S OPENING CREDITS

AMANDA ANN KLEIN

Though there is little critical work devoted to the study of opening credits, they are arguably one of the most important segments of the text, both in film and on television, because they are the first images the viewer encounters. The original purpose of a film's opening credits was mostly utilitarian (i.e. to "credit" all of the individuals who contributed to the production of the film), and so it is not surprising that style, usually plain typography over a still image, reflected function (Haskin 10). By the 1950s, filmmakers were beginning to realize that they could use this obligatory segment in service of the film as a whole—to set up the film's overall themes or images, provide a prologue for the narrative, or establish a mood.[1]

Until recently, US television credits also served a simple function, namely to introduce the show's cast, creators and guest stars, usually against the backdrop of a few images representative of the series. The credit sequences which open *Friends* (1994-2004) and *The Cosby Show* (1984-1992), for instance, have their primary cast members dancing in various locations as the show's theme song plays, while *The Sopranos'* (1999-) opening credits depict Tony Soprano (James Gandolfini) driving through New Jersey, past locations which feature prominently in the series.[2] While these segments certainly work to establish a mood for the program which follows, the images we see are primarily lifted from the diegesis of the series. In recent years, however, the opening credits to several acclaimed television series, including *Deadwood* (2004-), *Desperate Housewives* (2004-), *House* (2004-) and *Six Feet*

Under (2001–2005), among others, have replaced this traditional format with a sequence of disconnected, "dreamlike" images that are more "generic" than specific, more connotative than denotative. These credit sequences clearly borrow their stylistic cues from music videos, which employ chains of disparate images that stress discontinuities in time and space to evoke abstract concepts (Kinder 3).

HBO's *Deadwood* is a prime example of how opening credits can set up the broader themes, concerns and narrative goals of a television series. Rather than editing together shots of the series' main characters along with images from the 1876 settlement of Deadwood, *Deadwood's* opening credits combine a chain of generic, often highly abstract images of life out West: a wagon wheel pushing through the mud, a block of ice splashed with the blood of freshly slaughtered meat, fingers raking through a pan of pay dirt in search of gold, a prospector pulling a rotten tooth from his mouth, a buxom woman sinking into a tub of water, and so on.

These images are intended as bursts of instantly recognizable, multilayered meanings, culled from almost two hundred years of Western tradition, both in print and on film. The close-up of a wooden wheel, for example, acts as both a metonym for the covered wagon, as well as the great Westward migration of the 1800s in general. This simple image represents the arduous journey made by Eastern adventurers as they sought a new life in the West.[3] Likewise, the scruffy man who inspects and then disposes of his tooth serves as visual shorthand for the prospector's mentality. During the first years of the gold rush, when a man could uncover incalculable fortunes at any moment, a rotten tooth is of little consequence. His face, creased from hard prairie living and toiling in the sun, is that of a man intent on striking the bonanza he knows must surely be waiting for him in the next pan of pay dirt. Finally, the image of the bathing woman, drawn in a few bold strokes, conveys a wealth of information to the viewer. "Proper" Eastern ladies, as we are told in Westerns like *Stagecoach* (John Ford, 1939), *My Darling Clementine* (Ford, 1946), and *The Harvey Girls* (George Sidney, 1946), wear dark suits, high, starched white collars and tight corsets. These women, who represent culture, education and domesticity, have difficulty understanding the Western hero's "uncivilized" way of life,[4] and as a result, spend much of their screen time attempting to "Easternize" him. In contrast, the bathing woman's nudity, griminess and lack of modesty (we can see men milling around her open door) point to her status as a prostitute, a woman who understands and embraces the Western mentality. Though we only see this woman from behind, the simple act of sinking into the tub, presumably after a long day's "work," illustrates the weariness that comes with her independence from the feminine codes of the East. As Robert Warshow explains in his seminal essay "Movie Chronicle: The Westerner" (1954), "nobody owns [the prostitute], nothing has to be explained to her, and she is not, like a virtuous woman, a 'value' that demands to be protected" (108).

Beyond providing the viewer with a glimpse into the difficult, dirty living conditions of life in the Old West, this opening sequence also efficiently establishes the central syntax of the Western genre, namely the archetypal struggle between civilization and savagery. As numerous film scholars have noted, the Western (and all film genres for that matter) revolves around a binary opposition reflecting an irresolvable contradiction entrenched within the American psyche. Each new entry in the genre represents another attempt to negotiate and resolve the particular cultural conflict generated by these opposing forces.

In *Hollywood Genres* (1981), Thomas Schatz explains that "In addressing basic cultural conflicts and celebrating the values and attitudes whereby these conflicts might be resolved, all film genres represent the filmmakers' and audience's cooperative efforts to 'tame' those beasts ... which threaten the stability of our everyday lives" (29). Thus, a particular genre's longevity is often a sign that its conflict is of fundamental social interest—that both sides are appealing. While we demand, on the one hand, the establishment of law, order and democratic regulation in order to build a stable society, we also chafe against these restrictions and long for the anarchy, independence and freedom associated with America's frontier days.

These two sides of the Western's central conflict can be represented by numerous antimonies: East versus West, government versus self rule, white man versus Indian,[5] lady or schoolmarm versus prostitute, homesteader versus rancher, garden versus wilderness, compromise versus integrity, etc. (Belton 254-5). As an example of a "genre of order" (Schatz 35), the Western resolves its central conflict through the violent elimination of one side of this binary, rather than through the integration of these opposing forces.[6] In the Western, it is almost always the savage side of the conflict, typically embodied in the character(s) of an outlaw, a hostile Indian tribe, or an entire depraved community, which must be eliminated in order to make way for the establishment of social order.

Indeed, it is because of this ability to address social conflicts and then resolve them in simplistic ways that genre films are thought by many critics to be structures through which dominant ideologies flow. In her article "Genre Films and the Status Quo" (1986), Judith Hess Wright examines the way in which enduring American film genres, namely the Western, the science fiction film, the horror film, and the gangster film, help to reinforce the status quo by "produc[ing] satisfaction rather than action, pity and fear rather than revolt" (41). In other words, if social conflicts are given a satisfactory solution, audiences are pacified and, consequently, deterred from the desire for social change. For this reason, Wright argues, genre films almost always conclude with a re-establishment of the status quo.

Having the Western conclude with the triumph of civilization over savagery, culture over nature, and democracy over solipsism, allows audiences to continually work through and thus "naturalize" the violence of Manifest Destiny (Schatz 47). John Belton, author of *American Cinema/American Culture* (2005), supports this theory:

> Ever since the closing of the frontier and the disappearance of the old West, contemporary American audiences have needed the Western to provide them with a mythical, quasi-utopian past in which they are empowered as individuals and become members of a society whose values and beliefs are rooted in the stable realities of the land itself.
>
> (267)

The Western thus implies that, while the Westward expansion was a violent process, this violence was ultimately justified. The true Western hero, as we are frequently reminded, never draws first, though he always draws the quickest.

Of course, many Westerns, particularly those released in the 1960s and 1970s when the concepts of "civilization" and "progress" began to lose their sparkle—*The Man Who Shot Liberty Valance* (John Ford, 1962) and *Ride the High Country* (Sam Peckinpah, 1962)—also lament this transformation of wilderness into garden. However, even these Westerns, which are nostalgic for the disappearance of the American frontier, admit that its eradication is/was inevitable and necessary. In fact, such a perspective is built into the genre: in 1893, two years before the invention of the cinema, Frederick Jackson Turner declared, in a famous speech entitled "The Significance of the Frontier in American History," that the Western frontier was officially "closed." Consequently, "[t]he birth of the Western film was inextricably bound up with the death of the West" (Belton 250). Every Western, whether on film or television, has been made in the aftermath of this "death," and is therefore always an attempt to justify, negotiate and/or understand the birth of America and the American character.

In *Deadwood*'s opening credits, the images of prospectors, prostitutes and covered wagons are all entities that brought "civilization" to the West or are the result of the arrival of civilization. Indeed, these images move in an almost chronological fashion—from the first wagon trains and prospectors, to the arrival of the women who keep said prospectors happy, to the establishment of businesses (signified by the image of a butcher reaching for a chicken in a wicker cage). Each represents a new, more enduring sign that the white man from the East has set up its claim on the West. The final images of the sequence are, significantly, all filmed indoors, indicating that permanent buildings, as opposed to tents, have been erected in Deadwood. We see a hand of poker, a line of shot glasses awaiting liquor on a gleaming mahogany bar, and a brass scale weighing a pile of fine gold dust. The existence of these spaces of leisure points to the establishment of a permanent civilization in the West.

This Western iconography, particularly the images of prospectors and prostitutes, can also represent the savage side of the Western binary, but only when opposed with a more obvious signifier of civilization such as the Eastern tenderfoot or the schoolmarm. Along the same lines, the aforementioned images only denote civilization when opposed with a clear signifier of savagery or wilderness, which is why, in the opening credits, they are repeatedly interrupted with shots of an unbridled horse, a classic symbol of the uncontainable frontier spirit, running through the landscape.[7]

It is important that these shots maintain a consistent screen direction (right to left and/or background to foreground) because it implies that this horse is running screen left, towards the wilderness of the West and away from the civilization of the East. Each time the viewer is confronted with an image of permanence, the camera cuts to the same horse, running, but always against a new background. In other words, the horse is continually fleeing the confines of law, order and community, only to find that civilization keeps catching up with him. This push and pull between wilderness and civilization is integrated into one shot towards the end of the sequence, when the horse runs through a makeshift prospector camp on the banks of a river. In attempting to flee society, the horse finds that he has run straight into it. There is nowhere left for him to run.[8]

The final shot of this opening sequence, of the horse coming to a stop in the settlement of Deadwood, is the most important thematically because it is the first *specific* image to be taken from the series itself (as opposed to the previous generic images of wheels and faceless women). Having the horse end its journey in the location where the series is based and then disappear creates the impression that the settlement of Deadwood marks the final disappearance of the frontier. Westward expansion is over, the wilderness is gone, and the white man is here to stay.[9] The reason we know that this final shot is filmed in Deadwood is because in a puddle by the horse's feet we see the distorted reflection of the Gem.

This brothel and saloon, owned by Al Swearengen, is a locus for the town's criminal elements, a place where men can revel in the most depraved forms of civilization. Within its wooden walls dope is purchased and distributed, women are sold and abused, and men are shot, stabbed, and impaled on deer antlers for offences big and small. "Civilization" has arrived in the West, this final shot implies, but it is hardly the civilization with which America wishes to identify itself. In fact, the civilization residing in the Gem, and Deadwood as a whole, can hardly be differentiated from the savagery it has supposedly replaced for the good of the community.

Here we can see how the carefully selected images of *Deadwood*'s opening credits provide, within a few minutes, the thematic progression of the classic film Western. Much like a shootout at high noon, these images represent the battle between the forces of civilization and savagery that are constantly at play in the Western. Of course, *Deadwood* is *not* a classic film Western; it is an HBO series. And as viewers know from previous encounters with programs created by that cable powerhouse, such as *The Sopranos* (1999–) and *The Wire* (2002–), HBO can never simply present a straightforward account of a seemingly straightforward genre.[10] *Deadwood*'s vision of the Western relies on the ambiguity, or perhaps even the impossibility, of morality and values over the traditional and more digestible binary oppositions of the classic film Western.[11] The opening credits foreground this opposition between civilization and savagery precisely because these concepts do *not* appear as oppositions within the series itself. They are, rather, the twin faces of America, past and present. Every episode of *Deadwood* opens with this "prehistory," this shorthand of the genre's central concerns, in order to further highlight the series' own deviance from the classic Western model.

Simply put, *Deadwood* is different from its televisual and even its filmic predecessors because it does not work to disavow what the viewer knows to be true—that the differences between civilization and savagery, which the Western labors to establish, are nonexistent. Robert Warshow argues that this generic disavowal is one possible explanation for the enduring appeal of the Western: "One of the well-known peculiarities of modern civilized opinion is its refusal to acknowledge the value of violence. This refusal is a virtue, but like many virtues it involves a certain willful blindness and it encourages hypocrisy" (121). In fact, one of the truisms of the Western is that progress, civilization, and, by extension, the creation of America, was only possible through the establishment of laws and government and the elimination of criminality and anarchy. This syntax is necessary in order to justify the American myth of origins and to rationalize capitalist development.

Since Turner delivered his turn-of-the-century lecture on the American frontier spirit, filmmakers and audiences have used the genre to romanticize and legitimize the nation's cruel and violent history (Saunders 6). Therefore, to deny the differences between civilization and savagery, to argue that these labels are arbitrary and imposed from without, is, in effect, to deny the nobility of America's mythologized past as well as its present. *Deadwood* implies not only that our present civilization was built on a foundation of savagery, but also that there was never a difference between the two in the first place. As Sol Star explains to his partner, Seth Bullock, who has reservations about using Swearengen's capital to back their banking venture, "If money had to be clean before it was recirculated we'd still be living in fucking caves" ("Requiem for a Gleet," 2.4).

Indeed, that the settlement of Deadwood exists at all is primarily the result of Al Swearengen, the series' unquestioned hero, and his ability to understand the symbiotic relationship between civilization and savagery and the necessity of violence in the past to the erection of the American democracy and capitalism we celebrate in the present. It is therefore fitting that Season Two concludes with Mr. Wu, who has just slaughtered all of his business rivals, cutting off his queue (a marker of his ethnic difference) and pronouncing to Swearengen, "Wu! America!" Recognizing Wu's meaning, that violence begets progress and ensures the future of a burgeoning nation, Swearengen smiles and assures him, "That'll hold you tight to her tit" ("Boy the Earth Talks To").

In his oft-quoted essay "Theses on the Philosophy of History" (1940), Walter Benjamin ruminates on the process by which history is understood and recorded. He points out that the past is regularly deployed as a justification for the present, that "[t]here is a secret agreement between past generations and the present one. Our coming was expected on earth" (254). The history of Westward expansion, as told by the Western, in print, in the cinema and on television, is that this expansion was inevitable, necessary, and justified. We see the violence of our past and the civilization of our present and conclude that one eradicated the other, and for the better. The secret of the Western, continuously disavowed in text after text, is that there is no difference between civilization and savagery—civilization *is* savage. As Benjamin argues later in the same essay, "There is no document of civilization which is not at the same time a document of barbarism" (256). *Deadwood* is one of the few Westerns to come to terms with the implications of this statement, that American society was built upon a foundation of inhumanity and bloodshed. In *Deadwood* this history, unlike the murdered corpses digesting in the bellies of Mr. Wu's hungry pigs, is left out in the open to bloat and decay before our eyes. The opening credits to *Deadwood* work to establish the supposed opposition and separation between civilization and savagery in order to prepare the viewer for a series that complicates and questions an often-romanticized period of American history.

CHAPTER 8

ROBERT PENN WARREN, DAVID MILCH, AND THE LITERARY CONTEXTS OF DEADWOOD

JOSEPH MILLICHAP

The enduring significance of Robert Penn Warren, Renaissance man of modern American letters, in our popular culture is revealed by the second movie adaptation of *All the King's Men* in 2006, a century after his birth and six decades after its first publication. The pervasive influence of his creative example is also demonstrated by the award-winning productions of David Milch, maverick genius of contemporary television. The second season of his popular and provocative HBO series *Deadwood* in 2005 occasioned a *New Yorker* profile by Mark Singer in which Milch revealed his profound respect for Warren both as a writer and as a man. From 1965 to his death in 1989, Warren successively acted as Milch's teacher, mentor, and colleague, but the profile also reveals that the senior figure still serves as a role model for the younger in terms of his life as well as of his work. Warren's creative canon demonstrates a number of influences on and intertextualities with Milch's diverse productions, providing insight into the literary contexts that make *Deadwood* high quality television.

At first glance, critical comparison of the Hollywood eccentric with the Yale conservative, of the self-proclaimed addictive Milch with the austere Warren, may seem something of a stretch, but their parallels prove too numerous to ignore. In addition to Milch's revealing commentary on Warren, the two writers also share many subjects, modes, and styles—albeit in differing genres. The film adaptations of *All the King's Men* in 1949 and 2006 provide a link here, however, especially when we recall that Warren wrote his own theatrical versions of his novel and assisted director Robert Rossen with its first movie production. In *Deadwood*, Milch presents a dramatized and filmed serial novel in one-hour installments while drawing on literary sources ranging from Shakespeare to Dickens to the classic movie Western, a genre Milch attributes to Jewish studio moguls (Havrilesky). While Warren is more concerned with popular culture than his academic critics have acknowledged, Milch is more involved in a high culture critique of the American experience than his reviewers have recognized.

Robert Penn Warren was born in 1905, the first child of Robert Franklin Warren and Anna Ruth Penn, devoted and ambitious parents who had recently settled in Guthrie, Kentucky. Warren's hometown was the thriving agricultural and railroad center of the Black Patch, the dark-fired tobacco country in Western Kentucky and Tennessee. Both Warren's parents were descended from established agrarian families, and, coincidentally, both of their fathers had served as captains in Nathan Bedford Forrest's Confederate cavalry corps. Warren grew up only a generation after the Civil War, and as a boy he lived through one of its many aftershocks in the bitter Tobacco Wars of his region during the early twentieth century. Wherever he would live and whatever he would write, Robert Penn Warren would remain a Southern writer at heart, if not always in mind.

Warren's literary genealogy was a great deal less regional, however. Both sides of his family were educated and well read; his mother was a schoolteacher before and after her marriage, while his father had studied the classics and published verse as a young man. Encouraged by his parents and teachers, Warren excelled at local schools, and he enrolled at Vanderbilt University in nearby Nashville in 1921. In some respects, the university was still a Methodist backwater, but no place could have proved better suited for the development of a young Southern writer. Although the burgeoning Southern Renaissance had its other outposts, the Nashville Fugitives were already in residence when Warren arrived there. No other venue was as amenable to the shock of modernity, as the younger Fugitives often considered Southern subject matters in terms of Modernist forms. In particular, the most important inheritance for Warren was T. S. Eliot's *The Waste Land*, as evidenced by his not only reading but also memorizing this Modernist masterpiece on its publication in 1922.

Perhaps the pure bravado of young Warren's appreciation reveals the intellectual intensity and the artistic ambition that would drive the public aspects of his career. Warren remains the only person to have won Pulitzer prizes both for fiction and for poetry, the former in 1947 for *All the King's Men* (1946) and the latter in 1958 for *Promises* (1957) and again in 1979 for *Now and Then* (1978). The Warren canon includes nine other novels, a volume of short fiction, a score of poetry collections, a verse drama, several plays and screenplays, as well as significant cultural criticism, such as *The Legacy of the Civil War* (1961). He also helped found the literary New Criticism that dominated American letters for a generation in a series of influential texts written with Cleanth Brooks. So Warren would have remained a formidable figure on the literary scene of mid-twentieth-century America, even if he had published nothing after reaching the customary retirement age of sixty-five in 1970. The writer he was at that point is the one recognized by the traditional criticism—the Renaissance man of American letters. Recently, readers have recognized that Warren's collections published between 1970 and 1985 reveal a different writer, a major twentieth-century poet; his later poetry is less derivative from the early Modernists and therefore more open in form, more evocative in tone, and more personal in subject matter.

A century after his birth, it becomes clearer that Warren's *alterswerk* (his "age work," to literally translate that useful critical term) forms only one part of his lifelong project of bridging the gulf between high and popular culture in America. This effort began as early as the 1930s when the economic and social dislocations of the Depression decade transformed the Fugitives, essentially an aesthetic gathering focused by the traditions of high culture, to the Agrarians, a broader intellectual grouping aware of popular culture as well. Warren's contribution to the Agrarian anthology *I'll Take My Stand* in 1931 was a conflicted essay on race in the South; written from the perspective of his Rhodes scholarship at Oxford and entitled "The Briar Patch" after a Brer Rabbit tale, the piece recognized regional injustice but offered only the impractical solution of agrarianism in an industrial age. Almost immediately, Warren published his first fiction, the long story "Prime Leaf" (1931), that clearly dramatizes the persistent failures of the Southern tradition in the depredations of nightriders during the earlier Tobacco Wars in the Black Patch.

In the 1930s and into the 1940s, Warren's impulses toward high culture were confined for the most part to his poetry and literary analysis, while his fiction and cultural commentary were involved to a greater extent with popular culture. Exceptions exist, of course, as with his long narrative poem "The Ballad of Billy Potts" (1944), which was based on a Kentucky folktale and popular history. His first published novel, *Night Rider* (1939), extends the compass of the earlier story "Prime Leaf," while *At Heaven's Gate* (1943), his second novel, dramatizes the turbulence of Tennessee politics in the preceding decades. It was only with his third and best-known novel, *All the King's Men*, in 1946 that Warren truly entered the realms of popular culture. Loosely centered on the historical figure of the colorful Louisiana politician Huey Long, Warren's narrative skillfully weaves the popular story of his political persona with that of a faintly autobiographical narrator who allows the incorporation of high culture perspectives on Southern history. The novel was chosen for a Book-of-the-Month Club selection, and then earned the Pulitzer Prize for Fiction; a movie adaptation of *All the King's Men* appeared in 1949, and it won the Academy Award for Best Picture in turn.

Born in 1945, a generation after Warren, David Milch grew up in suburban Buffalo, New York, where his father was a prominent surgeon and his mother a member of the city school board. As Milch told Warren's authorized biographer, Joseph Blotner, in a 1988 interview, he became "a Jewish country day school boy" (3). At Yale, Milch's major advisor in English was R. W. B. Lewis, an eminent scholar of American literature, and his teachers included Cleanth Brooks, theorist of the New Criticism, as well as Robert Penn Warren. Milch went on to earn an MFA at Iowa, later teaching there and at Yale while publishing poetry and fiction. During the early 1970s he assisted his three distinguished professors with the editing of their anthology, *American Literature: The Makers and the Making* (1973). About this experience, Milch says, "I never really got an education until I began to do that work for them" (Blotner 1). Careful considerations of his television productions, especially *Deadwood*, reveal not only how much Milch learned from his mentors by way of their own creative and critical legacies, but how much he is influenced by the great traditions of American literature he discovered through them. "Warren spread out all the literary artifacts of American culture for me to study, as part of my working for him on that history of American literature" (Singer 205).

In 1982, a former Yale classmate recommended Milch as a writer for the breakthrough television series *Hill Street Blues*; his initial script, "Trial By Fury," fictionalized the murder of a nun and earned him both an Emmy and the Humanitas Award. With this initial success, Milch left academe for full-time work on the series as a writer, an editor, and finally a producer. After *Hill Street Blues* concluded in 1987, Milch produced the unsuccessful spin-off *Beverly Hills Buntz* and the short-lived press drama *Capital News* (1989). In 1992, he once again teamed with *Hill Street Blues* producer Steven Bochco to create the highly praised and recently concluded series *NYPD Blue*. Milch came to control these productions to the point that he became their *auteur* in filmic terms, complicating the collective methodology of a television ensemble and culminating in his separation from *NYPD Blue* in 1997. After that, he was involved with a number of critically acclaimed projects, most notably *Big Apple* (2001), an sixty-minute drama series set in the New York City FBI office. Admitting that he struggled with personal demons including the abuse of multiple substances as well as compulsive gambling even while at Yale, Milch confesses that these problems were exacerbated by the entertainment world. His personal life did take a more positive turn after marriage to documentary producer Rita Stern and the births of their three children in the 1980s, though only health problems in the late 1990s scared him into sobriety. He still bets, though, often on his own horses.

Like the best of Warren's works, Milch's finest creations, especially *Deadwood*, employ a distinctive, diverse, and mannered style to delineate a harshly naturalistic vision of the dark and divided depths within the American national character, an identity simultaneously and paradoxically both innocent and corrupted. In an introduction to a selection of Herman Melville's Civil War poems for an American literature anthology, Warren characterized the nineteenth-century master's style as "metaphysical" in both poetry and prose. Warren recognized that like the English poets of the seventeenth century, Melville fused physical with psychological imagery. In describing and analyzing Melville's poetry, Warren really describes his own work as well: "[Melville] was aiming at a style rich and yet shot through with realism and prosaism, sometimes casual and open and sometimes dense and intellectually weighted, fluid and various because following the contours of the subject, or rather the contours of his own complex feelings about the subject" (*Melville* 12). Thus, Warren's formulations here might be applied to Milch's methods in *Deadwood* as well; the style Warren inherited from Melville he left in turn as his literary legacy for Milch.

The most notorious aspect of *Deadwood* has become its dialogue, a striking conflation of flowery rhetoric, often verging on Shakespearean verse or Victorian prose, with rough slang and crude profanity. *Deadwood's* negative critics have reacted to this torrent of vulgarity even more vehemently than to its callous depiction of sex and violence. One commentator counted the "f-word" used some 870 times in the twelve episodes of *Deadwood's* first season (more than once a minute), and this profusion is nearly matched by the plethora of other even more startling expletives. Both poles of his characters' speech have been challenged in terms of historical realism, but Milch resolutely defends his practice in recent interviews. While he probably is enjoying his freedom from the network censors who constantly snipped at *Hill Street Blues* and *NYPD Blue*, Milch also may be ensuring the attention of cable viewers already inured to shock from earlier HBO series such as *The Sopranos*, *Six Feet Under*, and *Carnivale*.

Milch is also following Warren's example in both fiction and poetry. For example, *All the King's Men* is narrated by Jack Burden, a failed scholar become cynical political operative, who combines philosophical terminology with tough-guy slang to tell the story of Governor Willie Stark. Warren also extended this practice into his poetry. Notable examples include "The Ballad of Billy Potts" (1944) and *Audubon* (1969), both narrative poems set on a Kentucky frontier of the early nineteenth century not so much different from frontier South Dakota in the later half of that century. The narrator of *Chief Joseph of the Nez Perce* (1983), a Western epic poem set like *Deadwood* in the same years of gold fever and Indian hysteria following the first strikes in the Black Hills and the Battle of the Little Big Horn, complains of how the frontier powerbrokers "slick-fucked a land" (*Collected Poetry*, hereafter *CP*, 520). Even in the more personal revelatory lyrics of his later career, Warren balances capitalized abstractions such as "Time" and "Truth" against vulgarities similar to those heard so often on the streets or in the saloons of Milch's fictionalized Deadwood.

Other than the characters' language, Western buffs have found little to complain about in *Deadwood's* recreation of the frontier West; indeed, several critics have proclaimed it the most realistic example of the genre ever made. Milch prides himself on the historical accuracy of his production, personally overseeing even the smallest details of sets and costumes. The overall effects of this surface realism mirror a deeper, more naturalistic vision of the human experience as seen on the frontier between wilderness and civilization. All aspects of the life process are presented in a somber naturalistic vision: birth and death, youth and age, sex and violence, illness and decay, even nutrition and elimination. Perhaps the most repulsive instance is the constant disposal of murdered corpses as fodder for the pigs of Deadwood's Chinatown. Again, all of these elements mirror Warren's own naturalism, even the flesh-eating swine are found in "Go It Granny—Go It Hog," in the deceptively titled collection *Promises*. *All the King's Men* is filled with other Darwinian examples, intertextual with the Realists and Naturalists Warren admired, from Stephen Crane and Theodore Dreiser to Ernest Hemingway and William Faulkner.

In *The Mind of the South* (1940), W. J. Cash speculates that Southern history was different from that of other American regions because it evolved through the frontier mode not just once, but twice—in the ante-bellum and post-bellum eras. Warren writes consistently about both Southern frontiers—other examples not mentioned above include *World Enough and Time* (1949), *Brother To Dragons* (1953), and *Band of Angels* (1955). Writing in the 1960s, no less a critic than Leslie Fiedler considered these narratives the heart of Warren's achievement: "Warren ... has attempted the risky game of presenting to our largest audience the anti-Western in the guise of the Western, the anti-historical romance in the guise of that form itself" (392). Warren's works also consider the Western frontier directly—from the Willie Proudfit plot strand of the early *Night Rider* to the lyrics focused by the Western landscape that predominate in Warren's last poetry collection, *Altitudes and Extensions* (1985).

Warren's later lyric poetry, so much admired by its contemporary readers including David Milch, likewise presents many examples of Western landscapes and Naturalistic visions. Warren's "Going West" (1981) provides a paradigmatic example, with its startling central image of a pheasant smashed against the windshield of a car speeding across the Great Plains, so that poet and reader can see the shining mountains only through a sudden curtain of blood:

> I have seen blood explode, blotting out the sun, blotting
> Out land, white ribbon of road, the imagined
> Vision of snowcaps.
>
> (CP 455)

As the poem's persona sums the experience up, "This is one way to write the history of America" (CP 455). In his 1974 Jefferson Humanities Lecture

"Democracy and Poetry," Warren characterizes the "corrosive" vision of America's history found in our art: "and man, moving ever Westward, was redeemed from the past, was washed in the blood of a new kind of lamb" (8). "Going West" also anticipates the manner in which David Milch would rewrite the accepted history of his America in *Deadwood*, moving from the decaying cities of the East to the final frontier of the great West, like Warren in this poem, but discovering the same patterns of human violence that deny the American Dream. The opening episode of *Deadwood*'s second season ("A Lie Agreed Upon" Part 1) is titled by Napoleon Bonaparte's skeptical yet fitting definition of history.

A powerful pattern of imagery in *Deadwood* presenting this reading of American history is the exploitation and betrayal of youthful innocence. Because few children were found in a mining camp such as Deadwood, they become natural points of narrative focus. In fact, two episodes are organized around this theme, as their titles indicate: "Suffer the Little Children" (1.8) and "Childish Things" (2.8) The most significant children are the orphaned Sofia Metz, discovered after her family's massacre in the first season, and the fatherless William Bullock, adopted in the second season by his uncle Seth who dutifully wed his brother's widow in an act of patriarchal piety. Both of these pre-pubescent children seem to represent the innocent hopes forfeited by almost all the adults in Deadwood, and in so doing they become bright little pawns in their elders' shady relations. Although Sofia's life seems constantly in danger from villainous Al Swearengen throughout the first season, it is William who is killed in the second season, seemingly by chance, though some suspect foul play. William's funeral provides a thematic focus for Season Two, somewhat the same way as Wild Bill's last rites served for Season One.

Another young pair just the other side of puberty from William and Sofia are the putatively innocent Miles and Flora Anderson, who arrive in Deadwood searching for their "lost" father—significantly from Buffalo—in "Suffer the Little Children." Although their Victorian names are realistic enough for the time period, readers of American literature will recognize that they are recycled from those of the lost children in Henry James's chilling story of psychological horror, *The Turn of the Screw* (1898). Interestingly, James's biographers reveal that the author set *The Turn of the Screw* in the English country house he had just purchased because he was working through his own unhappy youth in several fictions at that time. In Milch's intertextual retelling, the young pair, ostensibly brother and sister like James's earlier children, arrive already corrupted and attempt to seduce and swindle several of the adult denizens of Deadwood. Suspected and then detected by Machiavellian and murderous Cy Tolliver, Miles and Flora of Buffalo are savagely beaten, brutally slaughtered, and callously tossed to Mr. Wu's pigs as their episode ends.

Deadwood also develops this theme of innocence betrayed in many autobiographical revelations by adult characters, both female and male, of the youthful experiences that shaped their present lives. Almost all of those Deadwood residents capable of any self-awareness and self-expression have such moments. The major female figures—ranging from the barely reputable Alma Garret and Calamity Jane, to the completely disreputable Joanie Stubbs and Trixie the Whore—all imply duplicity and perhaps physical and/or sexual abuse by literal fathers or other patriarchal figures. Interestingly enough, many of these revelations between and among the women of Deadwood come as they flock together, reputable and disreputable, in protection of the orphaned Sofia Metz, as if to prevent their past fates from befalling her in the future.

The male characters prove more reticent, though their betrayed *naïveté* becomes apparent in their relations to these same women: Seth Bullock to Alma, Al Swearengen to Trixie, Cy Tolliver to Joanie, and Charlie Utter to Calamity Jane. The most significant of these confessions come in Al's drunken dialogues while being pleasured by Dolly, a barely post-pubescent substitute for Trixie, who can only grunt her response to his tortured monologue. In "Sold Under the Sun" (1.12), Al reveals that he too is an orphan, abandoned by his prostitute mother at a Dickensian workhouse in Chicago run by "Mrs. Fat Ass ... Anderson." After little William's funeral in "The Whores Can Come" (2.11), Al confesses that the family who purchased him from Mrs. Anderson beat him mercilessly after the death of their natural son from "falling sickness." Swearengen also calls the orphanage overseer a "pimp," probably because she sold him not just Dolly but other whores whenever he passed through Chicago to revenge himself on his own past (Havrilesky). Perhaps because he was sexually abused himself, Al's uncharacteristically benevolent attitudes toward both young Sofia and William therefore might be explained by the trauma of his own life journey at the same ages as these youngest inhabitants of Deadwood.

This thematic pattern may prove most important, however, in unraveling Al Swearengen's complex relations with Seth Bullock, the central conflict of character driving *Deadwood* as a series. Despite the fact that both men can be merciless killers if their circumstances demand it, both are strangely distanced from their base behaviors. Seth, in particular, often seems a *naïf* pulled between principle and pragmatism, though Al also is sometimes unaware of his motivations, especially his better ones as with Sofia and William or with the grotesques Jewel and the Reverend Smith. Milch has compared the complex characterization of Al Swearengen to the heroic if flawed Detective Andy Sipowicz of *NYPD Blue*—a drunk, a racist, as well as a character "very much like my dad, who was complicated and driven" (Havrilesky). Elmer Milch was not only a respected surgeon but also a compulsive gambler, who early on involved the young David with the manic part of his personality and through it with the seamier side of Buffalo. As Milch put it in the *New Yorker* profile: "I was the surrogate demon who was to act and sort of expurgate the demonic in my dad" (Singer 200). Milch also implies to his interviewer that he was sexually abused by a counselor when he was packed off to camp so that his parents could enjoy the racing season at Saratoga; as Singer sums it all up: "What Milch has made of such fraught relationships, betrayals, and traumas is, in essence, his life's work as a writer" (197). So, if Al Swearengen proves another imperfect father figure, Seth Bullock then becomes something of another betrayed surrogate son seeking out his place after the death of his own adopted boy, young William.

Such themes of disillusioned innocence can be found throughout Warren's voluminous canon, but particularly in his early short fiction and his late lyric poetry, as these both explore memories of his own childhood. Perhaps the finest example in fiction is his best-known and most often anthologized story, "Blackberry Winter" (1946). While many of the later poems Warren once called his "shadowy autobiography" (CP 441) might serve us just as well, a fine instance is the one most often quoted by Milch in interviews, "I Am Dreaming of a White Christmas: The Natural History of a Vision" (1973). The logic of this tripartite lyric involves the subconscious psychology of dreams, and its settings triangulate a dreary December in Western Kentucky during the 1910s of the poet's youth, a smoggy summer in the New York City of his 1970s present, and his timeless future as implied by the first snow of the season falling on the Nez Perce Pass between Idaho and

Montana, named after Chief Joseph's gallant flight and not that far from Deadwood in the real or the symbolic geography of the West.

The poem then evolves into a naturalistic "vision" through the process of finding consequential continuities among past, present, and future. In this grim, fairytale world, three small chairs are placed for the three Warren children, and under the desiccated cedar Christmas tree wait "three packages. / Identical in size and shape" (CP 278). Unable to open his present, the persona is fearful of the implication that his parents' primal legacy is only their mortality. Then the "brown-lacquered" scene of the Kentucky past and the hazy skies, "yellow as acid," of New York City's present are altered to the West's universal whiteness (CP 276, 279). Although he will never know the exact nature of his childhood gift, Warren realizes the true nature of his birthright from his parents:

> This
> Is the process whereby pain of the past in its pastness
> May be converted into the future tense
>
> Of Joy.
>
> (CP 281)

For the New Yorker profile, David Milch told Mark Singer that he embraced "this as a creative manifesto" (199); in fact, Milch entitles one of the chapters in his course on screenwriting "Future Tense Of Joy." Summing up his influence on him, Milch has said, "Mr. Warren maintained certain disciplines that were the best lessons he gave me. As a model he was crucially important" (Singer 127).

Thus, the most significant connections between David Milch and Robert Penn Warren are more deeply personal than simply professional. As Milch puts it, Warren taught him how to be a human being by giving himself up completely to his art. He told Joseph Blotner in the 1988 interview, "You had the sense in his presence of what it took, of just how whole-souled the commitment was ... and that it was a way to stand in the world" (2). Milch, like most of Warren's more recent critics, values his mentor's poems more than his fictions, and, though he left poetry early on in his own writing career, the television *auteur* frequently rereads Warren's poetic works.

Milch then emulates Warren's creative methods by preparing himself to be found by his muse, an aesthetic version of the religious spirit. So Friedrich Kekule's remark, after his discovery of the Benzene ring in a dream, that "Visions come to prepared spirits," made its way as a salient example from Warren's creative writing seminars at Yale to Milch's screenwriting classes in Hollywood (Blotner 5, Singer 195). After watching Milch's scripting sessions for *Deadwood*, Singer judges them "equal parts master class and séance—the comparison that strikes me as most apt is channeling" (195). Associating with Warren taught Milch that even careful research and preparation must inevitably give way to a psychological, moral, and artistic commitment that cannot be compromised by any consideration aside from the personal vision of the artist.

Moral commitment may seem an strange formulation to use in regard to *Deadwood*, yet Milch insists that, despite its vulgarity and violence, all his work, including *Hill Street Blues* and *NYPD Blue*, is "profoundly moral," judgments born out by his several Humanitas awards for his writing on these shows (Nyhuis). His next project, *Big Apple* in 2001, was so named he says "not for New York City, but for the fruit from the Tree of the Knowledge of Good and Evil" (Boles). Likewise, in his own historical notes for the *Deadwood* website, Milch characterizes the thematic premise of the show as "A kind of original sin—the appropriation of what belonged to one people by another people." Similar themes are found throughout Warren's canon in works of fiction, poetry, and cultural criticism as seen above—and in "Original Sin: A Short Story" (1942), *The Circus in the Attic* (1947), or *Segregation: The Inner Conflict in the South* (1956).

In *Deadwood*, one stylistic counterpoint to the characters' incessant profanity is found in the poetic diction of the King James Bible. To underline these contrasts, a preacher arrives in Deadwood for each season. In the first, Reverend H. W. Smith, a demented Civil War chaplain, preaches Wild Bill's funeral, reading from St. Paul's epistles comparing the community of the church to the human body: "And whether one member suffer all the members suffer with it." Later, Smith is doomed by a brain tumor and mercifully suffocated by Al Swearengen who secretly shares his suffering. In Season Two, Andy Cramed, a cardsharp abandoned by Cy Tolliver to die with plague, returns born again as a self-ordained preacher who conducts young William's funeral, reading extensively from the psalms. It is as if, through his art, Milch is exploring the possibilities of both individual and collective redemption in nineteenth-century Deadwood, the very place where it would seem least likely, as well as in contemporary America, where it often seems, if anything, even less so.

As Milch says of Warren in this regard, "his poetry is an expression of a unified state of being and really is ... As close to an exalted state as one who hasn't God can get" (Blotner 5). Thus Warren became not just a mentor for Milch, or even an "avatar" to use Mark Singer's formulation in the *New Yorker* profile (194), but a humane, artistic father figure who empowered his devoted surrogate son to find his own selfhood and to create in *Hill Street Blues*, *NYPD Blue*, and *Deadwood* some of the most real, complex, and memorable characters ever to grace American television. Milch's expanding canon continues to demonstrate a number of important influences from and intertextualities with Warren's diverse works, providing insight into the literary contexts of *Deadwood* as quality television. The carefully cross-cut conclusions of the second season—with its intricate weave of the wedding celebration in the muddle of Main Street, the territorial treaty signing in the depths of Al's Gem Saloon, and Wu's sacrificial slaughter of Lee in the shadows of Chink Alley—only promise more of the same for Season Three of David Milch's *Deadwood* as a developing part of Robert Penn Warren's literary legacy.

CHAPTER 9

OLD, NEW, BORROWED, BLUE

DEADWOOD AND SERIAL FICTION

SEAN O'SULLIVAN

"Why do I imagine a snake swallowing its tail, huh? ... Whereas the warp, woof and fucking weave of my story's tapestry would foster the illusions of further commerce, huh?"

Al Swearengen, "A Lie Agreed Upon," Part 2 (2.2)

In 1864, as he was writing his first multi-plot serial novel in seven years, Charles Dickens wrote a letter to his friend and fellow author Wilkie Collins, expressing anxieties about the task before him. "Strange to say I felt at first quite dazed," he explained, "in getting back to the large canvas and the big brushes; and even now, I have the sensation as of acting at the San Carlo after Tavistock House, which I could hardly have supposed would have come upon so old a stager" (Letters 10:346). The author's notorious penchant for figurative language lands him here in the middle of a mixed metaphor. On the one hand, the act of writing is like the act of painting; and Dickens' pictorial challenge lies in the shift from the recent maller-scale enterprises of A Tale of Two Cities (1859) and Great Expectations (1860–1861)–shorter works, issued weekly–to the "large canvas" of the new object, Our Mutual Friend, which would be revealed to the public in monthly installments over the course of a year and a half. On the other hand, the act of writing is like the act of theatrical performance; and Dickens' image of stage fright reflects the amateur productions he had indulged in at Tavistock House, his former home, opposed dramatically to the daunting venue of Naples' legendary opera building.

But mixed metaphors, whatever their reputation, are often the most effective way to convey transitional states, or conditions that are difficult to name, and in any case this heterogeneous formula proved entirely appropriate for the novel he was writing, a novel built on the foundation of a mixed metaphor. Unlike *Bleak House* (1852–1853), which privileged the theme and metaphor of the courts, or *Little Dorrit* (1855–1857), which privileged the theme and metaphor of the prisons, *Our Mutual Friend* would subsist on at least two simultaneous themes and metaphors: the river and the dust. One could argue that multi-plot serial fiction, as a genre, relies on mixed metaphor as its engine. If we think of mixed metaphor as two or more competing narrative models, as different but interwoven ways of conveying a single story, we are thinking of serial fiction's genetic predisposition for alternately separating and conflating its many strands of people and events.

Dickens' self-consciousness about the task before him—his awareness that he was now going to be examined by a new audience, but one that knew all his old tricks—illustrates that his stature as the world's most popular novelist did not exempt him from doubt. The nature of this self-consciousness, and of this doubt, had been central to the mechanics of his serial fiction for a long time. One key component of those mechanics is the gap, the space between publication of installments that differentiates serial fiction from every other art form. In his letter to Collins, that gap is articulated as the gap between the writing of his last twenty-part novel and the most recent one. The two other key components, and the two other key terms of this essay, are the new and the old. Dickens accents the new in phrases like "at first" or "getting back," words of initiation or renewal, and the sense of the perpetual newness of the job comes across in the present tense confession of "even now, I have the sensation." Dickens accents the old at the end of his self-description, in the characterization of "an old stager," a seasoned thespian who has done this kind of things many times before but who still feels disoriented by his labors. The symbiosis of new and old, as the defining dialectic of his enterprise, had occupied Dickens' thoughts from the time he was a young stager, when in 1841 he ceased publication of his weekly journal *Master Humphrey's Clock*, which had featured *The Old Curiosity Shop* and *Barnaby Rudge* in succession. In an open letter to his readers, in the last issue of the *Clock*, he lamented the brief, weekly installments as "jerking confidences which are no sooner begun than ended, and no sooner ended than begun again." He promised that, after a gap of one year, he would return to the monthly, thirty-two-page episodes that had made his name with *The Pickwick Papers* (1836–1837) and *Nicholas Nickleby* (1838–1839): "I purpose, if it please God, to commence my new book in monthly parts, under the old green cover, in the old size and form, and at the old price" (*Master Humphrey's Clock*, vol. 3, before p. 409). The new would be known by the old—the old wrapping, the old length, and the old cost of a shilling.

This was not just a matter of rhetoric or economics. Dickens understood how the serial, by its nature, exists at the crossroads of the old and the new. Unlike the stand-alone novel, or a feature film, which presents itself to us *in toto*, the serial offers constantly the promise of the new—the new installment next week or next month, often bringing with it a new plotline or character that will change everything. Given its leisurely unfolding, however, the serial also draws us into the past, as old characters appear and disappear, as old green covers pile up by our nightstand, or old episodes of a program burrow into our memory, creating a history commensurate with our lifespan, unlike the merely posited past and present of a text we can consume in a few hours or days. Every reading, or every watching, requires a reconnection of old and new, an iteration of past and present; and within a week or a month, what was new will get funneled into the old.

And, with *Our Mutual Friend*, Dickens would make this complex set of transactions—between author and public, between memory and sensation, or simply between installments—the very stuff of his novel. The first two chapters of the book make the struggle and confusion between old and new the focus of our attention, between a character who "was no neophyte and had no fancies" and characters who "were bran-new people in a bran-new house" (*Our Mutual Friend* 17). *Our Mutual Friend* is a serial novel about seriality. Even its less ostensibly metafictional themes, the river and the dust, themselves conflate the old and the new. The river mingles and dissolves, and it coughs up dead bodies (the old) that will serve new purposes for the living; the dust mounds, that is vast mountains of trash, prove to be immensely valuable, the old unwanted stuff of urban life recycled into new goods and livelihoods. In scope and substance, this was Dickens' most urban novel, his most explicit wandering through modern London, a city at once old, fraught with traditions desirable and undesirable, and new, bringing in fresh arrivals and fresh capital every day.

This chapter considers *Deadwood*'s relation to this fictional ancestor, and specifically it considers the second season as an allegory of seriality. Second seasons of television programs often make us aware of the peculiar parameters and difficulties of serial narrative, since both creators and viewers begin negotiating the tension between new and old more closely than at any time before. Every first season maintains the gloss of a new coat, even as its installments start to create a backlog of the old; and by the time the third season makes its appearance, the obligatory complaints about "jumping the shark" (a decline in quality) kick in, the gulf between the cherished old and the disappointing new turned into a dangerous chasm, rather than the negotiable gap that Dickens addressed. I emphasize *Deadwood*'s second season not simply for conceptual reasons but for specific, internal ones, since the season's structures and stories echo the connection between seriality *of* story and seriality *as* story that Dickens exploited in *Our Mutual Friend*.

Mark Singer's *New Yorker* profile of David Milch, *Deadwood*'s creator and chief author, provides one version of this issue. In a discussion with his writing staff that preceded the creation of the second season, Milch endeavored to hammer out the tone and arc of the new campaign. "The first season is about the individuals improvising their way to some sort of primitive structure," he explained. "There's a provisional sense of promise." This summary applies not only to the characters living in Deadwood but to the series itself; like all new series, a primitive structure is created—an edifice of plotlines, psychological conflicts, and narrative rhythms that will make a show recognizable and distinguishable, a house like and unlike other houses on the street. In the second season, by contrast, "what ought to haunt the atmosphere is that the gold may have dried up. ... What you want every character to be looking at is 'What's the worst-case scenario? What's the disaster scenario? They sink the shafts and there's nothing there'" (Singer 195). The new season will be about the old haunting the new, in other words, the fear that there is nothing new to find underground. That disaster scenario is also the disaster scenario of serial authorship itself, whether within one series or at the start of a new narrative. What if the writer sinks the shafts and there's nothing there? As Dickens' concerns about the large canvas and the San Carlo indicate, every new moment of art can be haunted by every old moment of art, and no art form bangs the old and the new together more forcefully and regularly than serial fiction.[1]

The situation of the second season of *Deadwood*, its crossroads of old and new, presents not just a generic aspect of seriality, but also a manifestation of the energies of this serial drama in particular. The series takes place in a town built as the crossroads of old and new, a locale defined by the daily influx of new people that transformed the local population, in the year between 1875 to 1876, from the hundreds to the thousands (Parker 228), and the friction created between locals and newcomers. Near the end of the first season, Tom Nuttall, the longest-serving resident among the recurring characters, tells Al Swearengen that he has lost touch, amid all the turnover: "I feel like the camp's getting away from me. ... I don't feel like I know anybody no more" ("Jewel's Boot Is Made for Walking," 1.11). *Deadwood* rubs explicitly against dominant narratives of the West, as either a virgin pastoral territory, a new and easily available geography championed by ideologies of expansionism, or as a space fit for new urban environments, deracinated from the past, exemplified later on by Las Vegas, a city that is all-new, all the time. The work of Deadwood, by contrast, is the work of unearthing the past: getting gold out of the ground, minerals that have rested out of sight for millions of years, old material—material given almost mythological embodiment in the person of George Hearst, whose status as "the boy the earth talks to" makes him a figure of ancient fable. In the second-season finale, he will descend upon the town as the experienced, older man, a fixed asset in this maelstrom of changing fortunes.

What is old and what is new in Deadwood is constantly up for debate. In the first season, Alma and Brom Garret seem to represent the older, established United States of America, the cultured Northeast; yet their hopeless newness in this unfamiliar setting makes them vulnerable. Al Swearengen, whose scheming mind and apparent lack of sentimentality align him with the new or the future, is rumored to be from England, a civilization even older than the Garrets'; when asked about his connections with British nobility, he claims, "I'm descended from all them cocksuckers" ("Deadwood," 1.1). The muddying of old and new defines the town of Deadwood, which is in fact not a town but a "camp," a word that connotes the temporary and which seemed entirely appropriate during the series' initial episodes. By the start of the second season, however, that designation is itself outdated, no longer useful in conveying the permanent (no longer primitive) structures that run along the thoroughfare. Deadwood's ontological fuzziness, as a place both new and old, and a place neither new nor old, serves as a major storyline in both seasons, as magistrates and commissioners from outside the camp seek to annex it, make it part of some older and recognized entity. The second season brings that fuzziness, that condition of being both and neither, even more to the forefront than did the first.

The fuzziness might be given another name, a name that Dickens provides in the very first paragraph of *Our Mutual Friend*, in a gesture that once more ties directly into the special practice of serial fiction. The novel opens on the Thames, in what might be called an establishing shot:

> In these times of ours, though concerning the exact year there is no need to be precise, a boat of dirty and disreputable appearance, with two figures in it, floated on the Thames, between Southwark Bridge which is of iron, and London Bridge which is of stone, as an autumn evening was closing in.
>
> (*Our Mutual Friend* 13)

This paragraph is a sonata of vagueness, from the lightly imprecise date of "these times" and the unnamed group that is "ours," to the blatant refusal to be "precise," to "a" boat with two "figures" (male? female? people at all?) seemingly without direction ("floating"). The fuzzy language is completed by the mood of an autumn evening—a moment of transition both in the seasons and the day—and in the final word, "in," which repeats the first word of the paragraph and moves us toward the fuzzy center rather than toward the sharper edges. We begin the book "between"—not just between two bridges but between day and night, between summer and winter, between some time and another—and between-ness will be a major preoccupation of the novel.[2] The most visceral manifestations of the between are to be found in Mr. Venus' curiosity shop, which features "a muddle of objects ... among which nothing is resolvable into anything distinct," among them the unresolved creation of "a Hindoo baby in a bottle," a variety of taxidermical items, and loose body parts, including the leg of his sometime associate Silas Wegg.[3] Between-ness also defines the novel's nominal and schizophrenic hero, John Harmon, who takes on three different names and identities and spends the book shuffling between one and the other; and the "mutuality" of the title points to a thing shared by, or between, two other things.

The between is another term for the gap, the third item of seriality, along with the new and the old. We are always close to the beginning or end of something in a serial narrative, and so the space between has its own special import, whether between one installment and another or in the space within an installment, when old and new are both temporarily at bay. I would argue that between-ness takes on an even more complicated role in a narrative that unfolds not patiently over twenty months but intensively, in three-month clusters separated by nine or more fallow months. The second season of an HBO serial draws us particularly into the between, since we have clearly moved away from the newness of the first year, and we may imagine that we are still several years away from the final episode of the series, a terminus invisible to us at this point. It is precisely the synthesis of old, new, and between that Milch examines in the second season, right from the start.

The first shot of the season opener, "A Lie Agreed Upon," Part 1 (2.1), shows us the stagecoach from Bismarck on the road, on its way to camp. We might say that a vehicle full of strangers, as a dramatic device, is itself a traditional hybrid of old and new, an ancient and familiar narrative technology for introducing a batch of unknown characters into a prefabricated situation. And the stagecoach, as a bringer of the new, will indeed play a major part in the season, its arrivals spaced out to push the plot along. To make certain that we understand the coach's structural purpose within the series, later in the episode we are given Cy Tolliver, spying the carriage on the horizon in the company of two of his employees, and underscoring its import: "Don't the kid in all of us look forward to the new arrival? ... Who could it be? President Hayes? Maybe it's jugglers, or face painters?" Tolliver's candidates for the stage's occupants are so unlikely as to make us wonder what they might connote; the jugglers and face painters suggest old-fashioned forms of entertainment, while the freshly elected Rutherford B. Hayes suggests a new era, and combined they suggest exactly what *Deadwood* is and is not at this moment, an entertainment both old and new.[4] The stagecoach motif will signify the new, much more than the old, in this new season. Its recurrence will be all the starker when we consider the stagecoach's virtual absence in the first season, as a system of introduction: the series' major characters either already live in Deadwood before the story begins (Al and Trixie; E. B. Farnum; Brom and Alma Garret; Doc Cochran; Ellsworth; Reverend Smith) or drive themselves to the camp, in their own wagons (Seth Bullock;

Wild Bill Hickok, Calamity Jane and Charlie Utter; Cy Tolliver and Joanie Stubbs).

The stagecoach, as a conveyance pursing a long journey broken up into parts, a contraption not unlike serial fiction, explicitly heralds a change of dramatic apparatus at the start of the second season, one that will regularly bring incarnations of the new into the camp, each new passenger or new piece of cargo automatically making every passenger or piece of cargo that preceded it a representative of the old. The occupants of that first coach of the season will offer the most complex mixture of new and old we will see. Three of the six passengers are new whores, headed for Joanie's new bordello; a fourth is Maddie, the new co-madam of that bordello who is also called an old friend of Joanie's, and who will slyly jest about how old and unfit for service she is; the fifth and sixth are Martha and William, Seth Bullock's simultaneously new and old wife and son, two people whom he barely knows but who have been part of his family for some time, as the widow and child of his brother. All six of these people, as alloyed harbingers of the new, will be radically and negatively transformed by Deadwood, either killed (Maddie and William) or traumatized by death (Martha and the other whores). Not for the last time in this season, the new will fall victim to the old, or to other harbingers of the new. If the second season of *Deadwood* could be said to play favorites on the serial seesaw, then the new fares far worse than the old, and the coach will bring many of the new to ruin in this town. Such a dynamic speaks not only to the way that some embryonic communities create identities for themselves by favoring tradition (however new that tradition might be) over innovation, but the way Milch uses labyrinthine plots and dialogue as hazing rituals for viewers, forcing us to become locals very quickly or get the hell out of town.[5]

While the truculent villain Cy Tolliver alerts us in this opening episode to the stagecoach, and the old and new—the violent struggle within serial fiction's DNA—his more ambiguous rival Al Swearengen alerts us to another device, one that announces the ambiguous third term of seriality, the between. The device in this case is the telegraph, the revolution in communication whose poles Al and his henchmen see sprouting up from their balcony, in a scene that anticipates, and clearly rhymes with, Tolliver's. Al fulminates at this intrusion, at the "messages from invisible sources, or what some people think of as progress ... wires to hurry the sorry word and blinker our judgments of motive." This outrage represents not the bitterness of a Luddite but the consternation of someone who knows a rival when he sees one. The telegraph has the ability to organize the disparate, to bring control to a sprawling landscape, a capacity for synthesis that is Al's chief talent. Even more specifically, the telegraph is an instrument for bringing information, information that must be interpreted by an adept in order to make meaning. Al's status in the camp rests largely on his ability to decode what no one else can; Dan's announcement to his boss in "Complications" (2.5) that "they's developments that need interpretatin' on every front," and Farnum's insistence in "Amalgamation and Capital" (2.9) that "something strange has happened that I need you to construe," are just two examples among many where Al's authority in the camp rests in large part on his hermeneutic brilliance.

All interpreters operate as go-betweens, to some degree. But the telegraph particularly imitates the between-ness of serial fiction; like the serial, it appears to us in parts (poles) and gaps (wires), pieces and spaces of narrative rather than continuous conduits such as roads or rails, and if we are in the middle of the country, in a between place like Deadwood, we can see neither the end nor the beginning of the telegraph's story. Instead, we lie in the middle, bobbing on the narrative like those floating figures at the start of *Our Mutual Friend*, between one terminus and another. And indeed it is in that between-state that we as readers or viewers do most of our interpreting—speculating about plot developments or resolutions, wondering about characters and their choices, luxuriating in the details of the story's construction. Swaying between the ignorance of the new and the knowledge of the old, we are most active, most enmeshed in the narrative—most like what Al Swearengen is every day. As I have noted, the stagecoach will serve as Charon's ferry for so many in *Deadwood*'s second season, conveying souls to their demise, or serving as an instrument of death. The two most prominent exceptions to this protocol are Blazanov, the operator for the Cheyenne and Black Hills Telegraph Company, and George Hearst, the man who has invisibly pulled the strings from a distance for the entire season, and whose eventual arrival is anticipated by a telegraphic message. In other words, the interpreter and the author, the reader and the writer, those who know how to negotiate the old, the new, and the between, are the ones who survive, after parents, children, and prostitutes are damaged or destroyed.[6]

Just as that first coach brought together disparate people who would find common cause in violent experience, Blazanov in "Childish Things" (2.8) arrives on the same coach that brings Tom Nuttall's velocipede, also known as the boneshaker. Like installments of Dickens novels, or of Milch serials, which contain clusters of putatively separate storylines that in fact comment on or reflect each other, each appearance of the coach brings with it a collection of objects that are in some kind of conversation. In this case, the conversation seems clear enough, since both Blazanov's telegraph and Nuttall's bicycle represent new technologies of a kind. Both require mastery of a particular set of instruments, although they seem to split evenly into work and play, into the adult world of power and commerce and the youthful world of innocence and freedom. That division is emphasized later in the episode, when Nuttall takes a ride around the thoroughfare, in a spectacle of entertainment that draws the attention of everyone in the camp. It's an odd moment in the series, not simply because the jollity feels a little forced, but because the vision of community it provides is so rare in a place, and a series, defined by faction and contest; as a reflection of viewership and the public, the bicycle ride represents a different kind of show from *Deadwood* itself—a giddy and easily mapped route that runs counter to the dark and tricky interstitial paths of the program.

The bicycle's second appearance, in the subsequent episode "Amalgamation and Capital," that is when the new technology has started to become familiar, will in fact offer something darker and trickier. Nuttall, rejuvenated and emboldened by his toy, invites William Bullock to share a ride; as the boy awaits his chance to hop aboard, a wild horse runs through the town and stampedes him, in a fatal accident. What kills William Bullock? Nuttall tries to assume the guilt, but in fact the combination of the camp's oldest mode of transportation (horses) and its newest (the boneshaker) have conspired to slay the boy—the synthesis of old and new, or serial fiction itself. Indeed, the boy's demise is a remarkable one in *Deadwood*: it is the only death, out of all the deaths over the course of two seasons, that is the result of a blameless accident. Milch, in the *New Yorker* profile, suggests that "coincidence is God's way of staying anonymous" (Singer 7). There is no starker moment of coincidence in the series, and therefore no more patent handiwork of an anonymous God, a God in this instance named David Milch, than William's unlikely death. Sometimes fiction, especially serial fiction with its roots in melodrama and the overwrought, needs to be pushed to its climaxes not by internal forces but by external ones.

The confluence of old and new technologies sometimes occurs not on the level of event but on the level of genre, or character. Clearly, *Deadwood* draws on one of cinema and television's oldest technologies, the Western, even if by 2004 the oater had virtually disappeared from the small screen. The traditional schemes of that convention, however, are made new in multiple ways, most obviously in the claim to a certain kind of realism, as evidenced by the recurrent nudity and by that most complicated of old/new technologies, the English language. The new words here, for television, are not just "cocksucker" or other obscenities for which the series has become infamous, but the new style in which Milch fuses the mannered sentence structure of Victorian speech with colloquialisms and "low" speech. (A joke about the alleged ahistoricity of the dialogue is included in the fittingly titled episode "New Money" (2.3), when Farnum expresses surprise at a profane expression that Francis Wolcott, Hearst's geologist and advance man, presents as an old Italian maxim. "Did they speak that way then?" Farnum asks.) Milch's language has been called "deliciously literary" (Feeney), a phrase that works to justify the series as high (old) art, without quite specifying what literary veins Milch might be tapping. The most surprising and perhaps oldest vein is the soliloquy, that chestnut of the Elizabethan theater (and beyond) that popped up only through the character of Farnum in the first season. The second season, by contrast, features a wide range of monologists: not only Farnum, but also Wolcott talking to himself as he prepares to kill the prostitutes, Ellsworth chattering to a dog, Jane discussing liquor, Alma (in voiceover) speaking to her dead husband Brom in the season finale and, oddest and most persistent of all, Al conversing regularly with the severed head of an Indian chief. The head itself is a relic of the old, since it made its first appearance in the fourth episode of the first season, and it requires an active, alert audience to stitch together the old and the new. The soliloquy represents Milch's version of what other prominent HBO series have also tried to pull off: externalizing consciousness, a notoriously difficult task for the predominantly literal medium of the filmed narrative. *The Sopranos* draws liberally on dream sequences, and *Six Feet Under* traffics in scenes where the living project the presence of the dead. Milch abjures those newer, twentieth-century approaches, in favor of the antique, and the collision between what reads as "fake" or theatrical (in the intimate medium of television) and what reads as "real" (the verisimilitude of the sets, and the absence of dreams or apparitions) represents yet another one of the series' violent syntheses.

Perhaps the oddest synthesis of all, the most curious amalgam of old and new, lies in the person of actor Garret Dillahunt. In the first season, Dillahunt played Jack McCall, the shambling, droop-eyed murderer of Wild Bill Hickok; McCall escaped conviction in Deadwood itself, only to be tracked down by Seth Bullock and Charlie Utter. Dillahunt returns in the second season in a very different role, the confident, worldly, menacing Francis Wolcott, bridging the old and new roles by his very screen presence, fusing characters that might otherwise seem to have nothing in common. Milch had been party to something loosely similar in the past, when Dennis Franz played a policeman, a minor character named Sal Benedetto, on *Hill Street Blues*, and then returned, two years later, as Lieutenant Norman Buntz—who would eventually morph into Andy Sipowicz, the central character in Milch's breakthrough show, *NYPD Blue*. But those Franz characters were, to some degree, all of a piece. Here, the huge leap in social power and sophistication between McCall and Wolcott, and the direct proximity of their appearances, one season after the next, makes this later juxtaposition particularly uncanny. In effect, Dillahunt enacts the mixed metaphor of serial fiction that Dickens invoked—two parallel and perhaps incompatible versions of the same thing, here represented not by two figures of speech telling the same story but two characters made flesh in one actor. That consubstantiation matters all the more because Wolcott is far and away the most important minor character in the second season—"minor" only because, unlike the incontrovertibly major characters, he does not yet exist in the first season, and because he fails to survive the second. Virtually all the chief plots and subplots of Season Two—the running of Joanie and Maddie's Chez Amis bordello, the orchestrated rumors about overturned gold claims, Al's machinations regarding annexation, the arrival of a new contingent of Chinese workers—flow through or refract off Wolcott; likewise, the peculiarity of his past (including that prior avatar, Jack McCall) infiltrates his present. Once we are invited to consider this combination of old and new, we can, as operators and interpreters, glean connections and decodings that might otherwise seem invisible.[7]

McCall and Wolcott are both foolish and violent gamblers; McCall's boasting at the card table gets him in everyone's bad graces, while Wolcott jeopardizes his livelihood through his sadistic treatment of high-end prostitutes. More importantly, each is linked with a single dominant male figure, one who looms over his respective season of *Deadwood*, as much by absence as by presence, that is to say by the defining alternations of serial fiction: Wild Bill Hickok and George Hearst, each of whom represents a claim to authority and reputation that far exceeds anyone else's in the camp. The first season could be seen as Hickok's season, even though he is killed one third of the way through, because the recklessness and independence that he embodies articulate the early story and situation of Deadwood itself. The second season could be seen as Hearst's season, even though he does not appear until the final episode, because the corporate interests and territorial acquisition that he embodies articulate Deadwood's adolescence, the transition from tribe to system. Dillahunt's reappearance allows the series to bring the two giants into close contact, these two Americans with competing narratives about America.

McCall and Wolcott also escape punishment for their crimes, or at least punishment at the hands of Deadwood proper; McCall is last seen trussed up and headed for trial in Yankton, and Wolcott hangs himself in the closing moments of the season finale. Their evasions of the law speak to Deadwood's fear of naming itself, of becoming something definable. Swearengen conspires to get McCall acquitted in the courtroom improvised at the Gem, because he fears that any act of official justice will risk the camp's position with the US government; the magistrate tells the jury that they must use "common custom" to make their decision, putting instinct and emotion over law and civilization. The key element in Wolcott's case, in the wake of his triple murders, is not statutory governance but the pressure of economics, as Tolliver insists that the geologist be exonerated, because of the greater value, to the camp's prospects, of Hearst's beneficence; the only forceful dissenter is Charlie Utter, who delivers Wolcott a beating but does not reveal what he knows of the offense, since he has been told its facts in confidence by Joanie Stubbs. Two very different models of human relations, therefore, bear responsibility for Wolcott's acquittal: the realpolitik of big business and the personal bond between friends, each fighting for its place in the evolving scheme of the camp's way of life.

Finally, McCall and Wolcott share an affliction related to the eye. In McCall's case it is the droop, his most distinguishing physical characteristic, which a riled Hickok says looks "like the hood on a cunt" ("Reconnoitering the Rim," 1.3), an image that chillingly anticipates Wolcott's psychotic conflation of the organ of vision with the organs of reproduction. Wolcott indulges in his killing spree after he discovers that his predatory behavior toward women has been revealed to Tolliver; when Carrie, the prostitute imported precisely for his pleasure, and yet another person we have seen alight from the coach to her future demise, asks the motive for his crime, Wolcott says, referring obliquely to the fact that she has seen his genitals, "I don't want to have been seen." McCall inhabits an almost exclusively male world, in his scenes, while Wolcott's character, for all his many dealings with men, is sketched most fully in his dealings with women. The two roles provide a diptych of human behavior at its most feral, its most inexplicable, violence and sex as sources of destruction, and the watching eye, perhaps our watching eye, as implicated in both.[8]

The picture of the eye leads us into conclusion, or more precisely it leads us into introduction. The first episode of the second season finishes with Seth Bullock walking away from the house he has built for his new/ old wife and child, and we hear him read, in voiceover, the letter he wrote her describing the house's construction. Of the house's windows, he says, "being unfinished, they look like unfocused eyes." This is not a "primitive structure"—the phrase Milch used to explain the social architecture of the series' first season—but it is an unfinished one, as the second season of a continuing series is by its very nature unfinished. Seth explains that the sills and rafters of the house are made of pine, specifically "one-year-seasoned" pine—a wry indulgence on Milch's part, since of course *Deadwood* itself is made of one-year-seasoned material at this, the start of the second season. That new house, with its mismatched inhabitants, puts our eyes out of focus at the beginning of the season; but we are explicitly asked to focus back on it at the end of the season, when it has become a house filled with death, a house haunted by memories suddenly made old. The season wraps up with the wedding of Ellsworth and Alma, who marry to legitimize the child that she is bearing, produced by her affair with Seth. The wedding, in other words, encompasses the old (Ellsworth, a man of advanced years relative to his wife), the new (Alma, the widow returned to matrimony), and the between (the developing fetus in Alma's womb). Al Swearengen gets the final words on the clandestine romance that has roiled the camp all season, in the last pieces of dialogue distinct from the noise and huzzah of celebratory merrymaking. When he spies Seth drinking alone at the Gem, he bellows, "Don't you have a fuckin' home to get to?" And when he sees Seth hesitate on the way to that house, locking eyes with Alma, Al prods Seth again, though out of his target's earshot: "I believe it's to your fuckin' right." Sinister Al sends right-thinking Seth back to the uncompleted, unfocused structure that may never be a home, that may never be completed and focused, that may always hover between old and new. Seth retreats to the abode of serial fiction, seen here in that transitional state between beginning and end. All this will be old news, by the time the new season rolls around.

PART 4
THE FABRIC OF
SOCIETY IN DEADWOOD

CHAPTER 10

"LAWS AND EVERY OTHER DAMN THING"

AUTHORITY, BAD FAITH, AND THE UNLIKELY SUCCESS OF DEADWOOD

DAVID DRYSDALE

The first season of HBO's Western series *Deadwood* is framed with images of law and authority. In the opening sequence of the first episode, the audience meets Marshall Seth Bullock, who is staging an impromptu—but lawful—hanging of a horse thief to save the criminal from an angry lynch mob. The season ends with Bullock, who abandoned his post as a marshal in Montana to seek his fortune in Deadwood, angrily accepting the position of Deadwood's sheriff as the United States cavalry rides out of town. The overarching plot of the first season is resolutely concerned with bringing law to Deadwood. In the early episodes, the audience is repeatedly reminded that, since the camp is in Indian territory and therefore not part of the USA, there are no laws. However, as the season progresses, the imminence of law becomes quite apparent: in addition to the attempts of Deadwood's primary movers and shakers to establish an informal and expeditious local government and other institutions of governmental authority, the camp also has its own unwritten code of law, complete with its own procedures and punishments.

The interplay of competing expressions of law lies at the heart of *Deadwood*'s popular and critical success. With the Western considered by many critics to be all but dead, the program is an unlikely hit. Unlike other Westerns of the past ten years, most of which failed either critically or financially, *Deadwood*, I will argue, successfully feeds the audience's hunger for what Forrest G. Robinson terms "bad faith"—a covert discussion of

social injustices that a society or subgroup is uncomfortable with addressing
openly (78). It enables its audience to address its own complicity and guilt
regarding the nature of law and authority in the USA since the World Trade
Center terror attacks. The camp of Deadwood, with its precarious liminal
position between sanctioned political law and authority and the unofficial
law exercised by persons in the camp, becomes an analog for the USA and its
post-9/11 policies. Through this covert parallel, viewers can encounter their
own social guilt regarding perceived injustices born out of the Patriot Act
and the War on Terror. However, perhaps more significantly, *Deadwood* also
confronts its viewers with their fear that the American brand of democracy is
imperfect and not a government of the people but of the privileged.

I. DEADWOOD'S PLACE IN THE WEST(ERN)

As a genre designed to represent some concept of the past, the Western
is inherently linked to history. In 1953, Andre Bazin observed that the
Western's faithfulness to history was a little-known aspect of the genre. The
genre's historical accuracy, he wrote,

> is not generally recognized—primarily, doubtless, because of our
> ignorance, but still more because of the deeply rooted prejudice
> according to which the Western can only tell extremely puerile
> stories, fruits of a naïve power of invention that does not concern
> itself with psychological, historical, or even material verisimilitude.
> True, few Westerns are explicitly concerned with historical accuracy.
>
> (142)

Recognizing that the Western is not meant to be explicitly accurate, Bazin
nevertheless posits a dialectic link between the Western and history that
engages in "the opposite of a historical reconstruction" (143). He suggests that
the goal of the Western is not to reconstruct history but rather to take apart
the historical basis of the text and expose its inconsistencies and conflicts
with the public attitude. He emphasizes the Western's mythic role as a tale
meant to help its audience internalize historical matters surrounding the
creation of the text and the situation of its reception.

Since the publication of Bazin's essay, numerous critics have commented on the Western as a reflection of history. Various films have been linked to the Cold War, McCarthyism, the Vietnam War, and other American conflicts, internal and external. However, few have written on the Western in such historical terms since the end of the Cold War. Instead, theorists have focused on the postmodern nature of films as commentaries on the genre itself rather than as historical texts. Clint Eastwood's Oscar-winning *Unforgiven* (1992), for example, has been analyzed as a deconstruction of the genre, focusing on the film's presentation and ultimate rejection of classic Western archetypes of gender and justice. As interesting and significant as these theses are, they unfortunately do not address a larger issue surrounding *Unforgiven* and other recent Westerns: the question of why such a shift occurred.[1] While texts using the conventions of Westerns should be analyzed in terms of their generic implications, the historical circumstances that facilitate or inspire the reconstruction or deconstruction of the generic traits must similarly be examined.

The Western in the 1990s and early twenty-first century is a particularly interesting subject, as many critics have been eulogizing the genre since the 1980s. In 1989, a *National Review* article lamented the absence of Western films and series and suggested that the scant few that did appear were not advertised as Westerns but "as possessing qualities incompatible with the traditional form" (Lejeune 23). The early 1990s saw a small revival of the genre with films such as *Dances With Wolves* (1990), *Unforgiven* (1992), *Tombstone* (1993), and *Wyatt Earp* (1994) but, by 2004, Gary Hoppenstand felt moved to write in *The Journal of Popular Culture*, "The major A-list motion picture Western was not in cardiac arrest. It was long dead" (2). Hoppenstand observed a trend similar to the one the *National Review* reported in 1989: "the trick for producers who desperately need to market their product to those younger demographic groups is to define [the Western film] as something other than what it actually is" (3).

II. THE UNLIKELY SUCCESS OF DEADWOOD

Given this apparent public distaste for the genre, any Western that achieves any kind of popular and critical success is worthy of study. *Deadwood* debuted on HBO on March 21, 2004 and was an instant success, attaining the second-highest rating for any new HBO drama (Carter, "HBO"). A second season was ordered after only the second episode, and by the sixth episode of the series, the show occupied second place in the cable television ratings, tied with professional wrestling and close behind *The Sopranos*, HBO's flagship show (Oldenburg and Yancey). In the *New York Times*, HBO chairman Chris Albrecht speculated that *Deadwood* "feels like the new franchise we've been looking for" (Carter, "HBO"). The show also spawned multiple online fan communities and, perhaps surprisingly, resulted in a considerable boost in tourism for the real-world Deadwood, South Dakota: the small town's website hit count rose from an average between 2,000 and 3,000 monthly to 150,000. Furthermore, requests for tourist brochures about the town rose tenfold, and actual bookings saw a fifteen per cent increase (Oldenburg and Yancey).

Apparently, *Deadwood* is able to speak to audiences in a way that other Western projects have not. This success may have developed because, unlike Lejeune's Westerns "incompatible with the traditional form," the program does not seek to distance itself from the Western genre. Rather, it revels in it. The opening credits, however unique and artful, make it patently clear that the program is a Western: the sequence includes a horse running across open land, shots of alcohol being poured in a saloon, poker games, and prostitutes bathing in a metal tub. Much of the action in the show itself takes place in a saloon; and, if there were any further doubt of the show's generic affiliation, one of the primary characters in the first several episodes is Wild Bill Hickok.

Deadwood's use of Western generic conventions and its popularity lead to the question of why it has been so well received. Apparently the answer is not a general aversion to Westerns: while others, including *Open Range* (2003), have fared poorly, *Deadwood* has not, suggesting that the genre and its audience acceptance are not quite dead yet. The answer must be in the content of the program.

As has already been suggested, the popularity of the show may be explained in terms of its relationship to what Forrest G. Robinson terms "bad faith." Robinson argues that many popular texts include a covert subtext that addresses issues the society as a whole is uncomfortable with acknowledging openly (78). In American culture, this allegorical function often informs texts that deal with issues such as slavery, social stratification, and gender (80). The audience denies the presence of the covert narrative but appreciates the text's dominant, triumphal narrative. In this manner, it is able to subconsciously encounter troubling cultural or political issues while engaging with a text that is an apparent affirmation of its own values and beliefs (79). Robinson addresses the Western *Shane* (1953) specifically, noting its popularity and commenting that the reason readers return to the book and the film is "because the repression of what we have glimpsed ... keeps us coming back. These novels are popular because they enable movement toward a bearable angle of vision on matters that we can neither face for long nor fully forge" (84). Through texts like *Shane*, Robinson argues, the audience is thus able to confront its own guilt about its complicity in social injustices such as the treatment of women in American society (86). Robinson posits that this function is especially operative in modern American texts as the members of their audience

> perceive themselves as enfranchised, morally responsible actors in—and not merely passive subjects of—the world that unfolds before them. Thus their anxiety arises out of a feeling of inner complicity with power, and not from the spectacle of its threatening encroachment from without.
>
> (Robinson 87)

So, according to Robinson's theory, the success of a series like *Deadwood* may be attributed to the way it subtly addresses such social problems.

III. THE INTERTEXTUAL WEST

Superficially, *Deadwood* seems to follow the standard Western plot structure that Will Wright identifies as "the classical Western" (32). According to Wright, this is "the story of the lone stranger who rides into a troubled town and cleans it up, winning the respect of the townsfolk and the love of the schoolmarm" (32). *Deadwood*, after all, does involve a protagonist—Seth Bullock—who rides into a lawless town. A former lawman, committed at least to "the color of law" ("Deadwood," 1.1), he becomes the most morally admirable character in *Deadwood* as the series progresses. Along with Wild

Bill Hickok, he leads the posse that investigates a massacre of Norwegian settlers ("Deadwood") and establishes himself on the side of law and order when he hunts down Jack McCall, Hickok's murderer: rather than kill McCall outright, which would "be as fair a shake as [McCall] gave [Hickok]," Bullock turns the murderer over to the authorities at Yankton for a proper trial ("Bullock Returns to the Camp," 1.7). By the end of the first season, Bullock has not yet rid the town of its undesirable elements, but he does accept the position of being "the fuckin' sheriff" ("Sold Under Sin," 1.12), suggesting that he will indeed bring order to the camp.

Westerns have long been concerned with bringing order to wildness. Stanley Corkin argues that Westerns following the classical plot "portray the moment just before the 'incorporation' of the 'frontier' into the material, administrative, and ultimately ideological systems of the United States" (67). These Westerns, then, are not merely about the settlement of the West but also, as Patricia Limerick suggests, American imperialism after the Second World War (Corkin 71). Such films "bridge the gap between frontier mythology and Cold War imperatives" (Corkin 70). And Richard Slotkin contends that these Westerns "made the heroic style of the gunfighter an important symbol of right and heroic action for filmmakers, the public, and the nation's political leadership" (379–80).

While *Deadwood*'s "town-tamer" plot certainly did not emerge from a Cold War atmosphere, it nevertheless relates to a radical shift in American policy that occurred two years before its debut. The National Security Strategy, signed into law in September 2002, shifted American defensive stance from depending on "evidence of a credible, imminent threat" to adopting a preventative pose, resting "on the suspicion of an incipient, contingent threat" (Kegley and Raymond 385). The National Security Strategy emphasizes the USA's right to "stop rogue states and their terrorist clients before they are able to threaten or use weapons of mass destruction against the United States" and the importance of "advancing prosperity and freedom in the rest of the world" (*The National Security Strategy*). The language of the National Security Strategy, which paved the way for the American invasion and occupation of Iraq in 2003, is eerily reminiscent of Cold War containment policies intended to stop the spread of Communism through investment in Third World nations. If *Deadwood* is read as an example of the classical Western "town-tamer" plot, it may be a response to the re-emergence of such explicit American interventionism abroad. As Slotkin suggested after the first Iraq War, Saddam Hussein "was the perfect enemy for a modern Frontier-Myth scenario, combining the barbaric cruelty of a 'Geronimo' with the political power and ambition of a Hitler" (651). The rhetoric of George W. Bush after the terrorist attacks of 9/11 continued this myth, characterizing terrorists as bandits who are wanted dead or alive.

As a Western, *Deadwood* is an ideal text through which to address concerns related to the US role in the contemporary world. In the show's version of the past, authority is consistently morally compromised: Bullock is only able to be sheriff because Al Swearengen, ever the powerbroker, allows it. This depiction suggests that the role of the lawman come to "civilize" the town is not necessarily a positive one. In order to put himself into a position whereby he might perform his proper function, Bullock has allied himself with the very elements he should be seeking to expel from civilization. Furthermore, Bullock's reasons for "cleaning up" the camp—to make it safe for the arrival of his wife and child—are undermined by his affair with Alma Garrett. By consummating his relationship with Garrett, Bullock weakens his ties with the outside world and strengthens his allegiance with the chaotic and sexually promiscuous camp he is supposed to liberate. Through this deconstruction of Bullock's motivations and means, *Deadwood* interrogates the position of the Western hero, and, by proxy, that of the USA in contemporary politics. The series seems to suggest that in order to redeem the world, the Western hero must become one with the world's most corrupt elements.

Additionally, *Deadwood* distances itself from the themes and cinematography that usually characterize the classical Western structure by drawing more heavily on the darker, more "realistic" spaghetti Westerns of Sergio Leone. The cinematography in *Deadwood* is a departure from that of the Ford-style classical Western, which tended, of course, to favor grand, panoramic landscape shots, emphasizing the sheer size of the West. As Bazin writes, "The [classical] Western has virtually no use for the close-up, even for the medium shot, preferring by contrast the travelling shot and the pan which refuse to be limited by the frame line and which restore to space its fullness" (147). Writing in 1953, Bazin could not have anticipated Sergio Leone's use of the close-up in his 1960s spaghetti Westerns—the paradigm that *Deadwood* builds upon. In *Deadwood*, Ford-style traveling shots and extreme long shots are quite rare. Most of the story takes place within the confines of the camp, and even when characters travel, the directors instead prefer medium shots. Instead, the cinematography is often claustrophobic. Most scenes take place inside the cluttered camp, where there is barely room to move in the midst of crowds of people, businesses, and mines being built in the middle of the street.

Deadwood's mise-en-scène acts as intertextual references, connecting the text to the Westerns of the late 1960s and 1970s, heavily influenced by the Vietnam War and, amidst political and social turmoil, dedicated to deconstruction of the Western's triumphalism. As previously mentioned, Sergio Leone altered previous generic standards, using formalist cinematography that was new to the Western. He was also instrumental in popularizing a new type of hero for the Western: the anti-hero, exemplified by Blondie in Leone's "Man With No Name" trilogy. Other directors, especially Sam Peckinpah, continued what Slotkin terms "the demoralization of the Western" (591). Peckinpah's The Wild Bunch (1969), Slotkin suggests, expressed "the cognitive dissonance that afflicted contemporary ideology and [developed] responses (of a kind) to the attendant demoralization of American politics" (591). His exaggerated violence exposed the brutality of the American Western myth for an audience that was now becoming aware of the moral ambiguity of American involvement abroad. As Slotkin points out, "Instead of protecting women and children from 'the horror,' [American troops had] become 'the horror'" (585).

Deadwood is further connected to the Westerns of this period through its characterization and morality. Seth Bullock borrows mannerisms from Clint Eastwood's portrayal of Blondie, including Eastwood's trademark single-word affirmative sentence "Yeah." Additionally, as in the pictures of Leone and Peckinpah, in Deadwood there are no such things as "good" or "evil" as absolute categories. In some cases, the heroes' actions can be as suspect as the villains: even Seth Bullock performs acts that are morally troubling, such as his support of Bill Hickok's preemptive attack on Tom Mason, whom Hickok had anticipated as a threat. Deadwood also engages in the deconstruction of the Western hero: Hickok himself is a far cry from the gunfighter ideal; rather, he spends his time gambling and earning money for saloon appearances, uses his name and reputation to gain free drinks, and is wanted for "professional vagrancy" ("Deadwood").

Like Deadwood's use of the classical Western plot structure, the show's uses of the cinematography, devices, and thematics of the formalist Westerns act as allusive tools. Such devices connect *Deadwood* not only to the Westerns of the late 1960s and 1970s but also to the era's historical situations of protest and mistrust of the government. *Deadwood* becomes associated with the deconstruction and demoralization of the Western: through its cinematic referents to films that participated in a cultural reckoning of American involvement in overseas wars, *Deadwood* questions contemporary American interventionism. *Deadwood* points its readers to countercultural texts and protest movements from the past and consequently connects current acts of American adventurism—namely, the war in Iraq—with the Vietnam War.

Deadwood is thus a hybrid text, combining the structure of the classical Western with the cinematography, morality, and characterization of more formalist Westerns. Yet these elements of the text do not exist on the surface. Rather, they operate covertly in the manner Robinson describes as his "bad faith" principle: the audience participates and enjoys the dominant literal narrative that sees *Deadwood* as a triumphal story of a frontier town conquered and tamed by "civilization." However, the more allegorical subtext, built upon these intertextual references, engages the audience in a very different story that questions American interventionism. The audience connects the older, expected structures with the contemporary environment in which *Deadwood* is viewed, and through this subtle intertextual mechanism is able to encounter the problematic nature of American foreign policy and its own complicity in it as enfranchised citizens.

IV. HONEST ABE IN THE WHORES' QUARTERS

Deadwood not only confronts its audience with its involvement in American foreign policy; the program also addresses domestic politics. As the show progresses and Deadwood moves toward creating a government, additional critiques of the American situation become evident. The various exercises of law that the town engages in are examples of this: the only trial held in the camp is a sham, and the government that the people in the camp create borders upon farce. Other demonstrations of legal authority—including the connived appointment as sheriff of the "shitheel" Con Stapleton and the town meeting regarding the outbreak of smallpox in Deadwood—are equally ludicrous.

Significantly, all of these acts of law take place in Al Swearengen's Gem saloon. This is not for a lack of a better place to hold the proceedings: when a location is discussed for the trial of Jack McCall, Cy Tolliver defers to Swearengen because Al is his senior in the camp, and when the camp's civic leaders meet to discuss the forming of an "informal municipal organization—not government," the larger Bella Union saloon is rejected simply because Swearengen called the meeting ("No Other Sons or Daughters," 1.9).

Despite its status as a den of iniquity and chaos, however, the Gem is visually connected with law and order to some degree, due to a picture of Abraham Lincoln that hangs above the bar. According to Michael Bohnke, images of Lincoln in Westerns are iconic, drawn from the tradition of John Ford films. Lincoln appeared in seven Ford films, though rarely as the primary character,[2] usually representing "certain abstract terms like idealism, human rights, equality, or consciousness" (51-2). Böhkne argues that "Abraham Lincoln always stood at the top of Ford's hierarchy" and that in his films, Lincoln was the "best representative" of "certain ideal qualities of American law" (50).

Given this visual allusion, it is striking that the two choices of location for town meetings are both brothels. These settings connect the authorities in Deadwood with prostitution, a point that is exemplified during the trial of Jack McCall, when Swearengen asks the jury to retire to "the whores' quarters" to deliberate their decision. Throughout the series, money is constantly connected to law. When Bill Hickok tells Bullock "Pretty soon you'll have law here, and every other damn thing," Bullock replies by saying that he'd "settle for property rights" ("Here Was a Man," 1.4). Offers of money and goods are frequently used as a method of keeping the peace: Sol Star placates an angry customer with a free commode, and Al Swearengen frequently offers his customers free drinks and discounted prostitutes to preserve order in his saloon and in the camp in general. *Deadwood* continually suggests that money is the primary means of maintaining structure in a community; as Farnum says at the meeting that creates Deadwood's first government, "Taking people's money is what makes organizations real" ("No Other Sons or Daughters").

Money is also the prime motivation for the creation of the municipal government. In "No Other Sons or Daughters," Al Swearengen proposes the "informal municipal organization" in order to raise funds to improve the camp's esteem in the eyes of the government at Yankton. The group that meets to discuss the fundraising makes it clear that the money is not to go to civic improvements but to bribes; Bullock's suggestion of actually providing services in exchange for the money seems somewhat ludicrous in this context. Indeed, in "Mr. Wu" (1.10), Bullock's proposals to improve the camp's waste management are met with disdain by Mayor Farnum, who is troubled by the idea that the money will go back into the camp rather than to government officials in Yankton. Additionally, the sole motivation for annexation is monetary. There is no suggestion in the show that annexation will improve the camp by bringing "civilization" to Deadwood; rather, the civic leaders desire annexation because it would be good for business. Swearengen worries that the creation of the municipal organization will suggest to the United States government that Deadwood considers itself a sovereign political entity, resulting in the camp being seized rather than annexed. The result of such action would be the seizure of all assets in Deadwood. Furthermore, money motivates Swearengen to influence the decision of the court in the trial of Jack McCall. He warns the judge that he has had a vision of "government vipers" descending on Deadwood should a guilty verdict be passed. Even Sol Star speculates that "hanging [McCall] here is opening a can of worms" ("The Trial of Jack McCall," 1.5). Swearengen covers the picture of Lincoln during the trail, accentuating the absence of political idealism and equality, and the trial is clearly not a fair one: Swearengen easily exerts his influence on the verdict. Significantly, Swearengen wonders after the trial whether he should remove the picture of Lincoln from the wall.

The emphasis on money as the means and end of a political system is rampant in *Deadwood*, providing a critique that is similar to many liberal criticisms of the Bush administration. Liberal filmmakers, artists, and commentators decried the Bush administration as a government of the rich, complaining that the administration favors the wealthy. Other critics suggest that, like the municipal administration in Deadwood, the American government uses its wealth to influence other political bodies. Some, including Senator and Democratic presidential candidate John Kerry, have referred to the allies of the USA in the War in Iraq as the "coalition of the bribed" (Beaumont). Once again, *Deadwood* is drawing attention to the nature of the American political animal. The show is demonstrating the integral role of money in American politics and subtly suggesting that a system that requires capital to attain any political success may be doomed to corruption.

Ultimately, *Deadwood* presents its audience with a text that addresses their concerns about the current state of American law and politics. Most importantly, the program allows the audience to encounter its fears about its own nation. While presenting a story in the classic Western mold, *Deadwood* uses generic techniques of other Westerns as well as plot structures and characters that serve to question the triumphal nature of its own story. The end result is that audience members are encouraged to reflect upon their own fears. While it may not be true that the rich run America or that government exists to serve business, the fear that this is the case still exists, and it is this concern that is being addressed through *Deadwood*'s covert allegorical text.

CHAPTER 11

PIMP AND WHORE

THE NECESSITY OF PERVERSE DOMESTICATION
IN THE DEVELOPMENT OF THE WEST

G. CHRISTOPHER WILLIAMS

The manner in which community is formed and order becomes necessary in a lawless land has been of interest to the Western genre prior to a show like *Deadwood*. While the Western seemingly privileges independence over codependence and wildness over the civilized, consider how Stephen Crane's short story "The Bride Comes to Yellow Sky" (1898) serves as a parody of earlier dime novel Westerns by marrying off the sheriff and thus ending the rough and tumble rivalry of that sheriff and his outlaw nemesis. The outlaw, Scratchy Wilson, shuffling off into the sunset after meeting the sheriff's bride and observing, "I guess it's all off then," marks the end of the myth of the rugged, individualistic cowboy of the Old West (258), or, as Mary Lawlor puts it in "Stephen Crane's Literary Tourism," denotes the "domestication of male anarchy" in the Old West (144).

The Clint Eastwood canon would seemingly serve as a rebuttal to the claim that the Western supports domestication, since, in almost all of his Westerns, Eastwood plays an unmarried drifter who either brutalizes women (as he does in *High Plains Drifter* [1973]), disrupts a domestic situation (as he does in *Pale Rider* [1985]), or plays a widower who can re-embrace his pre-marriage savagery due to the loss of his domestic situation (as he is and does in both *Unforgiven* [1992] and *The Outlaw Josie Wales* [1976]). Yet, the presence of the domestic and the order it represents become the very focal point of many of these films. If William Munny is "unforgiven" and the violence and bloodthirstiness of the gunslinger is exposed at the film's end, it is the loss of his wife that has been the catalyst for his return to savagery. Likewise, the necessity of a domestic situation for the taming of the gunslinger is represented by Josie Wales's efforts to help a young woman and her mother find their home at the close of *Josie Wales*. It is only through such a homecoming that Wales regains his role as protector and provider for a newly formed family and is reintegrated into civilized society.

Critics like André Bazin (*What is Cinema?*) and John Cawelti (*The Six-Gun Mystique*) have simplified such themes of the Western by describing them (respectively) as concerning "the relation between law and morality" (145) and "affirm[ing] the necessity of society" (80). In an interview with Heather Havrilesky on Salon.com, *Deadwood* creator David Milch discusses a seemingly different and more complex approach to showing the development of a social order in the West. Using the same words of Saint Paul quoted by Reverend Smith at the funeral of Wild Bill Hickok in "The Trial of Jack McCall" (1.5), Milch compares a community's formation and ultimate organization to the "organism" of the body:

> But Paul says, "If the hand shall say, 'Because I am not the foot, I am not therefore the body of Christ,' is it not of the body?" In other words, because we misunderstand our natures, does that exclude us from the community of spirits? And the answer is no, it just means we misunderstand our natures. So many of [*Deadwood's*] characters misunderstand their natures, but that does not prevent us from recognizing that they're of the body of Christ. My feeling about "Deadwood" is it's a single organism, and I think human society is the body of God, and in a lot of ways it's about the different parts of the body having a somewhat more confident sense of their identity over the course of time.

In *Sixguns & Society*, Will Wright suggests that most Westerns contain an "estrangement-acceptance pattern" (74) between the Western hero and his society and that he most often acts because "the act that harms the hero also harms society." Milch's more organic notion of communal development—with its roots in religious philosophy and its odd resemblance to the fascistic metaphor of the organic body politic—may relate to Wright's sense of the individual's relationship to the larger "body" of society in the Western and the necessity for domestic organization in the interpretations of the West described earlier more so than may be readily apparent.

While it may seem that it is only in the second season of *Deadwood*—through its exploration of the awkward relationship between Seth Bullock and his wife—that the series first approaches questions about marital relationships in addition to the sociopolitical relationships of the town, I would nevertheless argue that depiction of marriage and domestication has been one of the chief means of exploring on a more individualized level the sociopolitical implications of Milch's "community as body" throughout the series. Particularly, in the first season, domestication is bizarrely represented through the symbolic marriage of the pimp, Al Swearengen, and his whore, Trixie.

While in "The Whores Can Come" (2.11), Trixie explains her inability to leave Swearengen despite his violence towards her, saying that "I've lived most of my life a whore, and as much as he's her misery, the pimp's a whore's familiar, so the sudden strange or violent draws her to him," nevertheless, the first season suggests an even more mystical and more "familiar" role between pimp and whore—that of man and wife. This seeming perversion of the biblically defined marriage of two becoming "one flesh" (Genesis 2:24) may seem the antithesis of marriage, nevertheless, if such a relationship can be reasonably seen as a "marriage," Swearengen and Trixie's domesticity as it develops in the first season certainly maintains the metaphor of the body that Reverend Smith suggests in his funeral oratory if only at the microcosmic level. Viewing the first season of *Deadwood* through this relationship then becomes a way of understanding the negotiation, reciprocity, bribery, and violence necessary to turn an anarchic group into a community at the sociopolitical level. Additionally, though, it maintains the genre's interest in how such negotiation, reciprocity, bribery, and violence become the means of turning two self-interested individuals into domestic partners who can tame their own uncivilized selves.

That Swearengen and Trixie relate through a kind of perverse marriage represented by the licentious reality of their occupations as pimp and whore as well as the biological representation used in Milch's religious language only emphasizes his need to present such a relationship in this manner. Law and legality are the stuff of political culture—the sphere that normally defines the rules of domestic relationships and marriages. Biology and organism exist outside the boundaries of such social institutions, so the singular flesh is represented through a lawless relationship based on vice. Thus, I plan to show how the bodies (or more appropriately the united flesh of their shared "body") of Swearengen and Trixie become the guiding metaphor for the first season of *Deadwood*'s exploration of how the organism of community can grow outside the boundaries of law.

Swearengen, along with the other citizens of Deadwood, certainly seems to see the world largely through a series of bodily metaphors as is made clear through the use of metaphoric and often lewd language. For Swearengen, most people seem to be categorized as "cocksuckers," "cunts," "cunt lickers," and the like. Al's cursing is fairly indicative of his character and seems to reveal a great deal about how he views others in relation to himself. Counting its usage in the transcripts of the show's first season, the word "cocksucker" or "cocksuckers" is used 126 times. Swearengen is the third character to use the word and is accountable for 71, or well over half, of the usages of the word. Both "cocksucker" and "cunt" are rather fascinating word choices given both the occupation of the man using those words as well as their meaning. Swearengen generally refers to men as "cocksuckers" and "cunts" and largely to describe those he finds beneath himself (which likely includes every citizen of Deadwood). This reference to those beneath him, though, can hardly be seen as a surprise given Swearengen's occupation as pimp. Those who serve him directly—prostitutes—are, indeed, literal "cocksuckers" and the expression, enlarged to include his male lackeys and anyone else "other" to himself, such as his political enemies or the Native Americans in the territory, allows himself to enlarge his own position as boss of his own whores to boss of all those around him, who are after all simply there to suck his cock either literally or metaphorically. Calling a man a "cocksucker" or a "cunt" feminizes that individual, weakening him within the male-dominated culture of the West, while also weakening those individuals as servants more specifically of Swearengen's cock—perhaps, in Swearengen's mind, the only "real" cock in town. In other words, Swearengen divides the world into two groups—his own cock and those who suck it.

While it may not at first be obvious how a whore sharing this pimp's bed makes any sort of difference to the bodily metaphor for power that Swearengen sees himself as representing, it is interesting to see how early Milch alters this kind of relationship between Swearengen and one of his whores, Trixie, in the show. Given the above context, Trixie could be seen as a simple "cocksucker" in his employ in the first episode, "Deadwood" (1.1), yet, she shares his bed, not as simple "cocksucker" but as a lover by the close of that episode. The act of consummation implied between Trixie and Swearengen is rather unique to the show. Besides Trixie, Swearengen's sexual relationships to his whores are shown as exclusively consisting of oral sex acts on Swearengen while his bed (barring one exception that will be discussed later) is never shared with another. At the close of this episode, a strange kind of marriage bed is made, based very much on the traditional notion of marriage represented by the Genesis dictum of two becoming one flesh. Trixie makes the move across Swearengen's social divide from the group that sucks his cock to the cock itself—indeed, if she has become his flesh, she must be all of his body—cock and all.

This transformation begins with a move on Trixie's part that seemingly implies a challenge to Swearengen's brutal power. Trixie's first appearance on the show is in a scene in which she has just shot and killed one of her (or more appropriately from the pimp's mindset, one of Swearengen's) clients. Swearengen is not swayed by Trixie's explanation that she told the client to stop beating on her during their encounter, thus precipitating the shooting in self-defense. Swearengen's orders to Trixie are short and clipped in this scene, treating his underling as if she were a dog to command, "Come here" and later, regarding the particulars of events, "Tell me in my office." In his office, Swearengen tells her that she should have called his muscle, Dan Dority or Johnny Burns, when the client became violent. "You don't shoot nobody 'cause that's bad for my business and it's bad for the camp's reputation," he scolds, before seemingly growing somewhat sympathetic as he examines her bloodied face, "He beat the living shit out of you, didn't he?" This compassion is short-lived, though, as Swearengen appears ready to strike her himself. Trixie's physical responses to her master are clearly instinctive and submissive throughout the scene as she cowers and tells him to, "Do what you gotta do to me." If Swearengen views his whores as beneath himself, Trixie's behavior is testimony to that as well as Swearengen's rapid response to this seeming acquiescence to her need for punishment. He knocks her down, saying, "Don't tell me what to do" and places his boot at her throat. If Trixie is submissive like Swearengen's animal in this scene, she is also submissive like a child: "I'll be good." Throughout this first episode, though, the viewer finds Trixie to be positioning herself to reclaim some of her dignity.

Shortly after experiencing this violent display of her pimp's power, Trixie requests that Jewel, the crippled barmaid at Swearengen's Gem

Saloon, purchase another gun for her to replace the one Swearengen took following the shooting. Later, Dan suggests to Swearengen that Trixie may be a danger, and throughout the episode we witness Trixie's newly acquired gun tucked seemingly in readiness to repay Swearengen's violence against her. If Swearengen's power is tied to his physical body as cock and also as violator of the body through physical violence, Trixie's new gun seems a challenge to both his orders for her to allow his male lackeys to defend her as well as an equalizing agent of physical violence.

Trixie's quest for some level of equality with her master takes an odd turn at the close of the episode. As she enters his room and draws the weapon, rather than fire it, she simply places it at his bedside. The nature of this physical confrontation changes as he watches wordlessly as she strips off her dress, offering not only the gun, an emblem of physical power, but her naked body, an emblem bare and exposed to the weapon that is his body, and climbs into bed with him. Swearengen's expression is unchanging as she curls up next to him and the episode ends; a physical pact between the two has been created through these covenantal physical acts. Through her submissiveness Trixie has shown Swearengen her loyalty to him, giving up her weapon and her body to his care. Such a covenant is physical, matrimonial, and political, particularly given the fact that she has not joined Swearengen on her knees as "cocksucker" but cuddled up next to him as equal sharing her pimp's bed.

Physicality is clearly important to organization—be it matrimonial or political. As E. B. Farnum, Swearengen's stooge and the execrable mayor of Deadwood, observes in "No Other Sons or Daughters" (1.9), when discussing the importance of providing governmental services to the people of Deadwood, "More than providing services to 'em, taking people's money is what makes organizations real, be they formal, informal, or temporary." While Farnum's description of power regarding governance is rather minimalistic, he nevertheless recognizes that the loss of a physical object or the need to pass on an important physical object is the tie that binds people together—the physical symbol that represents the abstraction of organization. Thus, the importance of Trixie's physical representation of submission, through gun and body, to Swearengen mirrors, more than any ring, this organizing principle much as a ring and physical consummation normally embody the abstraction of marital organization. Farnum's statement diminishes the notion of service and responsibility to the community, but

Swearengen will soon reveal that reciprocity and the need to protect the one who has placed herself under his authority are compelling needs for those in whom authority is placed.

The scene immediately following Swearengen and Trixie's act of consummation may seem to belie this notion. The first scene of the following episode, "Deep Water" (1.2), begins the morning after that event as Swearengen and Trixie awaken in their bed. Swearengen, indicating the gun, asks, "Is this for me?" to which Trixie responds, "Brought it for you." While Swearengen seems to want to acknowledge his new partner's gift to him, the swaggering pimp cannot allow this challenge to his unfettered authority to stand despite its reciprocal insinuations. He places Trixie in an exposed position; again, by throwing the covers back off her body, this time refusing to allow his body to be used as a bulwark for his partner. "Get out," he insists, angrily. While the equality of the domestic situation established in the previous episode seems to have been brutally and quickly terminated in this scene, Swearengen's later actions in this episode reveal that a clear change has occurred in his relationship to Trixie.

When one of his lackeys, a highwayman named Tom Mason, enters the Gem, Swearengen offers him some female companionship. When Mason spots Trixie and says, "I'll take her," Swearengen curiously but importantly tells him to "Pick another." This moment marks a notable change in Swearengen and Trixie's relationship and in their roles as pimp and whore throughout the majority of the season. While Swearengen seems not to have noted the symbolic act that Trixie's sacrifice of gun and body implies, nevertheless, their organization and the exclusivity of their relationship becomes apparent. For at least the next eight episodes, Trixie will share Swearengen's bed exclusively and become not simply a bed buddy but his confidante, again, echoing a strangely domestic and marital relationship between pimp and whore.

While in "Suffer the Little Children" (1.8) Trixie seems to be considering betraying Swearengen by leaving Deadwood and is even given by Alma Garrett (a rich woman widowed due to Swearengen's machinations) a rather large nugget of gold from Garrett's property, the scene from the first episode is re-enacted when Trixie returns to Swearengen. Like the gun, the gold nugget becomes emblematic of Trixie's submission to Swearengen when she returns to his room at the close of the episode and places it next to his bed. Unlike the first scene, though, Swearengen's response has become softened to his lover and confidante, and his response is anything but the stoic stare away from Trixie that marked the first time she brought him a gift. When faced with the possibility of betraying Swearengen's wishes earlier in the episode, she apparently attempts to kill herself through an overdose of laudanum. When Swearengen forces her to show him her wounds, she slaps him. Rather than attack her back, Swearengen accepts his punishment and, as she undresses, throws back the covers of his bed to invite her back to her place with him. Despite her potential betrayal of him, it is he who humbly renews their relationship through this action, even allowing her to turn her back to him as she climbs into what is now clearly *their* bed, since she is allowed now not merely to supine her body towards him but use the bed as she sees fit to make her anger and distaste clear.

Likewise, in "No Other Sons or Daughters," a re-enactment of the two waking together is again played out with significant changes. Swearengen immediately establishes his swaggering pose despite the previous night's challenges to his decision-making ability as he goes to use his chamber pot and sarcastically observes, "Her Majesty awakes, huh?" However, rather than kick her out as he did in the previous enactment of this scene, he immediately falls into discussion of his plans regarding the recent arrival of a government official that spells trouble for the camp as a businessman might normally do with his wife before departing for work. Though he does attempt to reinstate his power and diminish the symbolic meaning of the nugget as he indicates it, saying, "I can hope those'll be appearing on a regular basis," her response, "No," reinstates its meaning as a symbolic renewal of their partnership, as does his curiosity-laden response, "No?"[1] Rather than argue this point of contention, Swearengen moves the subject instead to a concern for Trixie, and that solicitude sends a clear message of his consideration that their "partnership" continue:

> Swearengen: How's your arm?
> Trixie: It's alright.
> Swearengen: Don't fucking try it, doin' away with yourself again, huh?

That these scenes mirror the earlier ones is, of course, no accident, nor is the meaning that they suggest—the clear sense of the evolution of the domestic partnership that has been forged between a man and woman and the clear degradation of authority and power that the relationship between pimp and whore is normally based upon. Again, the symbolic relationship that this reciprocity is based on is made through a physical object as well as through the two's own bodies. The wounds become the shared burden of both parties, particularly if the organization that Swearengen and Trixie have forged is more that of an organism, a shared body. Clearly the risk of death threatens a shared body, destroying the literal life of one and also literally dissolving the forged bond of partnership that "one flesh" is intended to represent. That Swearengen is willing to be struck by one who has threatened this body through suicide is a clear recognition of the necessity the relationship between the two has become.

Thus, the series allows this domestic organism's development to mirror the development of the political organism of Deadwood itself. If Swearengen and Trixie's relationship is consummated rather quickly, this parallels the altogether rapid and awkward affair of the camp's organic development. Much like the marriage of this pimp and whore, the marriage of the various elements represented within the camp—the law through Bullock, business interests through Sol Star, competing business interests with Cy Tolliver, ethnic concerns through Wu, the criminal order represented by Swearengen himself, etc.—are not easily bound within a single body. If Swearengen initially is unwilling to reciprocate his responsibility to Trixie, neither do the various officials, like Seth Bullock as sheriff, initially feel comfortable with their responsibilities. If Tolliver represents a challenge to the authority and business opportunities of Swearengen, so too do Swearengen and Trixie challenge one another's position within their union. But if Tolliver and Swearengen must eventually get along for the organism of the camp to survive, as they find they have to in episodes like "Plague" (1.6), so, too, must the partnership of Trixie and Swearengen survive in order for their organization to survive, since their lives are bound to the fate of one another. Thus, it is also unsurprising that near the close of the season when the sovereignty of Deadwood is challenged from without by the potential betrayals of citizens of the camp's interests to their own (like Cy Tolliver's),[2] and the entry of a "foreign" body like Yankton, so too is Swearengen and Trixie's "marriage" also challenged by an alien to their own organic unit.

At the height of the citizens' uncertainty about the sovereignty of the camp in the penultimate episode of the season, "Jewel's Boot Is Made for

Walking" (1.11), the series parallels this civil instability with the instability of the union between Swearengen and Trixie. Indeed, in the initial scene in that episode, once again we find Swearengen bouncing ideas about how to deal with a significant threat to the town's stability (in the form of the warrant that threatens his own freedom to operate) off of his bedmate. He then gives Trixie "half a day off," confirming her uniqueness as a whore in his employ. The manner in which the day is spent by Trixie, though, manages to also generate a significant threat to the organism that the two have come to represent. Based on Star's previous overtures to her, Trixie arrives at his and Bullock's store to offer Star a "free fuck." Swearengen's inadvertent discovery of this non-work-related sexual encounter due to an injudicious comment by Bullock hits Swearengen hard. Upon hearing from Bullock that "my partner's fuckin' that whore," Swearengen is left speechless. Ironically, as he goes to his balcony in a daze, Reverend Smith stands below, and Swearengen listens raptly to his sermonizing about love: "Who shall separate us from the love of Christ?" Given Smith's earlier sermon on the body of Christ, the logic of the inseparability of being between God and man is compelling. One body cannot be separated and still be operable. Swearengen's attentiveness and anger at Trixie's betrayal is compounded by Smith's declarations of ideal love—in particular the inability of any natural or human obstruction to sever the bond of love between Christ and man. Therefore, it is unsurprising that while Swearengen does not initially confront Trixie directly about her liaison, when he summons Star to pay for Trixie's time, he allows her to overhear his comments to Star about the need for exclusive and non-obligatory love:

> Trixie! Don't you think I don't understand? I mean, what can any one of us ever really fuckin' hope for, huh? Except for a moment here and there with a person who doesn't want to rob, steal or murder us? At night, it may happen. Sun-up, one person against the fuckin' wall, the other may hop on the fuckin' bed trusting each other enough to tell half the fucking truth. Everybody needs that. Becomes precious to 'em. They don't want to see it fucked with.

The clear description here of the relationship between Swearengen and Trixie as bedfellows and confidants clarifies even more clearly that Swearengen has seen Trixie as more than a whore. His insistence on payment from Star may both serve to obviate his sense that a romantic rendezvous took place between Star and his "woman" and at the same time reveal that "his woman" has been transformed once again into simply "his whore"—no longer the confidante, no longer the "one person against the fuckin' wall" that allows them to trust "each other enough to tell half the fucking truth."

Later that evening a parody of Swearengen and Trixie's relationship is played out as Swearengen retreats to bed with a bottle and another whore, Dolly, as if to replace the missing Trixie and re-simulate their marriage (again, a kind of re-enactment of the final scene of the first episode). Dolly is allowed in his bed in this scene (although the next morning there is no evidence that she has slept there as Trixie's body would have served as evidence to) and allowed to be a sounding board for Swearengen's plans, but his language betrays the sham of this relationship as being anything like his previous one:

> Now, I see what the fuck's in front of me, and I don't pretend it's somethin' else. I was fuckin' her and now I'm gonna fuck you, if you don't piss me off or open your yap at the wrong fuckin' time. The only time you're to open—you're supposed to open your yap is so I can put my fuckin' prick in it. Otherwise, you shut the fuck up.

While Swearengen claims that he will "fuck" Dolly, he quickly moves her into her position as "other" to him by describing her not as a lover but a "cocksucker." Swearengen claims that he now sees what is in front of him, as if he was blind to Trixie as a whore and now he has come to his senses to see what whores are: those who suck his prick and remain quiet while he makes his plans, offering no advice or opinions as inferiors.

Clearly, the "marriage" has been dissolved when Swearengen tells Trixie, "You sleep tonight amongst your own," remaking Trixie into a whore and depositing her back with those who are not him—"your own." Interestingly, in this scene, Swearengen also reveals a sense of his inability to trust women stretching all the way back to his childhood and his abandonment by his own mother: "And my fuckin' mother dropped me the fuck off there [Mrs. Fat Ass Anderson's orphanage] with 7 dollars and 60 some odd fuckin' cents on her way to suckin' cock in ... in Georgia." Swearengen sees even in his own mother only a whore and, thus, only a cocksucker.

The other interesting subject matter raised in this dialogue is the "problem" that Swearengen is brainstorming to his pseudo-confidante about (Smith's precarious physical and mental state brought on by seizures and a tumor). Again, his problem with organism coincides with a consideration of Smith. The oddest thing about the dialogue is its insistence that "no one gives a fuck" about such a man and, yet, Swearengen's insistence that the "minister's gotta fuckin' die" is based on his sense that "he's makin' a fuckin' jerk of himself," implying that Swearengen cares about the dignity of this man. Even as his trust is shattered, Swearengen believes in the necessity of community. His question regarding the benefits of such indignity—"who's gonna benefit from that, huh?"—implies that existence is only meaningful if others can benefit from your actions. Thus, while Swearengen may seem like a predator within Deadwood, his decisions in these closing episodes to protect the town reveal this same concern for the dignity of the members of this body of people. While Swearengen's relationship to Trixie is sundered by infidelity and the camp is threatened by similar infidelities to the principles of organism, in the closing episode of the season, Swearengen kills Smith quietly to end his misery and indignity.

The manner in which this mercy killing is intercut with a prayer from Doc Cochran that God would "relent" in allowing what he sees as meaningless "protracted suffering" suggests a kind of divine intervention of sorts in the form of Swearengen as a necessary member of the body of Christ.[3] Even the body needs killers—antibodies and the like. While Swearengen's final failure with personal relationships reflects some of the failings of the camp to act as a unified organism, the season's climax proves that the body will take care of itself and that at least some dignity and honor still exists in the personal bonds of friendship and love—even if terminating love is the only means of protecting the body.

CHAPTER 12

DIVINING THE "CELESTIALS"

THE CHINESE SUBCULTURE OF DEADWOOD

PAUL WRIGHT AND HAILIN ZHOU

INTRODUCTION

America was never innocent. We popped our cherry on the boat over and looked back with no regrets. You can't ascribe our fall from grace to any single event or set of circumstances. You can't lose what you lacked at conception. Mass-market nostalgia gets you hopped up for a past that never existed. Hagiography sanctifies shuck-and-jive politicians and reinvents their expedient gestures as moments of great moral weight. Our continuing narrative is blurred past truth and hindsight. Only a reckless verisimilitude can set that line straight. ... It's time to demythologize an era and build a new myth from the gutter to the stars. It's time to embrace bad men and the price they paid to secretly define their time. Here's to them.

James Ellroy, American Tabloid

Like the work of James Ellroy, David Milch's historically ambitious and brilliantly coarse *Deadwood* pursues "reckless verisimilitude" in its discomfiting embrace of "bad men and the price they paid to secretly define their time." *Deadwood*, both as an historical stage and in the unflinchingly Hobbesian imagination of show-runner Milch, offers us a fascinating, disquieting glimpse into a cauldron of civic ambition, predatory avarice, Machiavellian statesmanship, and unrepentant vulgarity—all of which fueled the American project to transform an untamed frontier into a domesticated heartland.

Deadwood's byzantine and un-sanitized look at the American West chips away at the pieties of the "melting pot" narrative of American history. And like Ellroy's dyspeptic meditations on the racism, corruption, and "Imagineering" of 1950s Los Angeles,[1] Milch's series unapologetically explores the darkest aspects of American expansionism and economic adventurism.

This chapter will shed light on the role in *Deadwood* of the town's Chinese immigrants, and in particular of their deceptively muted public representative, Mr. Wu. We will also reflect on the thematic uses to which the "Celestials"[2] are put in the show and in the historical literature surrounding the town. A case in point is the relationship between Wu and Al Swearengen. As reigning avatar of the show's political and criminal consciousness, Ian McShane's Swearengen is a most menacing power-player—aggressively vulgar pimp; calculating manipulator; cyclically abusive civic father; and yet at the same time an almost Byronic soul, self-conscious that he is both a denizen and an architect of his own backwater Hell-on-earth. The show's developing dynamic between Wu and Swearengen trades on their parallel roles as community leaders and criminal overlords. In some respects, their relationship is as close to a grudging and professional friendship as any other on the show.

Aside from Wu's fascinating doppelgänger to Swearengen, the anonymous Chinese of *Deadwood* who serve Wu are equally compelling in the brief glimpses we get into their misery and subjection to the "civic father" of their own subculture. It seems that through the Chinese community of the show, Milch is evolving both a rival to and a microcosm of the political landscape of the town at large. This demimonde is worth exploring as it hints at an understanding of the Chinese experience in America that is refreshingly candid and unusually rich. Milch confronts both the shameful oppression and the abiding complexity of the Chinese pioneers who journeyed to and through the American West. Like Ellroy's celebrated "bad men" of the "gutter" who made America, the Chinese of *Deadwood* are seen not only in the light of their all-too-real victimization, but also in the shadow of their collaboration with the darker genius of the American frontier spirit.

This chapter will focus solely on the HBO production; online, we also touch on scholarly and archaeological efforts to unearth evidence of the vibrant, three-dimensional human beings who comprised Deadwood's Chinatown[3]—and on how the town's project of historical preservation is affected by legalized gambling and a tourist industry now driven in part by the HBO production. We end by returning to Milch's vision and what it might mean for reconstructing a frontier-Chinese identity—an identity deployed by *Deadwood* as a unique, pop-cultural instance of "Wild Western" Orientalism.[4]

AMERICA AS NURSEMAID AND THE BLOODY FOUNDING OF DEADWOOD'S CHINATOWN

> When did you start thinking every wrong had a remedy, Wu? Did you come to camp for justice or to make your fuckin' way?
> *Al Swearengen, "Sold Under Sin," 1.12*[5]

In "Sold Under Sin," the closing episode of *Deadwood*'s first season, Al Swearengen asks this of an incensed Mr. Wu, Chinatown's first citizen and resident counterpart to Al. In essence, Wu and the denizens of *Deadwood*'s Chinatown have spent the first two seasons in the life of the show attempting to answer that very question. We know very well what Al's personal answer to that question has been: "Every fuckin' beatin' I'm grateful for. Every fuckin' one of them. Get all the trust beat outta you. And you know what the fuckin' world is" (1.3). This encapsulates Swearengen's philosophical outlook on both his own miseries and those he inflicts, his profession of exclusive faith in the Nietzschean dictum that what fails to kill him outright makes him strong enough to see the world clearly. And yet there is a deeply political dimension to Al's thinking, a way in which the clarity he seeks in a good beating is ultimately a means to avoid beatings in the future—and hence pass them on to the next dreamer in the circuit foolish enough to think the unfairness of the world matters. Of all the delusions that forestall the full absorption of this lesson, justice ranks highest on Al's list.

This is precisely why Seth Bullock both intrigues and disturbs Swearengen. To the extent that Bullock takes justice seriously, even when he fails to reconcile its dictates to his passions, he remains an enigma to Al—a "priggish fucking douche bag ... who only wants to sell pots and pans, fan his pretty face and hold his nose from the stench of our fuckin' sordid carryings on over here ... all the time thinking he can protect the meek and innocent" ("Suffer the Little Children," 1.8). Al calculates, however, that it is precisely the distasteful, hypocritical naïveté of Bullock that makes him "the perfect fucking front man" for the camp as it navigates the treacherous waters between assimilation into the USA and genuine autonomy. In his inimitable locution, Al sums up the camp's dilemma: "Our moment permits interest in one question only: Will we of Deadwood be more than targets for ass-fucking? To not grab ankle is to declare yourself interested. What's your posture, Bullock?" ("Childish Things," 2.8).

In the wake of the various crises that consume the town in Season One (the murder of Wild Bill Hickok and the trial of his assassin; the outbreak of plague; the threat of domination by political hacks in Yankton), Al becomes ever more active in trying to engineer Deadwood's political destiny. As a result, he comes to acknowledge the need for that defensive "posture" to be coupled with at least the appearance of civility and order. As the absurd E. B. Farnum reminds the first assembly of the town council, "More than providing services to 'em, taking people's money is what makes organizations real, be they formal, informal, or temporary" ("No Other Sons or Daughters"). Taking money quietly and under the veneer of municipal efficiency becomes the parallel formula to Al's criminal interest in doggedly mining the miners of Deadwood, the so-called "hoopleheads." To satisfy both of these agendas increasingly demands the cooperation of the town's Chinese community, which entails regular negotiation with their taskmaster Wu. In fact, it is precisely Al and Wu's intertwined interests and often-murderous exchange of professional courtesies that fuel many of the show's central conflicts, as well as its brutal and blunt depiction of racial politics.

Initially, Swearengen's relationship to the Chinese is defined by Wu's ability to dispose of the bodies of Al's enemies and failed lieutenants in his pigsty. The gruesome image of Wu's pigs devouring bodies is a macabre running joke in Season One, and for a time seems to be Wu's only dramatic purpose given his lack of English and his existence on the cultural periphery of town. Al's major concern with Wu is making sure that he is not overcharged for the use of the pigsty: "Don't want to be suckin' hind tit on disposal fees" ("Suffer the Little Children"). Two key developments move Wu to center stage, or rather, to the revelation that he was there all along. The arrival in Deadwood of Cy Tolliver, Swearengen's more polished and arguably more brutal rival, fosters an ongoing antagonism between the two pimps that highlights their competing visions for the camp's future. Where

Al finds himself gradually evolving into a perverse, yet savvy statesman for the town, Tolliver eschews politics for real estate, angling to establish new brothels that will exploit anticipated new markets—namely, Chinatown itself. When Al discovers that Tolliver has purchased lots in "Chink Alley," he must credit Tolliver's ingenuity: "Nonetheless it says the man sees the fuckin' possibilities of things. I mean to come up at this fuckin' juncture, with the idea of creatin' an emporium for the fuckin' chinks takes brass fucking balls, and a long term vision for the future" ("Plague," 1.6).

This move on Chinatown combines with another explosive turn in the relationship between Al and Wu in episodes 10 through 12, which proves to be a defining arc in the series. Opium destined for Wu's organization and earmarked for Al to distribute is stolen by a pair of opportunistic addicts, one of whom works for Swearengen while the other has cast his lot with the Tolliver camp. The desperate theft sparks a now archetypal confrontation between Wu and Al which is at once abrasive and comical, and which illustrates a deepening relationship that transcends the vulgar pieties of racism itself. What is most revealing is how Wu for once initiates the conversation, while boldly refusing to make his way to Al's office by the usual backdoor route reserved for Chinese or African-Americans. Instead, Wu barges loudly into the Gem Saloon and into Al's inner sanctum, making his complaint in a surreal, almost primal combination of stick figure drawings and curses directed at the "white cocksuckas" who have stolen their opium (1.10).

As Al's dimwitted aid Johnny Burns attests to co-worker Dan Dority, "Those are the first 'cocksuckers' I have ever heard shouted from that room, Dan, that didn't come from Al's mouth that wasn't followed by Al comin' over to that railin', pointin' at you and beckoning you up them stairs with your fuckin' knife." Although Johnny dismissively adds that Wu's "people worship a fat man seated on his ass" (1.10), Wu's arrival on the scene of *Deadwood* as something approaching an equal has been made apparent. David Milch has said the following about the power and the limits of language with respect to these recurring exchanges between Al and Wu:

> The generation of words is an expression of electrical energy. The reason storytelling engages us perhaps more fully than other kinds of communication is because the words in a story can mean in different ways. They contain their opposites. In that scene—"Swearengen!"

"Cocksucker!"—we understand how provisional the meaning of a word is and that its fundamental meaning is contingent upon the energy with which it's endowed by the speaker. Energy is a gossamer and intangible and variable commodity, and words in a story are more clearly contingent and variable than words in a proof.

(*quoted in Singer 203–4*)

Al's grudging decision to give Wu one of the addicts presents him with a new dilemma: should he execute Tolliver's man and preserve his own, or surrender his own in order to avoid a conflict with the rival pimp? Swearengen pursues the seemingly safer course, only to find that Tolliver exploits the execution of Al's man in order to stir up resentment towards the Chinese—whose land Tolliver would like to see usurped and, ultimately, in his hands. Tolliver claims to Al that he stands "on principle," namely that "A white dope fiend's still white; I don't deliver white men to chinks." Swearengen responds to Tolliver's disingenuous suggestion that he get out of the business of "traffickin' in fuckin' junk" with his own mission statement: "I'm a purveyor of spirits, Cy, dope fuckin' included, and when chance affords, a thief, but I ain't no fuckin' hypocrite" ("Mr. Wu," 1.10).

Tolliver subsequently orders the surviving addict, Leon, to publicize his story of indignity suffered at the hands of Swearengen and an uppity "Celestial," of the devouring of his fellow dope-fiend as "a hell of a way to treat a white man" ("Jewel's Boot Is Made for Walking"). Leon enacts his criminal, race-baiting passion play, making his melodramatic case for the moral (i.e., racial) high ground: "Are we that far west that we've wound up in fuckin' China? Where a white man kowtows to a celestial like that arrogant cocksucker Wu!" Other incidents are staged for the benefit of propagandizing Deadwood, portending a near race-war in the town. Leon accuses an uninvolved Chinese launderer of trying to douse his eyes with lye, and then publicly abuses Wu, reminding him, "You may be a big shot in this alley, but you are less than a nigger to me!" ("Sold Under Sin"). The brutal incident ends with the death of Wu's underling and to Seth Bullock's horrified decision to become sheriff.

These conflicting agendas and acts of violence are tied brilliantly together in the complex denouement of Season One, which dramatizes the intrigues surrounding Deadwood's potential incorporation into the USA. The backdrop for the unfortunate murder of the Chinese launderer is provided by elements of the US cavalry billeting in the town, fresh from a war of brutal retribution on Native Americans in the aftermath of Little Big Horn. The murder is intercut with General Crook delivering an oration celebrating the restoration of white order in the Black Hills, "to the progress of the United States, of which I am certain this camp will soon be a part" (1.12).

The second season complicates and raises the stakes of this relationship between white and Chinese Deadwood, as Wu endures a rival Chinese leader entering the scene—the more polished, English-speaking Mr. Lee, who clearly plays Tolliver to Wu's Swearengen. Lee's "juice" and native intelligence are impressive enough to bring Al to remark half-jokingly to Wu that "Maybe you and me should be working for him" (2.18).[6] He has arrived at the behest of interests tied to George Hearst, father of William Randolph Hearst and eventual chief officer of the enormous Homestake mining concern. The Homestake "open-cut" mine heralded the end of small-scale entrepreneurship among the original miners drawn to the Lead-Deadwood region. As "amalgamation and capital"[7] exert a new stranglehold over Deadwood, Al is torn between maintaining his connection to Wu and severing it in the interest of preserving the camp's and his own autonomy. The camp is under assault on multiple fronts, from one-sided offers to join the Dakota Territory to the machinations of Hearst's disturbed proxy, Francis Wolcott, who employs Tolliver to spread panic that will encourage cheap sales of existing gold claims to the Hearst interest.

Tolliver is also commissioned by Wolcott to co-administer with Lee a band of Chinese sex-slaves brought in as bargain prostitutes for the increasingly underpaid miners, many of whom have been tricked or coerced into abandoning their old claims for lives as wage-laborers in the Hearst orbit. These miserable women are systematically and openly degraded, living like animals in cages and with barely enough food to survive ("Something Very Expensive," 2.6). Part of Wolcott's ultimate strategy is to introduce male Chinese laborers into the camp down the road, virtual slaves who will work under deplorable conditions and for lower wages that will drive the price of white labor down or eliminate the need for it altogether; as Wolcott writes to Hearst, "Anxious as I know you to be ... to move to 24-hour operation, until workers at wage outnumber individual prospectors in the camp, the matter of Chinese labor remains delicate of introduction" ("Childish Things").

In the interim, the Chinese sex-slaves are the symbolic vanguard of this dehumanizing project to undermine labor standards, earning power, and entrepreneurial confidence in the camp's existing arrangements.

In a show such as *Deadwood*, already unflinching in exploring the dark violence of which our language is capable, what is said of these anonymous and debased women is striking for its utter inhumanity. Tolliver suggests to his stooges that they sell the white miners of the town on the Chinese prostitutes by appealing to the exoticism and mortal danger of their very flesh: "I'd go with the strangeness, boys. Take it head on, turn it to your fuckin' advantage. Ah ... 'among humans, for grip, the Chinawoman's snatch has no peer. In all of nature, the python is its only rival, though few have lived to tell the tale'" ("E. B. Was Left Out," 2.7). The repulsive Stapleton complies, telling barflies that "the Chinese whore has a ancient way of milking ya of yer sorrow, your loneliness, and that awful feeling of bein' forsaken," to which bartender Tom Nuttall glibly replies, "Seems to me that'd leave you with nothing." When the reliably decent Doc Cochran angrily challenges Tolliver on the appalling conditions endured by the sex-slaves, Tolliver conveniently lays the blame at the doorstep of the Chinese: "I ain't one, Doc, holds the white man's as the sole and only path. I strive to tolerate what I may not agree with. But those people's culture, their women are disposable" ("Childish Things").

If Wu and the male Chinese of the first season of *Deadwood* had to suffer indignities in relative silence and anonymity, this is still more the case for the voiceless women in the second. In fact, it is their suffering that ultimately galvanizes Mr. Wu to the murderous action that may cost him everything. When Lee begins burning the ravaged bodies of prostitutes who have failed to survive, thereby ruling out any proper burial in China, Wu calls on Al to sanction his intervention ("The Whores Can Come," 2.11). Al, faced with a choice between Wu and Lee's backers, a choice not unlike that between the two addicts in Season One, is uncertain how to proceed. Seeing advantages in either course, his gut leans towards Wu since "Hearst's chink bossin' that alley ain't to my fuckin' taste." If only because of the social capital Al has invested thus far in Wu, he opts to delay the "battle of the chinks" and put Wu "on ice" until further notice. Al exploits the occasion of the death of Sheriff Bullock's son, telling Lee there will be "no violence between you and Wu while the grievin' goes on. My God, act civilized even if you ain't" ("The Whores Can Come").

In the second-season finale, Wu nearly undoes all the groundwork Al has laid for ultimately backing him by breaking the imposed truce in a street fight that ends with dead foot soldiers from both Chinese factions. Despite his irritation at Wu and his fears that he may have backed the wrong side in the Chinese conflict, Swearengen expresses a bemused respect for Wu, who "forsakes safety and even odds in a future fight for immediate fuckin' dubious combat" ("Boy the Earth Talks To," 2.12). Al is left baffled by "what gets into people's heads," but one begins to suspect that admiration mingles with bewilderment in his assessment of Wu. In order at last to confidently loosen the reins on Wu, Al must strategically subject him to one final, humiliating test of restraint and loyalty.

When the formidable George Hearst arrives in Deadwood to survey his newly won assets, he parleys with Swearengen to discuss the Lee/Wu clash and its ramifications for the new economy. Al trots Wu out like a degraded zoo curiosity, with his Chinese braid or "queue" leashed in Al's hands:

Al: This yellow monkey's Wu.

Hearst: Older fella. Not often you can tell how old they are.

Al: Done a turn or two for me, Wu has. And well-liked enough
         among his own. His display against *your* chink was my first
         fuckin' inkling that he's irrational.

Hearst: Mr. Lee, the man he tried to kill, has worked well for me in
         several camps.

Al: Then God bless Lee and off with fuckin' Wu's head! You've
         got your finger on the cause of it too—your chink bein' forward-
         looking. "Set the bodies ablaze, on with the day's trade!" This
         one bein' longer in the tooth—

Hearst: Set what bodies ablaze?

Al: Custom holds stronger to what passes for his mind.

...

Hearst: Do you know prospecting, Mr. Swearengen?

Al: Fuckin' nothin' of it.

Hearst: And the securing of the color once found?

Al: Not a fuckin' thing.

Hearst: All I really care about.

("*Boy the Earth Talks To*")

With Hearst's summary judgment that only the "securing of the color" ultimately matters—and that it absolutely depends on stability and the illusion of propriety—the subtle, rigged game being played for Wu's livelihood and life concludes. Key to the infernal bargain struck, however, is that "Wu will staff your mines. And those [Chinese] that survive the explosions, he can place in laundries or kitchens." Hearst and Al also demand of Wu a decisive, personal reckoning of his mettle—Wu, to use a "fuckin' mining term" Al has actually heard, must "prove out" by ritually murdering his competitors, and in particular the now expendable and embarrassing Lee.

In the closing moments of *Deadwood*'s sophomore season, Wu joins Al's white lieutenants in a *Godfather*-style assault on Lee's headquarters, where Lee is slaughtered in the grips of a sex- and opium-driven haze. As in the Season One finale, the massacre is intercut with other key developments in town, including the marriage of wealthy Alma Garrett, the suicide of the homicidal Wolcott, and the drafting of documents to incorporate Deadwood into the Dakota Territory. When Wu emerges victoriously from the carnage, he cuts off his queue in a public demonstration of defiance, autonomy, and—according to Al—his bloody purchase of an authentically American identity. Holding up what remains of his braid, Wu shares his triumph with his mentor, who presides not only over the marriage of Deadwood to the Dakotas, but of Wu and the Chinese to the USA:

> Mr. Wu: Wu! America! (*his braid in hand*)
> Al: That'll hold you tight to her tit!
> Mr. Wu: (*holding crossed fingers up to Al*) Heng dai! [loosely
>   translated, "Brotherhood!"]

> (2.12)

In a moment that is imagined as both birth and death, as nursing at the bosom of America and sacrificing at the altar of her cult of success, Wu has murdered both his rival and, symbolically, his Chinese identity in amputating his queue, the conventional symbol of subjection to the Manchurian emperors of the Qing Dynasty. He makes a primal bargain with assimilation—to the Hobbesian ethos of survival and the American ethos of prosperity at any cost. Held tight to America's "tit," Wu has finally answered Al's question in Season One, opting to make his way in a world where justice is too tall (and too white) an order. In correspondence with the authors, actor Keone Young was asked whether he thought his character's choice was in any way a betrayal of his heritage; Young's answer speaks volumes:

> There is a lot to articulate about Wu and why he cut his queue. It is as complex as the whole Chinese in America question. All I can say is that at some point we ChinaMEN [sic] decided that we would stop being sojourners in this country and become part of America. The queue was some kind of passport for us. Imposed on us by the Manchu's [sic] the queue would make us different from them. To make us look like animals or their horses when we prostrated before them. If we did not wear it we would be beheaded and so if we had come to America and cut it off we would not be able to go back home. Wu by cutting it off swears not only his allegiance to his newfound home but flies in the face of all those that want to colonize him and his people. I believe he finally finds that like all Americans to be free from tyranny is the appeal that this new country has. Even though it was rife with chauvinism and race prejudice. It was a country that was screaming and groaning for freedom. It is the sacrifice that one must make in order to be free is what Wu swears he will do. ... Hopefully if all goes right [in Season Three] Wu will make the next step up in the history of the "new" in America. I repeat from last season: "WU–'MELICA–HENG DAI!"[8]

In his *Pioneer Days in the Black Hills: Accurate History and Facts Related by One of the Early Day Pioneers* (1939), John S. McClintock, "meditating on the present physical status of our thin, gray line of Black Hills pioneers of '76," glumly observes that "there are few surviving members of that one time vigorous and venturesome band of indomitable Argonauts." McClintock thus concludes his history of the Black Hills gold rush era, carrying himself back one last time "in vivid remembrance and serious thought to an epochal period of time long past; a time when there assembled in virgin forests a mighty host of civilian immigrants." "This great army of agitated humanity," he muses, "apparently all of one accord, had arisen simultaneously from all sections of the country and from all walks of life" (253). McClintock's history shines in many respects, and it includes gems such as Deadwood's first directory of commercial services (the town's *Yellow Pages* in essence) and a grim, but informative "Summary of Early Day Fatalities" (202-6; 269-74). And yet for all of the insights and memories preserved in McClintock's sweeping memoir, his book scarcely acknowledges the existence and importance of the Chinese community to Deadwood's economy, culture, and overall prosperity. Neither his directory nor his fatality lists include a single reference to a Chinese merchant or combatant. McClintock's account leaves unspoken a key presumption—that enlistment in this "great army of agitated humanity," ranks swelling with "indomitable Argonauts" who despite all their differences tamed a frontier rich in "color"—was in fact the exclusive province of whites.

Thoughtful historians of Deadwood and the Black Hills have been wrestling with omissions such as these ever since, and we hope it is now clear that Milch's *Deadwood* is a compelling intervention in this developing conversation, which asks us to mine the town for its real color—for something both more real and ephemeral than gold—its cultural memory of Chinatown.

PART 5
THE BODY IN DEADWOOD

CHAPTER 13

"WHAT'S AFFLICTIN' YOU?"

CORPOREALITY, BODY CRISES
AND THE BODY POLITIC IN DEADWOOD

ERIN HILL

The climactic scene of "Requiem for a Gleet," the fourth episode of Season Two of HBO's dramatic Western *Deadwood*, is as exciting and action-packed as any in the series, holding the life of a central character in the balance and filled with guttural screams and violent movements not unlike those of the hand-to-hand combat or shootouts that characterize the Western genre. But, surprisingly, what is being depicted onscreen is not a fistfight or a showdown, but rather, a man passing kidney stones. This scene, which effectively ends the sickbed stint of Deadwood's favorite son and First Villain, saloon owner Al Swearengen, is neither the first nor the last in the series in which the body and its limitations take center stage, not in the aftermath of some central crisis that has been resolved with fists or guns but as the crisis itself.

A comprehensive list of bodily ailments exhibited on *Deadwood* would comprise dozens of complaints, ranging in seriousness from toothaches to brain tumors and in duration from one scene to an entire season of the series. While even medical dramas, which make the human body the site for their spectacle, tend to relegate bodily trauma to secondary characters, leaving their doctor protagonists unfettered by their own flesh, these ailments on *Deadwood* strike central characters down for episodes at a time. And perhaps more interesting than the sheer number of bodies and ailments displayed in the series is the diversity of purpose for which these ailments are put on view, from sketching the character of the Deadwood camp, to engineering change in its residents through crises of the body, to molding Deadwood's community into an organized political body with all of its accompanying disease and, in so doing, reflecting the larger questions posed by the series.

DEADWOOD'S CORPOREALITY

"Next one who farts in here is going out of the window into the muck."
Al Swearengen, "Reconnoitering the Rim" (1.3)

From the first moments it appears onscreen, its thoroughfare crowded with sweating, filthy men, the Deadwood camp is marked as a place of the body. The prospectors who make up much of the camp's population spend days at hard, manual labor on their claims, and return to the camp for the express purpose of tending to their bodies: washing the dirt from their skin in rented baths, filling their empty bellies with the sweet and the savory, numbing their aching joints with shots of whiskey and balls of opium, and draining the tension from their muscles with the more pleasurable exertions of dancing, dice, sex, fistfights, and other forms of carousing. Along with the Deadwoodian's healthy respect for the wants of the body comes an equally high regard for its emissions. Bargains in Deadwood are sealed with spit-lubricated handshakes, and bowel movements are treated with the utmost esteem, as evidenced by the attitude of Swearengen protégé Silas Adams who, returning from a business trip, insists that he must "take a shit" before he can report to his boss, maintaining that the bowel movement is "not the type that can be put off" ("Advances, None Miraculous," 2.10). Body functions are so well understood by the residents of Deadwood that they are often used to communicate in lieu of words, which are considered far less expressive—and concrete. Thus a prospector, angry over a decision made by Sheriff Seth Bullock, plans to ejaculate on the lawman's horse in order to express his displeasure, and A. W. Merrick, Editor of the *Deadwood Pioneer*, finds his printing press defiled with human feces after publishing an unpopular story. Even when words do not fail the inhabitants of the camp, their language usually makes reference to the body. Wild Bill Hickok, a refined man by Deadwood standards, cannot resist setting down Jack McCall with a little of this "body language," when he says to the parasitic gambler, "that dropped eye of yours looks like a cunt to me, Jack. When you talk, it is like a cunt flapping" ("Reconnoitering the Rim").

Those who come to Deadwood unprepared or unwilling to embrace its corporeality find a rude awakening there. Alma Garrett's intelligent, conman father, Otis Russell, makes no bones about wanting to leave the corporeal camp almost as soon as he gets there, claiming, "my olfactories are keen to the smell of shit." He is brought down to Deadwood's bodily level, however, when, after he attempts to establish dominance over Seth Bullock verbally, Bullock beats him bloody and knocks out several of his teeth. The following season, it is Bullock's wife who is initiated into the camp's corporeality when she arrives in Deadwood to find her husband engaged in hand-to-hand combat with Al Swearengen in the main thoroughfare. Looking up from the bodily struggle, Swearengen's greeting to Mrs. Bullock is the equally bodily exclamation, "Welcome to fucking Deadwood!"

AILMENTS AND BODY CRISES

"There you are, chokin' and coughin' just like the rest of us."
Calamity Jane, "The Trial of Jack McCall" (1.5)

Almost more noticeable than the primacy of bodies and their functions in *Deadwood* is the show's frequent depiction of bodily dysfunction. That both Seth Bullock and Wild Bill Hickok are ailing when they are first introduced to viewers in the pilot episode (Bullock with a gunshot wound, Bill with a headache) is an indication that in *Deadwood*, characters are as likely to be "poorly" as they are to be well. Over the course of the show's first two seasons, nearly every major character is afflicted with some sort of bodily ailment, many more than once. Whether big or small, most of these ailments seem to say something about their sufferers. In *Illness as Metaphor*, Susan Sontag discusses how, in literature, tuberculosis has often been treated as the product of the "inward burning" of someone "'consumed' by ardor" (20), and how cancer "is now imagined to be the wages of repression" (21). There is some affinity between the depiction of illness in the literature of which Sontag speaks and the representation of ailments on *Deadwood*, which tends to saddle its afflicted with bodily troubles that match or force to the surface the troubles of their souls. E. B. Farnum, perhaps the most corrupt member of the Deadwood citizenry, is afflicted with bodily ailments of a corresponding rottenness in the form of a decaying tooth and the putridity of the intestines associated with diarrhea, while A. W. Merrick, Deadwood's most cerebral citizen, suffers from hypochondria, his overactive brain creating in him the sensation of pain and illness where there is none. These ailments, fitting their sufferers as they do, reveal village idiot Richardson to be unintentionally profound when, finding Farnum choking on a clove soap remedy for his tooth, he exclaims "What's killin' you? What's afflictin' you?" ("Childish Things," 2.8). Indeed, in Deadwood, what afflicts residents' bodies is often a good indicator of that which is afflicting their souls.

Nowhere in *Deadwood* is the correspondence between outer, physical ailments and inner, psychic dysfunctions made plainer than in the case of what, for the purposes of this essay, will be called *body crises*. Writing in *The Body in Pain*, Elaine Scarry describes the isolation inherent in physical pain, which, seen in another person, "may seem to have the remote character of some deep, subterranean fact, belonging to an invisible geography that, however portentous, has no reality because it has not yet manifested itself on the visible surface of the earth" (3). Pain, according to Scarry, is so unshareable because it shatters language, resisting objectification and therefore separating the sufferer from others via an invisible barrier. Sontag touches on a similar sense of separation in her discussion of illness, calling it a "night side of life" and adding that "everyone who is born holds dual citizenship in the kingdom of the well and the kingdom of the sick. Although we all prefer to use only the good passport, sooner or later each of us is obligated at least for a spell to identify ourselves as a citizen of that other place" (3). Characters in *Deadwood* who experience a body crisis are those who enter this night side of life, taking leave of their reality to inhabit a separate realm of bodily pain for a period of time, and returning from it changed in ways that go beyond the physical. By facilitating the crossing of psychic barriers that seem otherwise insurmountable, these body crises make possible rapid character evolution on *Deadwood*, each season of which takes place over an extremely compressed period of time. Indeed, the swift development of character these body crises precipitate in their sufferers mirrors the development of Deadwood itself, which goes from being a rudimentary camp consisting of tents and few residents to being a bustling town with its own telegraph and local government in the space of a few months.

Alma Garrett experiences a body crisis when she gives up opium after her husband's death. She had used the drug to numb herself to her own powerlessness in her marriage to a man she did not love, and to whom she was mentally superior. Ironically, her withdrawal from the drug makes her more powerless than she has ever been, and at times she is unable to speak, hold down food, or control her body's tremblings. However, when Trixie, Al Swearengen's whore, explains to Alma that Swearengen is trying to control her by keeping her addicted, Alma is able, by sheer power of will, to exert enough control over her body to fake addiction in the presence of Farnum, who serves as Swearengen's spy, convincing his boss that she's not a threat and thereby maintaining indirect control over her husband's finances. The success of this charade constitutes the beginning of the end of Alma's powerlessness. As her body becomes clear of the drug on which she depended, the clarity of sobriety awakens Alma to what she is capable of, and gives her the confidence to take over her business affairs outright, a confidence she might not have found had she never had to struggle with the addiction. In the second season, Alma's struggle against powerlessness is recalled for her when she experiences the loss of control that comes with pregnancy. Visiting the gravesite of her dead husband, she remarks, "I am so afraid my life is living me and will soon be over without a moment of it having been my own." But though she fears a loss of control, Alma's experience with addiction and withdrawal has also taught her to trust her body's instincts which, now that they are unmediated by drugs, convince her to keep the baby, evidenced by her admission that "my body now tells me that this is fine and right" ("Boy the Earth Talks To," 2.12).

Some struggles with inner demons are not only played out during body crises, but, through these crises, are also written into the sufferer's flesh. Seth Bullock is a man constantly pulled in two different directions by, on the one hand, his desire not to become an instrument of the law and, on the other hand, his hatred of the mob justice that takes over when there is no law. Watching the comings and goings of the trial of Jack McCall for the murder of Wild Bill from his store, Bullock fears justice will not be served by the trial. When McCall is found innocent and set free, Bullock decides to create justice according to the dictates of his rage by chasing down and executing the murderer. However, this chase is interrupted by Bullock's encounter with an Indian, with whom he is forced to fight to the death ("Plague," 1.6). Though Bullock emerges victorious from the encounter, he is by no means unharmed. The injuries he has sustained, in the form of bruises, cuts, and a gaping wound above his eye, leave him unconscious until Charlie Utter revives him and tends to his wounds. Utter tells Bullock that the man he fought was simply trying to honor his own dead comrade when Bullock intruded on their holy ground. Bullock, traumatized by his injuries, recalls the senselessness of his violent, bodily struggle with the Indian, and the sheer luck that allowed him to land a deathblow. Through this experience, Bullock seems to recognize that his own mission was not governed not by justice but by personal vengeance, and, when he finally catches McCall, decides to turn him over to the US authorities instead of killing him. Bullock's battle scars remain visible for the six episodes of *Deadwood* that follow his injury at the hands of the Indian and, in those six episodes, Bullock becomes more willing to take part in the business of bringing order to the Deadwood camp, leaving some of his reluctance to take a leadership role in the community behind. His scars serve to remind the audience that, though Bullock doesn't speak directly of the body crisis that awakened him to the moral peril of living by his own rules, it is never far from his mind.

Other characters, both major and minor, experience body crises similar to Alma's and Seth's, during which their bodies become a site for both physical and psychic struggle. Mose Manuel's survival of gunshot wounds to his belly provides him with a psychic catharsis, ridding him of the guilt that was festering in his gut over his murder of his brother. Andy Cramed, a conman, finds his guilt over past bad acts forced to the surface of his feverish skin by a bout with smallpox, his illness sending him so far into the alternate universe of body crisis that he spends days there, writhing and incoherently blathering, "I apologize" to an unseen victim. When he returns to the kingdom of the well, Andy finds himself incapable of resuming his former profession and devotes himself to ministering to the fellow men he once sought to rob. His nurse during his illness is Calamity Jane, a character whose own body crisis, alcoholism, is ongoing in the first two seasons of *Deadwood*. Jane, possibly a survivor of childhood abuse, cannot bear to "stay fuckin' sober" ("No Other Sons or Daughters," 1.9) and live with the memories that plague her when she's lucid. Thus drunkenness is a fitting crisis for Jane, providing a painful respite from those memories through blackouts, which return her body to her in bruised and bloody condition.

But of all of the body crises in *Deadwood*, the one that perhaps fits its sufferer the best is Al Swearengen's bout with kidney stones. Prior to being incapacitated by the malady, Swearengen is driven daily by a need to know about and exert control over everything happening in the camp. Though his minions, Dan Dority and Johnny Burns, are loyal to him, he has little faith in their abilities, or in the loyalty of anyone else who serves him. As the camp grows and other citizens and outside forces begin to grab power there, Swearengen's worries about what he cannot control increase, and his tension can only be released physically, through his nightly blowjob from Dolly. It soon becomes clear that Swearengen will never be able to keep the firm hold on the camp he had during its early days, or to know everything that happens outside of his earshot, and so his anxiety over his slipping command builds until it seems to take over his body, clogging his "prick" via the kidney stones, preventing his nightly release, and ultimately reducing him to a twitching, incoherent body on the floor of his office. After his collapse, Swearengen is unable to run his operation himself and has to rely on and communicate through Dan and Johnny until the stones finally pass. When Swearengen returns to consciousness to find Dan smiling over him, he remembers little of his ordeal, but his first question—"Did you fuck me while I was out?" ("Requiem for a Gleet")—nonetheless indicates his recognition that, by leaning on Dan and Johnny during his body crisis, he has effectively yielded some of his control to them. What's more, following the ordeal, Swearengen, who had been unwilling to appear as ailing in front of Bullock following their fight in the street, now calls Bullock to his sickbed, revealing the extent of his illness to his sometime adversary and begrudgingly acknowledging his own weakness when compared to Bullock by saying "you got gall, coming before me prettier than ever" ("Complications," 2.5). Swearengen's body crisis has revealed to him his own limitations: he will never be able to fully control either his body or the camp without depending on others. Only by accepting these limitations and reaching out to Bullock, Dority, Burns, and later Silas Adams, Sol Star and Mr. Wu, is Swearengen ultimately able to become the agent of Deadwood's annexation, thus maintaining some of his original control over the camp. Still, he remains nostalgic for the days when he stood on his own, not limited by his own body, which is perhaps why, during his convalescence, Swearengen chooses a bodiless Indian head as his confidant.

COMMUNITY CRISES

"From one spirit are we all baptized into one body."

Reverend H. W. Smith, "The Trial of Jack McCall"

During his eulogy for Wild Bill Hickok, Reverend Smith compares mankind to a human body, saying,

> "The eye cannot say unto the hand, I have no need of thee; nor again the head to the feet, I have no need of thee." Nay, much more those members of the body which seem to be more feeble ... and those members of the body which we think of as less honorable—all are necessary. He says that there should be no schism in the body but that the members should have the same care one to another. And whether one member suffer all the members suffer with it.
>
> "The Trial of Jack McCall"

Smith is trying to ward off more senseless killing following Bill's murder by reminding his parishioners that they are a community and should take comfort in one another. A lesson that runs counter to the founding principles of the camp, which are lawlessness and an every-man-for-himself modus operandi, it seems to be lost on many of the mourners. One such mourner is Bullock who, frustrated as usual at being caught in a tug-of-war between law and lawlessness, exclaims afterward that the sermon was "pure gibberish," seeming to take the Reverend's meaning, but not wanting to admit that he has to do "any fucking thing that I don't want to do" with regard to the care and safekeeping of his fellow man. However, as the series continues, it becomes clear that the Reverend's point is a salient one, and that, when one member of the Deadwood community suffers, the community suffers as a whole.

Indeed, it is the Reverend Smith's own body crisis that convinces many in the camp of the truth in his sermon. Symptoms of Smith's brain tumor first present themselves only minutes after the sermon. As members of the camp begin to gather that Smith is sick, witnessing his partial paralysis, seizures and incoherent ramblings, his helplessness makes them so uneasy they can hardly bear to look at him. In effect, Smith has himself become the more feeble part of the communal body referred to in his sermon. Swearengen, whose own brother suffered from seizures similar to the Reverend's, tells Smith he must not come inside the Gem, rationalizing his refusal by the fact that the Smith is a man of the cloth. But as Smith's condition worsens, it becomes clear that Swearengen, his whores, and their customers simply cannot stand the sight of the ailing man in his pathetic condition. Bullock and Sol, though more sympathetic to Smith, also have difficulty interacting with him. And Doc Cochran, raging at God's senseless infliction of suffering on the Reverend, can barely stand to be in his presence. But, just like the other, stronger members of the communal body in his sermon, these stronger members of Smith's community cannot tell him they have no need of him. He is a reminder to them of the helpless who are present in every society, even a rough one like Deadwood, and who require the care of their fellow man. Thus, Cochran arranges for Smith to be cared for at the Gem, Trixie stays with the Reverend as his caretaker, and later Swearengen, having recognized that he must act where the Reverend's God will not, "takes care" of the Reverend in his own way, suffocating him and thereby ending his misery. In this way, Doc, Al, Trixie, and others in Deadwood are united around the Reverend's body crisis. The parts that the characters play in caring for Smith in what Doc calls "his last extremity," which Swearengen, in typical Deadwoodian style, equates to "a bag of shit" ("Sold Under Sin"), complicate their existences, making them realize that they have obligations to one another they would not have recognized had the Reverend stayed well.

While the Reverend's body crisis is shared by several of the show's main characters, the body crisis of Seth Bullock's son, William, brings Deadwood together as a community on an even larger scale. William, kicked in the head by a horse, goes into a coma and never returns from the "night side of life" that is his ailment. His thoughts, emotions, and even his pain remain veiled as he lies unconscious on his sickbed, his life ebbing away. But that pain can be read everywhere else in Deadwood as the community takes on William's body crisis as its own. The whores in the Gem are inconsolable, as is Tom Nuttall, who was looking after William at the time of the accident. Even the most hardhearted residents of the camp, such as the murderous Francis Wolcott, inquire as to the health of the child. William's body crisis ends with his death, but the crisis of the community continues through his funeral, during which nearly every resident of Deadwood files by the child's casket, needing to view his body in order to come to terms with the idea of such an innocent being killed. The body crisis of the child unites Deadwood in a way that all of the bodily pleasure that the residents have experienced there could not. Again, Smith's sermon about the weaker and less honorable members of the communal body is recalled. Though a weaker member of a society, a child like William can also be seen as the emblem of all that is and can be good there. It is clear from their reaction to this death that the residents of Deadwood have some common beliefs about what their community is and can be, but it isn't until those beliefs are shaken by William's body crisis that these residents realize these beliefs even exist.

DIS-EASE AND THE BODY POLITIC

"You call the law in, Sampson, you can't just call it off."
        Seth Bullock, "Deadwood" (1.1)

Deadwood's creator David Milch has said:

> The modern situation is predicated upon the illusion of the self's isolation—that business of 'I'm alone, you're alone, we can bullshit each other when we're fucking or whatever else, but the truth is we're alone. Right?' Well I believe that *that* is fundamentally an illusion.
>
> (Singer 192)

This idea—that human beings are not alone—informs much of the action in *Deadwood*, the purpose of which, as evidenced by the body crises discussed above, often seems to be to force a similar realization on the camp's inhabitants. But the realization is forced in a different way during the smallpox epidemic, a body crisis which takes the form of contagion, and which mobilizes the camp not as a body-like community sharing the suffering of one of its members, but as a politically organized body of people under one government or, in other words, a body politic.

In truth, there is nothing more symbolic of community than disease, which can only be spread by people who are not isolated from one another, but rather, who are living *together*. Additionally, as Elaine Scarry puts it, "In the isolation of pain, even the most uncompromising advocate of individualism might suddenly prefer a realm populated by companions" (Scarry 11). Thus, in coping with the smallpox contagion, residents of Deadwood are backed into the realization that, no matter how intent they are on being autonomous individuals, they will always be connected by uncontrollable elements such as communicable disease, and will have to depend on one another to survive as a community. Though there is some talk of annexation and government in Deadwood before the smallpox outbreak, it is only the outbreak itself that is able to force the more prominent citizens to form a town council, the first semblance of a government in Deadwood, to map out the ways in which the disease will be combated. This council is proven necessary by the very actions of the residents who claim that they do not need government, such as Cy Tolliver, who conceals the first cases of the plague by dumping a sick employee in the forest and only sending for vaccine when Doc Cochran bravely blackmails him into it. The opposing behavior of these two residents contains an answer to what is perhaps the central question of *Deadwood*, which is whether or not residents can be trusted to handle their business themselves without being regulated by a larger power, or, put more simply, whether order is possible without law. The answer, as provided by the plague outbreak, seems to be that, though some members of a society can be counted upon to behave decently, in order to ensure against the Tollivers of the world, some sort of institutionalized government, and the laws that accompany it, is necessary. In light of the fact that it is contagion that first forces the issue of law on the people of Deadwood, it is probably no mistake that Seth Bullock, the character in the series who is inexorably drawn to the role of lawman, is named the first health commissioner.

Throughout *Deadwood*, ambivalence is expressed, both by Doc Cochran and by his patients, about the limitations of the institution of medicine. Jane, Swearengen, Trixie and others all take turns telling Cochran that the fact that he cannot do more to heal patients like Reverend Smith, William Bullock and Mose Manuel, is a disgrace. Cochran, who lost faith in both God and his profession during the Civil War, when his patients all died for a purpose he couldn't understand, often echoes this sentiment. Just as the smallpox outbreak reflects the series' central question of law versus order, this dis-ease over the limitations of modern medicine, reflects a corresponding dis-ease at the coming of law. The institution that Cochran represents, like the law, seeks to bring order to unruly bodies, in the case of medicine through scientific knowledge and methods applied equally to all. Through this brand of order, the institution of medicine eliminates some unorthodox, unethical, and oftentimes malignant methods of dealing with illness, such as Cy Tolliver's decision to abandon his sick in the wilderness. But the same institutionalized order necessarily reigns in many benevolent forms of healing, such as Jane Cannery's unique brand of nursing, which restores Mose Manuel to health when Cochran, a practitioner of institutionalized medicine, has given up on him. The same is true of the law, which, while ensuring against catastrophes that may befall the town, also creates red tape that is an unnecessary hardship to residents like Tom Nuttall, who have come West to escape just such bureaucracy.

Still, as the coming of the epidemic demonstrates, law, with its regulation of the interdependent functionality of the community, is the only way to make sure that the weaker members of society are carried along with the strong. Additionally, the self-governance decided on by the residents during the plague eventually becomes the camp's only defense against the threat of the larger bureaucracy of the outside world. In a way, this struggle becomes *Deadwood*'s largest body crisis of all, with the camp itself as a body, its thoroughfare veins, its residents blood, its center (the Gem) a heart. The crisis is hinted at by Swearengen's continual comparison of the camp to a body ("they're going after our nuts") that the lawmakers in Yankton want control of like "runts or two-headed calves or pigs with excess legs for a good fuckin' grinding up" ("Childish Things"). As the forces of the outside world seek to gain controlling interest in the camp, their rumors of devalued claims spread among the residents much like a virus and it is up to Swearengen and Bullock to regain control over the town and its residents in the same way that they struggle for control over their own unruly bodies. This control is eventually regained, in part through the camp's body politic.

DEADWOOD AND ITS GENRE

"And though after my skin worms destroy this body, yet in my flesh I shall see God."

Andy Cramed, *reading from Job 19:26, "The Whores Can Come" (2.11)*

Many elements of *Deadwood* represent a departure from the traditional Western, not the least of which is the series' disposal, through body crises, of the notion of the truly stoic Western Hero, uncontrolled by bodily demands, untouched by illness and pain. But is it accurate to characterize *Deadwood*'s use of body crises as a complete departure from the genre of the Western? In *A Certain Tendency of the Hollywood Cinema, 1930–80*, Robert Ray identifies a central anxiety of the Western as being the closing in and eventual regulation of the West and its "individualistic, outlaw hero" (Ray 75). This anxiety is definitely present in *Deadwood* and is consistently echoed by the series' body crises, which warn of the inevitability of law and even precipitate its coming. Seen in light of Ray's observation, the body crises in *Deadwood* seem not to be a departure from the themes of the Western at all but, rather, a method through which the series reconnects with its genre. And, if viewed as a metaphor for the closed frontier, these crises and the institutionalized order that they necessitate can be seen as an extension of the trajectory of the Western into a kind of post-Western in which the worst fears of the genre are realized and escaping from law or even from one's fellow man into the unknown and unruly wilderness is no more possible than avoiding the common cold.

CHAPTER 14

DEADWOOD DICK

THE WESTERN (PHALLUS) REINVENTED

David Scott Diffrient

In the days immediately following the March 21, 2004 premiere of *Deadwood*, David Milch's revisionist Western series set during the 1870s, dozens of American newspaper critics pontificated on the merits and shortcomings of this latest entry in HBO's stellar Sunday night lineup. Of the many contentious aspects of the program, which, paradoxically, takes poetic license in de-romanticizing the exploits of Wild Bill Hickok, Calamity Jane, Seth Bullock, and other inhabitants of the titular South Dakota gold-mining camp, none generated so fierce a public outcry or so spirited a defense as its profanity-sprinkled dialogue. Laced with flamboyantly vulgar expressions unique to that lawless era as well as anachronistic neologisms, the scripts and spoken lines themselves became sites of critical discourse about the historical accuracy of a program otherwise beholden to cultural verisimilitude and meticulous attention to detail at the scenographic level.[1]

This initial (and ongoing) interest in the colloquial malfeasance of *Deadwood* is understandable; for never before had a TV Western unleashed such a torrent of profane yet florid prose, much of which leaps off the tongue of Al Swearengen, ruthless proprietor of the Gem saloon and its brothel upstairs, whose baroque turns of phrase are often punctuated with sudden eruptions of physical violence. One expletive in particular—"cocksucker"— became the focal point of many viewers who either condemned it for being inaccurate and distracting or expressed shock, disappointment, and disgust in their online harangues about its casual usage, failing to grasp the multivalent meanings of this quaintly passé if not totally obsolete word.[2]

Significantly, the many figurative references to male genitalia and the lower bodily stratum in the first episode are consolidated and literalized—indeed, visualized—in a scene from the show's second episode, "Deep Water" (1.2), when Tom Mason, one of Swearengen's criminal road agents, bursts into his boss's office buck-naked, holding his erect penis firmly in hand. Telling Tom (who is about to receive sexual gratification from an unnamed prostitute) to put his "iron" away, Al utilizes a word that highlights the symbolic slippage in most Westerns between *weapon* and *phallus*, something similarly articulated in the Season Two episode "A Lie Agreed Upon," Part 1 (2.1), when the brothel owner tells laconic yet love-struck Seth (who is having an affair with the recently widowed Easterner Alma Garrett), "Sheath your prick."[3]

Strangely enough, this intentionally "shocking" moment of full-frontal nudity in *Deadwood*, coming just two months after the Janet Jackson/Super Bowl debacle known as "Boobgate," went relatively unnoticed by TV journalists, congressional representatives in Washington, FCC chair Michael Powell, and message-board contributors, who all seemed more preoccupied with the show's linguistic fixation on the word "cocksucker" than with the flaunting of an *actual cock*—the most taboo of masculinity's "anatomical referents." Indeed, in those early weeks of the series' run, many viewers who had been anticipating its arrival—the first significant television Western since the six-hour miniseries *Lonesome Dove* (1989) and *Dr. Quinn, Medicine Woman* (1993–1998)—compared it unfavorably to such classic precursors as *Gunsmoke* (1955–1975) and *Bonanza* (1959–1973), male-focalized programs that, if unsullied by vulgar slang and corporeal abjection, nevertheless helped to sediment the phallic symbology of the genre.[4]

In the following pages, and with apologies to Nat Love (the *real* "Deadwood Dick," who gained fame throughout the Dakota Territory in the 1870s as an African-American rodeo star and cowpuncher on the Chisholm Trail before becoming a Pullman porter late in life),[5] I mobilize a conjoined term that speaks volumes about the phallocentric tendencies of the Western genre, which has largely been the domain of stories about all-male groups, fathers and sons, or lone riders whose "flight from commitment" and the trappings of feminized civilization parallels their acceptance of brutalization as a means of retaining the "natural" state of things. Indeed, the "Deadwood dick" that appears in "Deep Water," although dispatched along with its owner by episode's end, continues to haunt the series as an emblem of male power (much as Wild Bill Hickok remains an enduring if spectral presence in the town months after being shot dead by Jack McCall), and thus demands scrutiny as a material metaphor of masculinity; or rather, as a physical expression of masculine force made immaterial yet more threatening in its immateriality.

This notion—that what has disappeared or simply been hidden is more ominous as a sign of phallic dominion—is suggested in several other scenes throughout the series, including one from the second season, when Francis Wolcott, a kinky and conniving advance man working for George Hearst, attempts to have sex with his penis inside his pants, suppressing in one somatic arena what he unleashes in another as the brutal slayer of three prostitutes (in "Something Very Expensive," 2.6). By using a single shocking scene in Milch's series to elaborate a set of critical inquiries about the phallocentric disposition of the Western as a whole, I hope not only to contribute to the already considerable body of analyses about the genre, but also to illustrate just how sophisticated *Deadwood* is in negotiating and problematizing some of its time-honored tropes.

"AN INTERESTING PIECE OF STRANGE": MEN AND WOMEN IN DEADWOOD

Before elaborating the aforementioned scene in which Tom Mason is (to quote the dependably uncouth Cy Tolliver) about to "put a stink on his johnson," it will be helpful to place it and the surrounding scenes comprising episode two into historical and narrative contexts. The episode immediately preceding "Deep Water," simply titled "Deadwood" (1.1), is set in July of 1876, a period when the titular town was on the verge of transforming from a makeshift settlement of canvas tents to a thriving if still dangerous community filled with commercial buildings, including saloons, hotels, hardware stores and a working sawmill. Only two summers before, in 1874, did Colonel George A. Custer lead twelve companies of cavalry and infantry into the Black Hills, then part of the Great Sioux Reservation. Searching for an appropriate spot to erect a military post in this otherwise "uninhabited gulch," he and his men instead discovered gold in the creeks coursing through the hills.

By the time the famed gunslinger Wild Bill Hickok and his own party (including Pony Express rider Charlie Utter and the buckskin-wearing pioneer Martha Jane Canary-Burke, better known as "Calamity Jane") arrived in Deadwood in 1876, hundreds of prospectors had already begun pouring into the Black Hills, turning the town into a "quagmire of piss and bullshit," to quote hotelier E. B. Farnum—one of the many characters in the HBO series based on real people. Besides these prospectors, there was a wave of so-called "stagecoach aristocrats," people like former Montana Marshall Seth Bullock and his entrepreneurial partner Sol Star, who would, in the years to come, alter the appearance of Deadwood even further.[6] These and other historical figures are among the two dozen main characters populating *Deadwood*, a series in which the flamboyantly festooned Hickok and the virtuous yet short-fused Bullock stand out amongst a dizzying array of social misfits, greedy gold miners, skinflint card sharks, ballyhoo artists, and other grubby lowlifes.

As an ensemble series featuring some of the most talented character actors in Hollywood, *Deadwood* is an inherently discursive text, amenable to the diegetic dissemination and development of multiple, parallel or intersecting plotlines, periodically tracking the exploits of everyone from brown-nosing barkeep Johnny Burns to honorable doctor Amos Cochran to physically crippled broom-pusher Jewel. These potential pluralities can puncture the text, disturb its linearity, and offer myriad openings through which the reader-spectator is free to enter into and negotiate the world David Milch has so carefully created. Yet it can also be argued that, as the series has progressed, and despite the arrival of additional characters, one figure has acquired an auratic presence, lording over both the town and the text in a way that suggests that the *name*, *law*, and *word* of the "father" have been indelibly imprinted on this otherwise lawless community (not to mention the bruised faces of its prostitutes). That person, of course, is Al Swearengen, in reality one of the first men to have entered Deadwood after Custer,[7] the chief architect of its ad hoc municipal organizations, and someone who exerts editorial influence on newspaperman A. W. Merrick. He is someone whose ascendancy, as I hope to presently show, is consistent with the genre's privileging of patriarchal figures yet, from time to time, is undercut if not completely thwarted by a troubled corporeality that—although not apparent in the first or second episode—becomes prominent in the show's second season.

The first episode, "Deadwood," directed by Walter Hill and written by Milch, not only introduces Swearengen and most of the other major characters in the series (with the exception of Cy Tolliver and Joanie Stubbs, who make their initial appearances in "Reconnoitering the Rim" [1.3]), but also culminates with a gunfight between three men in the thoroughfare.

Although a standard plot device found in traditional Westerns, one that allows the binary tension between opposing forces (hero vs. villain) to be resolved in the form of a kinesthetic spectacle (complete with onlookers who act as spectator-surrogates), the showdown in the penultimate scene of this episode—rendered in classical shot-reverse-shot—is here invested with moral ambiguity and emotional gravity due to the ghastly circumstances leading up to it.

The men in question are lawman-turned-gambler Wild Bill Hickok and marshal-turned-merchant Seth Bullock, together squaring off against Ned Mason, a highwayman who staged a raid against a Swedish family on the Spearfish Road to Minnesota, making it look as if they had been attacked by Sioux Indians so that he could steal their money. When Hickok and Bullock discover that Mason is the man responsible for the Metz family's massacre, they confront him on the street outside of the Gem saloon and the Grand Central Hotel. The accused, still on horseback, draws his gun, but is shot dead by Hickok, whose bullet pierces Mason's left eye. This grisly climax to the first episode leads to a brief, wordless coda in which Al Swearengen receives his most valuable asset—a prostitute named Trixie—in his bed, where he has been waiting for her with his six-shooter under the covers. The gun, hidden from sight, is merely a phallic precaution, noticeably located near a region of his body that is regularly "serviced" by this bruised and beaten woman, who, earlier in the episode, killed an abusive customer there in the saloon. Significantly, she too had used a pistol in self-defense, putting a bullet into the man's brain—just to the side of his left eye—in a manner that is neatly replicated by Hickok at the end of the episode. Before joining Swearengen in bed, Trixie takes the gun that she has been hiding in her cleavage and deposits it on the nightstand before stripping off her clothes, thus relieving herself of this symbolic instrument of power, violence, and retribution, and reassuring her employer that her allegiance as well as her body still lie with him.

The final moments of this first episode introduce a theme that will be developed in greater detail throughout the rest of the season. Trixie, like the other "resident employees" at the Gem, has been disciplined into a passive and obedient servant, an object of male desire and sexual consumption whom Swearengen habitually ushers to the brink of death (earlier in this episode, he has put a boot to her nearly broken neck upon discovering the murdered customer). He will continue to exert his authority over Trixie, and each subsequent episode not only brings a mounting sense of her desperation but also ups the ante for her impending, if consistently deferred, escape. Thus, so long as she and the other prostitutes operate within a space of restraints and an economy of exchange as well as a symbolic order and ideological system opposed to female emancipation, Swearengen is able to ensure his unchallenged status as both pimp-patriarch and, by metaphorical extension, operator of gold claims for the town at large. Ironically, it is not through benevolent gestures but rather by insulting, humiliating, and sometimes killing those beneath him that he is able to shore up support from those who contribute to his commanding position. However, the commanding presence of this man, who hides his own pistol between his legs and—from his perch above Main Street—literally looks down upon the denizens of Deadwood (a town whose name alone connotes the end or expenditure of the phallus), will become destabilized as the season advances.

Like the wood floor of the Grand Central Hotel, which bears the bloodstain left by a previous occupant,[8] "Deep Water" is saturated with references to the previous episode. Picking up where "Deadwood" left off, it begins with Doc Cochran and Calamity Jane guarding the sole survivor of Ned Mason's attack, the youngest member of the Metz family whose name, we later learn (in "Suffer the Little Children," 1.8), is Sofia.[9] While the unconscious girl is being tended to, another innocent figure—New York dilettante Brom Garrett—begins working his recently purchased gold claim in the company of Dan Dority, Swearengen's right-hand man (and resident hatchet man). Finding neither flakes nor nuggets, the fastidious city dude believes that he has been duped by Swearengen, who brokered the $20,000 deal, and feigns back pain in hopes of selling the pinched-out claim to E. B. Farnum, scheming proprietor of the Grand Central Hotel. This is the first of many moments in the series when the *performance* of corporeal pathologies plays a role in pecuniary transactions with actual or metaphorical "prostitutes" (the hotelier is, after all, merely a pawn of the town boss, little more than a spying informant, even after E. B.'s promotion to Mayor). Swearengen, who pays little heed to the swindled Easterner's situation, shifts his attention to Tom Mason, brother of the recently deceased, when he and another road agent by the name of Persimmon Phil ride into town. Angered by his road agents' unauthorized attack on the so-called "squareheads,"[10] Swearengen ultimately opts to kill Persimmon Phil rather than permanently silence the Metz girl. He also sends Tom Mason to avenge Ned's death.

Before Mason makes an ill-fated attempt on Hickok's life, he is seen enjoying what little time he has left in his own life with a prostitute, his sexual gratification only momentarily preempted when—penis in hand—he flings open the door to Swearengen's office, proudly displaying his somatic pleasure to both diegetic and extradiegetic audiences while proclaiming, "That snatch is branded!" The "snatch" in question belongs to a prostitute positioned behind him, visible through the open door of the opposite room. This is the moment alluded to earlier in this chapter, a scene whose impact cannot be fully conveyed in writing. Its effect on the viewer depends on how prepared he/she is for so startling and narcissistic a display of virility. Nevertheless, in an attempt to sort through some of the implications of the image, a more elaborate description of this significant, if curiously overlooked, moment is in order.

First, it should be pointed out that Tom bursts in at the very moment when Al is threatening to slash Persimmon Phil's throat. Having backhand slapped the younger man onto the floor, Swearengen himself exudes vigor, rage, intensity, and authority in a space where nefarious schemes are habitually hatched and men are routinely murdered. His power over Phil—indeed, over the entire populace—is lent additional weight by the sudden appearance of Phil's burly cohort. Intruding on the scene, Tom fails to interpret Al's malicious intentions toward his friend, believing that Phil simply tipped over in his chair. Still grasping his penis, which seems to pull him, as if by magnetic force, back to the "action," he resumes having "sex with an unfamiliar woman" (to borrow the words of Bella Union owner Cy Tolliver in "Here Was a Man," 1.4).

The sight of Mason in apparent control of his libidinal urges, even as he appears to be on the verge of orgasmic release, at first renders this troubling image of male domination and female subservience as representative of the patriarchal structures and phallic narcissism embedded in the genre as a whole. However, because this moment ruptures the text and shifts spectatorial focus from the aural plane to the visual, from the "filthy" language of the soundtrack (otherwise composed of lilting fiddles and delicately strummed mandolins) to the filthy body of the disrobed outlaw, it not only lays bare certain ideological and narrative conventions of the Western but also challenges the genre's implicit male spectatorship by deflecting the active masculine gaze back towards itself, ironically calling attention to the ways in which women have long been the cinematic and televisual signifiers of passivity and spectacle.

Standing in the doorway during a moment of ecstatic rapture, this lumbering hulk of a figure in a liminal state is literally caught between thresholds (sexual and spatial), his body poised for ocular consumption and indicative of the ways in which Deadwood itself—as a combination of lawless frontier and settled township—is situated between two extremes. Similarly, as a "Darwinian universe" that, in the words of one reviewer, is "simultaneously familiar and utterly alien" ("an interesting piece of strange," to again quote Cy Tolliver ["Bullock Returns to the Camp," 1.7]),[11] the television series itself, torn between the chaos and order respectively personified by Swearengen and Bullock (who are constantly locking horns), oscillates between the earthy and the transcendent. Yet archetypal dichotomies and clearly delineated heroes and villains in this ultimately deconstructive Western give way to infinite shades of gray, so that the traditional dialectics of activity and passivity as well as masculinity and femininity become problematic.

Thus, this "baring of the device" renders the habitual utterance of the word "cocksucker" as mere pretext to a more profound engagement with corporeal pathologies and thematic binaries (exterior/interior, nature/civilization, individual/community, etc.) throughout the series. To put the matter simply, it *shows* what is so often hidden behind the façades of Hollywood's sanitized frontier towns, where gendered and/or racial violence is sanctioned under the rubric of "Manifest Destiny" and where metonymy and metaphor become necessary means of representing latent elements. In doing so, the very visible penis signals the demystifying agenda of Milch's series, thereby severing the latter's connection to classical TV Westerns like *Bonanza* and *Gunsmoke* while strengthening its links to such prostitute-filled films as Robert Altman's *McCabe and Mrs. Miller* (1971) and Clint Eastwood's *Unforgiven* (1992). Indeed, the town of Deadwood is not so different from Big Whiskey, the lawless community at the heart of Eastwood's magisterial yet mud-caked Western, where women are habitually made to bear the brunt of punishment for such "crimes" as giggling at a man's small penis. The fact that Delilah, the prostitute who fails to suppress her laughter in *Unforgiven*, is eventually mutilated by Quick Mike (the man whose diminutive member literally *engendered* the giggle to begin with) so as to make her sexually unattractive, suggests that what the penis lacks (or has lost) in potency can be compensated for (or reclaimed by) the phallus.

In *Deadwood*, however, phallic claims to power are constantly undermined by various forms of troubled corporeality, a theme clearly articulated in the first three episodes of Season Two. By the end of "A Lie Agreed Upon," Part 1, after a knockdown fight between Swearengen and Bullock that sends both men over the railing of the Gem's balcony and into the muddy street below (a descent that suggests Al's loosening grip on the town, his diminished control over its citizenry), they are each presented to the audience as a bloody mess: Swearengen's ribs are fractured in the fall and Bullock's nose is broken. Tended to by a prostitute named Dolly, who gives him a prostate massage to ease his pain, Al descends even deeper into physical anguish, becoming increasingly incoherent once his bladder begins to back up due to kidney stones. Momentarily out of commission, he endures even greater pain in "New Money" (2.3), when the appropriately named Doc Cochran runs a rod through Al's penis and into his bladder to relieve his debilitating kidney stones and septic shock.[12]

Similarly, another phallic instrument is turned against Tom Mason by the end of "Deep Water." As would-be-avenger of his brother Ned's death, Mason, thoroughly liquored up, is shot by Hickok's Colt revolver in Tom Nuttall's No. 10 saloon (ironically, the place where, two episodes later, droop-eyed poker player Jack McCall shoots the famous gunslinger in the back). In killing Mason, Hickok (who had anticipated the attack and asked Bullock, standing nearby, to watch his back) sets the stage for his own demise in "Here Was a Man," which plays out in a similar fashion, albeit with very different results (full of anticipation, although Hickok's back is turned toward the entrance of the saloon, as if he has given himself over to death). In each case, the gun, whether wielded by the unsuccessful Mason or the successful McCall, appears as a phallic manifestation of an instinctual drive, an id unfettered by the societal codes of morality and prudence that comprise what, in Freudian terminology, is the superego (the part of the unconscious that restrains and censors the ego).

A GENRE "STUFFED WITH PHALLUSES": GUNS AND VIOLENCE IN THE WESTERN

"I'd rather have Deadeye Dick than a female with a gun in her hand."

Line spoken by a cowboy in the musical-western The Harvey Girls *(1946), when Judy Garland's character—a bumbling restaurant waitress named Susan—enters the Alhambra saloon waving two six-shooters in the faces of the male patrons.*

Throughout the history of American popular culture, the gun has been a key component in the iconic constitution of the frontier cowboy, an indispensable tool in dispatching villains and meting out "justice" in a detached yet visceral way. From Edwin S. Porter's *The Great Train Robbery* (1903), which climaxes with a close-up of Broncho Billy Anderson firing his six-shooter point-blank at the audience, to the brutal films of Anthony Mann (*Winchester '73*, 1950) and Samuel Fuller (*Forty Guns*, 1957), this iconographic piece of hardware has not only occupied a pivotal place in the mythology of the American West, but also—as the penis' double—secured a privileged cinematic space for (white) masculinity to flourish amidst racial and sexual Others.

As richly associative symbols of sexual prowess, rifles and pistols are thus pictorial displacements of the actual male member as well as its material apotheosis.[13] In psychoanalytic terms, the penis is an externalized "sign of proactivity or authority" that provides man evidence of (or support for) his imagined freedom from castration—a perception that hinges on his continued exertion of power and privilege. Although theorists have articulated the lack of commensurability between *phallus* and *penis*, and have sought to underline the ways in which masculinity is but a societal construct through which to preserve the status quo, many would agree that—as a genre "stuffed with phalluses" (to borrow the words of Samuel Fuller)—the Western collapses epistemological distinctions between the two through the emphatic privileging of the gun as both a sign of sadistic male power and an emblem of libidinal expenditure. Indeed, the iconographic foregrounding of guns reveals the underlying patriarchal constructions of the genre, which revels in sexual subjugation and racial violence even as it endorses a form of homosocial bonding amenable to community-formation and integration.

When women take possession of guns, this "inappropriate" appropriation signals a potential to castrate, an ability to turn a tool of male violence against its ingrained impulses. This idea is literalized in the operatic 1946 Western *Duel in the Sun*, when Jennifer Jones's mixed-race character Pearl Chavez points a pistol at the crotch of a man who had earlier murdered her fiancé. However, as in *Duel in the Sun*, such maneuvers—perhaps indicative of a phallic narcissism—often result in either the expulsion of the female from the community and/or her death at the hands of a man whose libidinal drives spill over into violence, thereby disarming her castrating threat and rendering women's identification with such ill-fated protagonists as merely a masochistic play with culturally dominant forms of power.[14]

Not coincidentally, it is Calamity Jane, the mannish, tough-talking companion of Wild Bill Hickok, who has the most difficulty fitting in within Deadwood, and her temporary abandonment of the town is as much a rejection of traditionally coded gender roles as it is a reaction to her own inability to attain the motor efficiency and phallic drive necessary to stand up against Al Swearengen, in whose presence she unexpectedly crumbles as the weepy protector of Sofia ("Deep Water"). Calamity's androgynous claim to (phallic) fame is thus capsized by this image of feminine subordination. Although she is the target of belligerent stares as soon as she enters Deadwood and her very existence will be thrown into crisis once Hickok is gunned down, this loyal sidekick of the Western hero truly becomes a social outcast when she does what practically everyone else in town does: cower before Swearengen. Significantly, it is in the realm of spoken language (the very thing that seems to attract the most critical attention to the series) where Calamity—one of the most foul-mouthed frontiers-people of either sex—begins to rival and even surpass Al. But the profuseness of her profanity casts in relief the literal and metaphorical "lack" that is suggested by her willingness yet inability to employ a gun against the murderous, Machiavellian brothel owner.

Just as failed pioneer men are referred to as "limp dicks" in the series, this coarse, frequently inebriated woman (who in "Deadwood" proclaims to the all-male patronage of the whorehouse, "I don't drink where I'm the only fucking one with balls!") is forced to assert her physical if not sexual abilities by way of boastful tough talk and liberal use of expletives. Thus, she functions as a site of both internal conflict and external contestation, fluctuating between self-reliant and codependent, active and passive registers while remaining situated outside the two main categories of femininity established at the outset of the series. The antithesis of both the schoolmarmish Alma Garrett and the dancehall girl Trixie (both of whom are often shown passively peering through interior windows at the spectacle of male violence outside), Calamity must constantly reposition herself vis-à-vis the men and women with whom she comes into contact.

The liminal nature of Calamity Jane's butch-femme identity is therefore consonant with the notion, put forth earlier in this essay, that masculinity itself—linked to that most prominent of generic props, the gun—can be made to stretch in different directions, encompassing the personal ambitions of everyone from upright lawman Seth Bullock to downright villain Tom Mason. The fact that it is Tom, not Seth, who is shown flaunting his penis in "Deep Water," suggests that what Milch and his team of writers are trying to do is not only test the limits of what is permissible on television, but also reveal the extent and limitations of pure "evil" in *Deadwood*; for the bare-assed badman's own in-between-ness (as both subject and object, ready for action yet momentarily caught between thresholds) is a sign of things to come for Swearengen and his gun-toting cronies, who are all complex figures of contradiction (and occasionally compassion) and who—as the series progresses—appear to be increasingly willing to put down their weapons long enough to *talk*, to resolve problems in a non-violent, relatively peaceful manner.

THE FINAL FRONTIER: MALE GENITALIA ONSCREEN

"The eye cannot say unto the hand, 'I have no need of thee'. Nor again the head to the feet, 'I have no need of thee'. They much more those members of the body which seem to be more feeble. And those members of the body which we think of as less honorable, all are necessary."

Preacher Smith, *quoting First Corinthians to a gathering of mourners at Wild Bill Hickok's grave*, "The Trial of Jack McCall"

The kind of sexual symbolism that I have thus far been discussing has filtered into American popular culture for several decades and infiltrated genres besides the Western. In an episode of the coming-of-age high school dramedy *Freaks and Geeks* (1999–2000), Ken, one of the titular teenaged outsiders, refers to a girl who was "packing both a gun and a holster" at birth. This rather tasteless way of describing a hermaphrodite indicates just how deeply the gun-as-penis metaphor has seeped into the American cultural imagination. Not coincidentally, that episode's title, "The Little Things," connotes the manner in which sex organs are typically presented in cable television series these days. For example, one episode of *South Park* (1997–) features a scene in which an animated Osama bin Laden's miniscule member can be seen through a barrage of overlaid magnifying glasses. Another *South Park* episode, entitled "Good Times with Weapons," shows Cartman disrobing on an outdoor stage, exposing his "wee-wee" to the world. Although a tiny protuberance, the grade-schooler's penis causes uproar amongst the townspeople, who fail to even notice that his classmate, Butters (who is standing beside him on stage), has been stabbed in the eye by a ninja throwing-star. Their convenient oversight of Butter's flesh wound and exclusive focus on so small a thing as Cartman's genitals not only resonates with the moralistic tenor of public outrage following Janet Jackson's Super Bowl breast-unveiling, but inversely relates to *Deadwood* fans' and critics' near-exclusive focus on words like "cock" over the actual thing itself, the penis that Tom Mason parades before the camera in "Deep Water" as a sign of his virility and power over a prostitute.

Although full-frontal male nudity has long been a part of the European Art Cinema tradition, especially in the films of Rainer Werner Fassbinder, Pier Paolo Pasolini, Derek Jarman, and other filmmakers sensitive to the politics of gender and the erotics of (homo)sexuality, only recently has it begun to manifest in theatrically released American motion pictures like *Boogie Nights* (1997) and *Sideways* (2004). Such mainstream crowd-pleasers, which feature brief yet potent shots of men's genitalia, are nevertheless exceptions to the rule and are less interested in examining the correlations between scatological impulse, patriarchal authority, and social responsibility than HBO programs like *The Sopranos* (1999–), *Six Feet Under* (2001–2005), and *The Wire* (2002–)—the latter series featuring an episode (entitled "Ebb Tide") that at one point shows a scurvy pipe-cleaner of a man named Ziggy hauling his excessively large penis out to the amusement of his pub-mates.

As a pay-cable series less beset by fears of censorship and FCC regulations than its network competitors, *Deadwood* is able to push the limits of what is culturally permissible (in terms of profanity, sexuality, and violence) and—like *The Sopranos*, which frequently betrays a Rabelaisian fascination with excremental and digestive activities (from Adriana's irritable bowel syndrome to Uncle Junior's oral fixations)—paradoxically plumbs the depths of the lower bodily stratum while maintaining the high production values associated with quality TV. For example, in "Reconnoitering the Rim," Al—sniffing something in the air—asks his clueless colleagues, "Who cut the cheese?" Later, a faro junkie has a sudden attack of diarrhea in Swearengen's intimidating presence ("Mr. Wu," 1.10). The first sound and image in the Season Two episode "Complications" (2.5) is of Alma throwing up in a water jug.

Throughout the series, we are given a variety of views of both man's and nature's violence on the larger community, whose rising death toll or "body count" (tallied on the show's official website) is a testament to the difficulties of surviving in so wild and "uncivilized" an environment. Rotting corpses pile up, from Wild Bill's body—a magnet for swarming flies put on posthumous display outside Nuttall's saloon—to the pustule-covered victims of the latest "plague," smallpox. Significantly, when Al informs the Doc about the second victim of smallpox, he sarcastically jokes that the man "couldn't get it up." The fact that this highly contagious disease brought on by nature should be linked to a man's inability to sustain an erection is only further indication that the corporeal pathologies of the series are intricately intertwined with references to failed or troubled forms of masculinity.

Not coincidentally, *Deadwood*'s high-low approach to such themes is hinted at in the aforementioned episode "New Money," when Dan speaks for an ailing and incapacitated Al (who cannot utter anything beyond a grunt), telling the Doc that—between the "high" and "low" medical procedures available to him (entering above or below the penis)—his boss "wants the upper." This comment could be interpreted any number of ways. For instance, one might take Dan's comment as an indication of Al wanting to reclaim his superior position in the town once he has recuperated from this physical setback. Perhaps it anticipates the high road that Al takes in future episodes, reining in his rage to a degree and adopting a less caustic attitude toward Bullock and the others. I am inclined to read this emphasis on "the upper" or "high" method prescribed by Doc Cochran extra-diegetically, as a reference to David Milch's attempt to elevate his earthy material, to transcend the binaristic limitations of the Western genre and reveal the political intrigues, sexual indiscretions, and moral ambiguities that are not unique to that era of the late 1800s, but in fact can be found in the contemporary cultural climate.

In reconnoitering the Western and bringing twenty-first-century sensibilities to bear on its time-honored tropes, Milch should be commended for showing that this once popular genre—like the widow Garrett's gold claim—is not, as previously believed, "pinched-out." *Deadwood* not only makes a radical departure from the nostalgic impulses and sanitized mythos of traditional Westerns, but also invites allegorical readings through pandemic, profusely unbridled metonymy and metaphor—key components in the cinematic and televisual construction of masculinity. Moreover, if masculinity is, as stated above, a societal construct through which to preserve the status quo, then *Deadwood*'s openness in showing what is typically repressed in the Western can be seen as an extension of even broader satiric and deconstructive aims, delivered during a politically conservative, increasingly militaristic era—a time, I might add, in desperate need of such narratives.

DEADWOOD EPISODE GUIDE

#	Air Date	Title	Writer	Director
1.1	3|21|04	Deadwood	David Milch	Walter Hill
1.2	3|28|04	Deep Water	Malcolm MacRury	Davis Guggenheim
1.3	4|4|04	Reconnoitering the Rim	Jody Worth	Davis Guggenheim
1.4	4|11|04	Here Was a Man	Elizabeth Sarnoff	Alan Taylor
1.5	4|18|04	The Trial of Jack McCall	John Belluso	Ed Bianchi
1.6	4|25|04	Plague	Malcolm MacRury	Davis Guggenheim
1.7	5|2|04	Bullock Returns to the Camp	Jody Worth	Michael Engler
1.8	5|9|04	Suffer the Little Children	Elizabeth Sarnoff	Dan Minahan
1.9	5|16|04	No Other Sons or Daughters	George Putnam	Ed Bianchi
1.10	5|23|04	Mr. Wu	Bryan McDonald	Dan Minahan
1.11	6|6|04	Jewel's Boot Is Made for Walking	Ricky Jay	Steve Shill
1.12	6|13|04	Sold Under Sin	Ted Mann	Davis Guggenheim
2.1	3|6|05	A Lie Agreed Upon Part 1	David Milch	Ed Bianchi
2.2	3|13|05	A Lie Agreed Upon Part 2	Jody Worth	Ed Bianchi

#	Air Date	Title	Writer	Director
2.3	3|20|05	New Money	Elizabeth Sarnoff	Steve Shill
2.4	3|27|05	Requiem for a Gleet	Ted Mann	Alan Taylor
2.5	4|3|05	Complications	Victoria Morrow	Gregg Fienberg
2.6	4|10|05	Something Very Expensive	Steve Shill	Steve Shill
2.7	4|17|05	E. B. Was Left Out	Jody Worth	Michael Almereyda
2.8	4|24|05	Childish Things	Regina Corrado	Timothy Van Patten
2.9	5|1|05	Amalgamation and Capital	Elizabeth Sarnoff	Ed Bianchi
2.10	5|8|05	Advances, None Miraculous	Sara Hess	Dan Minahan
2.11	5|15|05	The Whores Can Come	Bryan McDonald	Gregg Fienberg
2.12	5|22|05	Boy the Earth Talks To	Ted Mann	Ed Bianchi

A DEADWOOD ENCYCLOPEDIA

COMPILED BY
DAVID LAVERY

This encyclopedia will continue to be updated throughout Season Three in a hyperlinked version on the book's website: http://www.davidlavery.net/Deadwood.

$7.60 Amount Al had to his name when abandoned at a Chicago orphanage by his mother.

$1,000 Amount paid to Al by Bullock and Star for a lot that will hold their hardware store.

$2,000 Amount Al pays Adams to kill Claggett (he asked for $20,000).

$5,000 Amount Al pays Miss Isringhausen for her cooperation; also the amount Magistrate Claggett demands to make a Chicago warrant against Al disappear.

$10,000 Amount E. B. wants from Wolcott for Wild Bill's last letter.

$20,000 Amount Brom Garrett pays for his gold claim.

$50,000 Amount Tolliver offers General Crook to garrison troops in Deadwood and Isringhausen offers Al for his cooperation in accusing Alma in Brom's death.

$200,000 Amount Wolcott offers Mose Manuel for his claim.

$300,000 Amount of capitalization Denver requires in order to open a bank in Deadwood.

A

Adams, Silas Played by Titus Welliver. Formerly Magistrate Claggett's right-hand man, becomes an advisor and enforcer for Al in Season Two after murdering his former employer. Frequently clashes with Dan Dority, jealous of his newfound importance to Al.

"Advances, None Miraculous" *Deadwood* Episode (2.10). The one in which Jarry returns and is manipulated by Al, Merrick, and Adams; Doc attends to William Bullock and Mose Manuel (at the Chez Ami); Hostetler and the Nigger General contemplate a return to town; Andy Cramed comes back as a minister.

Ajaye, Franklyn (1949–) *Deadwood* actor, playing Samuel Fields.

Almereyda, Michael (1960–) Director of "E.B. Was Left Out." Also directed a variety of short and feature films, including *Twister* (1990), *Nadja* (1994), *The Rocking Horse Winner* (1997), *Trance* (1998), *Hamlet* (2000), *Happy Here and Now* (2002).

"Amalgamation and Capital" *Deadwood* Episode (2.9). The one in which arrival of a safe with currency for the new bank is anticipated; Al reaches an understanding with Isringhausen; Mose Manuel is shot at the Bella Union; William Bullock is severely injured by a runaway horse.

Ambulators, the In "Mr. Wu" Merrick, distressed by the crowded conditions at the Grand Central, proposes formation of a club of walking, talking cogitators to be called the "Ambulators."

Anderson, Mrs. Fat Ass Proprietor of a Chicago orphanage where Al grew up after being abandoned by his mother.

Anderson, Flora Played by Kristen Bell. Young grifter who seeks to swindle Cy Tolliver and is brutally murdered by him.

Anderson, Miles Played by Greg Cipes. Brother and collaborator of Flora Anderson; murdered by Tolliver.

Anti-Semitism— Hostility and/or prejudice against Jews. Most prominently displayed in Deadwood by Al, who calls Sol a "Jew Bastard" ("Deep Water") and, after Sol is shot ("A Lie Agree Upon," Part I), tells Trixie "Wave a penny under the Jew's nose. If they've got living breath in them, it brings them right 'round."

Ass-Fucking All-purpose profanity figurative signifying being forced to do something one wishes not to do. For example Al's "Reconnoitering the Rim" observation that "Crazy Horse went into Little Big Horn, bought his people one good long term ass fuckin'."

Austria Country of origin of Sol Star.

B

Baseball In "Plague," Dan Dority laments not getting baseball scores from back east.

Beaver, Jim (1950–) *Deadwood* actor, playing Ellsworth.

Bell, Kristen (1980–) *Deadwood* actor, playing Flora Anderson. Later became the eponymous star of the UPN series *Veronica Mars.*

Bell, Marshall (1942–) *Deadwood* actor, playing Magistrate Claggett.

Bella Union Cy Tolliver's new, classier saloon, gambling emporium (offering faro as well as poker), and, of course, house of prostitution. Its opening in Deadwood comes as a surprise

to Al but not to "judas goat" E. B., who helped make it possible.

Belluso, John Writer of "The Trial of Jack McCall."

Bianchi, Ed (1942–) Director of "The Trial of Jack McCall," "No Other Sons or Daughters," "A Lie Agreed Upon," "Amalgamation and Capital," "Boy the Earth Talks To." Has also directed episodes of *Homicide, Law & Order: SVU, The Wire.*

Black Darjeeling The "fuckin" mountain-grown Indian tea, full-bodied but subtly flavored, specially requested by Al when he visits Alma Garret in "E. B. was Left Out."

Black Hills "[A] small, isolated mountain range rising from the Great Plains of North America in western South Dakota and extending into Wyoming, USA. ... The region is considered sacred by many of the Plains Native Americans. ... accurately described as an 'island of trees in a sea of grass'" [from Wikipedia].

Blazanov Played by Pavel Lychnikoff. Deadwood's telegraph operator, who arrives for the first time in "Childish Things."

Body Snatching Robbing of graves in order to procure bodies for medical dissection, a crime in which Doc Cochran is rumored to have engaged in the past.

Boneshaker, the Tom Nuttall's name for his velocipede bicycle.

Boothe, Powers (1949-) *Deadwood* actor, playing Cy Tolliver. His previous film and television roles include *Guyana Tragedy: The Story of Jim Jones* (1980), *Southern Comfort* (1981), *Nixon* (1995), *Frailty* (2001), *Sin City* (2005).

"Boy the Earth Talks To" *Deadwood* Episode (2.12). The one in which George Hearst arrives; Jane takes a bath; Alma Garret and Ellsworth are married; an agreement is reached with Jarry and Yankton; Andy Cramed stabs Tolliver; Wu is reinstated as the boss of Chinatown; and Wolcott hangs himself.

Bridgers, Sean *Deadwood* actor, playing Johnny Burns.

Brown, W. Earl (1963-) *Deadwood* actor, playing Dan Dority.

"Bullock Returns to the Camp" *Deadwood* Episode (1.7). The one in which Charlie and Bullock find McCall and take him to Yankton for trial; Flora and Miles Anderson arrive and begin their schemes; Brom's funeral is held; Rev. Smith is plagued by seizures; Bullock threatens Al (to harm Alma); Alma offers to pay Trixie's way out of Deadwood (with the Metz girl).

Bullock, Martha Played by Anna Gunn. Wife of Seth Bullock, who married her after the death of her husband, Seth's brother.

Bullock, Seth Played by Timothy Olyphant. Formerly a sheriff in Montana, comes to Deadwood to open a hardware store with Sol Star and becomes sheriff.

Bullock, William Played by Josh Eriksson. Son of Martha Bullock and Seth's late brother. Killed by a runaway horse.

Bummer Dan Shot by the bartender in Saloon #10 after he urinated in his hat ("A Lie Agreed Upon," Part 1).

Burns, Johnny Played by Sean Bridgers. Al's dim-witted, ass-kissing third-in-command.

C

Calamity Jane Played by Robin

Weigert. Profane, alcoholic former scout and fellow traveler of Wild Bill Hickok.

Callie, Dayton *Deadwood* actor, playing Charlie Utter.

Carradine, Keith (1949–) *Deadwood* actor, playing Wild Bill Hickok.

Carrie Chez Ami prostitute dangled by Maddie as bait in her blackmail scheme against Wolcott. Murdered by him (as is Maddie) in "Something Very Expensive."

Cat Piss In *Deadwood* an olfactory indication of lying, as when Al smells it (1) interrogating Jimmy and Leon in search of missing dope ("Mr. Wu") and (2) in the presence of Jarry, who has come to talk about annexation ("Boy the Earth Talks To").

Cedar, Larry (1955–) *Deadwood* actor, playing Leon.

Cheyenne City in Wyoming from which Wild Bill, Jane, and Charlie came to Deadwood and the latter operates a freight business.

Cheyenne and Black Hills Telegraph Company New Deadwood business represented by Blazanov. Its coming is cursed by Al.

Chez Ami New, pricey Deadwood bordello, opened by Joanie Stubbs (with financial backing from Eddie Sawyer) and her more experienced friend Maddie. The scene of Wolcott's murder of three prostitutes (including Maddie).

Chicago Illinois city, source of a warrant (for murder) against Al Swearengen used by Magistrate Claggett as blackmail in the negotiations over Deadwood's annexation. Al grew up there in Ms. Anderson's Orphanage.

Chief, the The severed head of a Cheyenne Indian, brought to Deadwood in "Here was a Man" by a Mexican seeking Al's bounty offer in the Pilot. In Season Two it becomes Al's constant ficele.

"Childish Things" *Deadwood* Episode (2.8). The one in which Al seeks Bullock's help with Montana; Doc seeks better treatment for the Chinese whores; Blazanov and Tom Nuttall's bicycle arrives; Al and Isringhausen negotiate; Mose Manual kills his brother; Nuttall takes bets on his bicycle exhibition; Jane befriends Joanie.

Chinese Prostitutes Brought to Deadwood as part of Hearst's plan to service the cheap Chinese labor he hopes will staff his mines. Cy Tolliver, assisted by Leon and Con Stapleton, tries unsuccessfully to market them to whites and shows no concern, despite Doc Cochran's protests, for their horrid physical conditions and short life spans.

Cipes, Greg *Deadwood* actor, playing Miles Anderson.

Civil War Though over a decade in the past when the series begins, its weight is still felt. Doc Cochran still carries bad memories of his service as a physician in the war.

Claggett, Magistrate Played by Marshall Bell. Double-dealing South Dakota politician who seeks to blackmail Al Swearengen with an old murder charge from Chicago. Murdered by Silas Adams.

Cochran, Doc Played by Brad Dourif. Deadwood's alcoholic, fascinated-with-anatomy (he has a history as a grave robber) M.D.

Color, the Slang (used by Wolcott and Hearst) for gold. Also "yellow," "the flake."

"Complications" *Deadwood* Episode (2.5). The one in which Al regains consciousness; Doc concludes Al has had a stroke; Tolliver learns of Wolcott's tendencies; Jarry gives Merrick a legal notice for *The Pioneer*, intended to frighten claimholders; Alma tells Trixie she is pregnant; Isringhausen seduces Adams; Al enlists Bullock to protect Jarry against an angry mob, which then turns its wrath on the Nigger General.

Corinthians 12 Reverend Smith quotes from this book of the Bible in the funeral service for Wild Bill.

Corrado, Regina Writer of "Childish Things."

Coyote, Peter (1942–) *Deadwood* actor, playing General Crook.

Cramed, Andy Played by Zach Grenier. Formerly an employee of the Bella Union, after almost dying of the plague he returns to town as a man of God. Knifes Cy Tolliver in the final episode of Season Two.

Crook, General Played by Peter Coyote. US Army cavalry officer who arrives with his troops seeking provisions in the camp during their mission to clean up the region in the wake of the massacre at Little Big Horn.

Crop Ear Earless, lowlife *Deadwood* character ("Requiem for a Gleet") seeking to deal with Al Swearengen during his illness. Has his throat slit by Dan Dority after insulting him.

Custer, General George Armstrong (1839–1876) US Army general, who died in the disastrous Battle of Little Big Horn in Montana, which took place just before *Deadwood* begins.

D

Deadman's Hand In poker, aces and eights, the cards Wild Bill was holding when murdered by Jack McCall.

"Deadwood" *Deadwood* Episode (1.1). The one in which Bullock hangs a man in Montana; Bullock, Sol Star, Wild Bill, Calamity Jane, and Charlie Utter arrive in town; Trixie kills an abusive trick; the conspiracy to dupe Brom Garret commences; the Metz family is massacred; Wild Bill and Bullock kill Ned Mason.

Deadwood Pioneer, The Deadwood's newspaper, edited by A. W. Merrick.

"Deep Water" *Deadwood*

Episode (1.2). The one in which Jane fails to protect Sophia Metz from Al; Charlie Utter arranges an appearance fee for Wild Bill; Brom checks out his claim; Tom Mason is shot down by Hickok; Doc stands down Dan Dority when he is sent to kill the Metz girl; Al kills Persimmon Phil.

Dickens, Kim (1965–) *Deadwood* actress, playing Joanie Stubbs.

Digestive Crisis Intestinal distress E. B. confesses to in "Boy the Earth Talks To": "Allow me a moment's silence, … I am having a digestive crisis. And must focus on suppressing its expression."

Dillahunt, Garret (1964–) *Deadwood* actor, playing Jack McCall (Season One) and Francis Wolcott (Season Two).

Dolly Played by Ashleigh Kizer. A Gem whore, who regularly services Al in Season Two.

Dope Deadwood's dope needs are supplied by Al, with the assistance of Wu, his supplier.

Dority, Dan Played by W. Earl Brown. Al's right-hand man and enforcer.

Dourif, Brad (1950–) *Deadwood* actor, playing Doc Cochran.

Busy film and television actor. Best known for his performance of Billy Bibbit in *One Flew Over the Cuckoo's Nest* (1976) and as the voice of the serial killer doll Chucky in a series of horror films. Also in *Ragtime* (1981), *Dune* (1984), *Alien Resurrection* (1997), and *Lord of the Rings: The Two Towers* (2002).

Driscoll, Tim Irishman used by Al in order to coerce Brom Garrett into buying a gold claim. Al has him murdered (by Dan Dority) in his room in the Grand Central.

E

"E.B. Was Left Out" *Deadwood* Episode (2.7). The one in which Tolliver disposes of the bodies of the whores Wolcott murdered; Charlie Utter beats Wolcott to a pulp; Al pays a visit to Alma Garret; a meeting of the town fathers is held (without E. B.); Chinese whores are marketed.

Ellsworth Played by Jim Beaver. A local prospector who becomes Alma's chief assistant on her gold claim and, eventually, her husband.

Engler, Michael Director of "Bullock Returns to the Camp."

Eriksson, Josh *Deadwood* actor, playing William Bullock.

F

Farnum, E. B. Played by William Sanderson. Slimey owner of the Grand Central Hotel and Swearengen minion.

Faro Game of chance at the Bella Union, introduced to Deadwood by Cy Tolliver.

Fields, Samuel Played by Franklyn Ajaye. AKA "Nigger General," an African-American visitor to Deadwood.

Fienberg, Gregg Director of "Complications" and "The Whores Can Come." Also executive producer of *Deadwood* and such other television series as *Twin Peaks*, *The Mind of the Married Man*, and *Carnivale* and feature films like *Candyman: Farewell to the Flesh* (1995) and *Gods and Monsters* (1998).

Fire Marshall Charlie becomes (in "No Other Sons or Daughters") Deadwood's first and takes his job quite seriously.

Flake See *Color, the.*

"Foraging in my remains" What Jane does not want Doc doing in her body (for the good of science) ("A Lie Agreed Upon," Part II).

Fort Kearney, Nebraska Riders are dispatched there to acquire smallpox vaccine.

G

Gant, Richard (1940–) *Deadwood* actor, playing Hostetler.

Garret, Alma Played by Molly Parker. The wife, later widow, of Brom Garret, Seth Bullock's lover, and the incredibly wealthy owner of the gold claim her husband left her.

Garret, Brom Played by Timothy Omundson. Eastern dandy, killed (at Al's orders) by Dan Dority in a failed attempt to acquire his gold claim.

Gem Saloon The popular bar and whorehouse (upstairs) owned and run by Al Swearengen.

Gimp, the Al's derogatory name for Jewel, the Gem's cleaning lady.

Grand Central Hotel Owned and managed by E. B. Farnum, Deadwood's most prominent place to stay, as well as home to an often frequented, though terrible, eatery.

Grenier, Zach (1954–) *Deadwood* actor, playing Andy Cramed.

Guggenheim, Davis (1964–) Director of "Deep Water," "Reconnoitering the Rim," "Plague," "Sold Under Sin." Also director of episodes of *NYPD Blue, Party of Five, ER, Alias, The Shield, Numb3rs,* and *24.*

Gunn, Anna (1968–) *Deadwood* actress, playing Martha Bullock.

H

Harris, Captain George Hearst's very large enforcer.

Hawkes, John (1959–) *Deadwood* actor, playing Sol Star.

Hearst, George Played by Gerald McRaney. Wealthy San Francisco mining entrepreneur who comes to Deadwood at the close of Season Two to look after his interests and further his pursuit of "the color."

"Here Was a Man" *Deadwood* Episode (1.4). The one in which Hickok visits with Bullock as he builds his store; Alma sees Brom's dead body; Tolliver hires Doc to look after his whores; Andy Cramed arrives and falls sick; Alma enlists the help of Hickok; Al considers killing Hickok; McCall shoots Wild Bill in the back of the head.

Hess, Sara Writer of "Advances, None Miraculous" (2.10). Has also written for *House.*

Hickok, Wild Bill (1837–1876) Played by Keith Carradine. Legendary gunfighter and lawman who arrives in Deadwood with his entourage seeking his fortune and is murdered by Jack McCall.

Hickok's Last Letter Wild Bill's final missive to his wife comes into the possession of E. B., who tries to swindle Wolcott with it.

Hill, Walter Director of "Deadwood" (1.1) and writer, director, and producer of numerous feature films, including *The Warriors* (1979), *Southern Comfort* (1981), *48 Hrs.* (1982), and *Wild Bill* (1995).

Hooplehead Al Swearengen's designation for a member of the largely unthinking, easily manipulated masses. Presumably refers to the city of Hoople, North Dakota.

Hostetler Played by Richard Gant. African-American owner of a livery stable in Deadwood. A runaway horse being castrated at his establishment kills William Bullock.

Hume, David (1711–1776) Scottish philosopher, author of such books as *Treatise of Human Nature* and *Inquiry Concerning Human Understanding*. In "Amalgamation and Capital" Wolcott blames Charley's economic notions on him, Karl Marx, and Adam Smith.

I

Irons, Jimmy Deadwood dope addict, killed by Al after he steals from Wu ("Mr. Wu").

Isringhausen, Alice Played by Sarah Paulson. Pinkerton agent who comes to Deadwood pretending to be a tutor to Sofia while under the employ of interests seeking to acquire the Garret gold claim.

J

Jarry, Hugo Played by Stephen Tobolowsky. South Dakota Commissioner who comes to Deadwood seeking its annexation.

Jason, Peter (1944–) *Deadwood* actor, playing Con Stapleton.

Jay, Ricky (1948–) Writer of "Jewel's Boot is Made for Walking" and *Deadwood* actor, playing the part of Eddie Sawyer.

Jewel Played by Geri Jewell. A crippled Gem Saloon janitress.

Jewell, Geri (1956–) *Deadwood* actress, playing Jewel.

"Jewel's Boot Is Made for

Walking" *Deadwood* Episode (1.11). The one in which Jewel asks Doc to make her a leg brace; Otis Russell arrives; Al hires Adams to kill Claggett; Con Stapleton becomes sheriff; Trixie offers Star free sex; Rev. Smith sermonizes to the oxen; Al is furious at Trixie for her infidelity; Tolliver hires Leon to spread bad blood about Al and the Chinese; Al tells a whore about his childhood.

Jews Sol Star, Bullock's hardware store partner, is the only identifiable Jew in Deadwood and the recipient of many anti-Semitic remarks, especially Al's.

Jones, Jeffrey (1946–) *Deadwood* actor, playing A. W. Merrick.

Juice Slang in Deadwood for clout or power. When Al discovers Lee has "juice," he surmises (correctly) that Hearst must be backing him.

K

Kidney stones Medical ailment afflicting Al in the early episodes of Season Two.

Kizer, Ashleigh (1983–) *Deadwood* actress, playing Dolly.

Krige, Alice (1954–) *Deadwood* actress, playing Maddie.

L

Laudanum Opium-based drug, to which Alma is addicted when she comes to Deadwood.

Lee Played by Philip Moon. "San Francisco cocksucka" sent by Hurst to gain control of Deadwood's Chinese population and concerns, including prostitution.

Leon Played by Larry Cedar. A dope-addict minion of Cy Tolliver.

"Lie Agreed Upon, A," Part 1 *Deadwood* Episode (2.1). The one in which Bullock and Alma's affair continues, even as Alma's gold readies for shipment to Denver; Al is upset that the new Black Hills commissioners are all from Yankton and with the coming of the telegraph; Al publicly insults Bullock; Bullock and Al come to blows (Star and Charlie are wounded while backing Bullock) and plunge over Al's balcony into the thoroughfare, just as Bullock's wife and son arrive by stagecoach; Alma pays an awkward visit to Bullock and his family; Tolliver is furious at the arrival of new whores who will staff Joanie Stubbs' Chez Amis.

"Lie Agreed Upon, A," Part 2 *Deadwood* Episode (2.2). The one in which Bullock demands Alma either leave Deadwood or end their affair; the Chez Ami is established; Bullock prepares to demand the return of his gun and badge, backed again by Star and Utter, as well as Jane; newly returned to the camp, Adams kills Slippery Dan at the Gem; Al returns Bullock's belongings (including his hat) and makes peace with his enemy because he needs him.

Lila Played by Meghan Glennon. Bella Union prostitute, sometime lover of Cy Tolliver.

Lychnikoff, Pavel (1967–) *Deadwood* actor, playing Blazanov.

M

MacRury, Malcolm Writer of "Deep Water" and "Plague." Has also written for *Earth: Final Conflict*.

Maddie Played by Alice Krige. Old friend of Joanie Stubbs and fellow prostitute who comes to Deadwood as a partner on Chez Ami with the secret motive of blackmailing Francis Wolcott but is instead killed by him.

Malcomson, Paula *Deadwood* actress, playing Trixie.

Manchester, England Al imagines himself running a brothel, "catering to specialists exclusive," in this English city in his old age.

Mann, Ted Writer of "Sold Under Sin," "Requiem for a Gleet," and "Boy the Earth Talks To." Has also written for a wide variety of other series, including *Miami Vice, Wiseguy, NYPD Blue, Millennium, Brooklyn South, Judging Amy,* and *Andromeda*.

Manuel, Mose Played by Pruitt Taylor Vance. Hulking gold prospector who murders his brother in order to sell his claim to Wolcott and Hurst's interests.

Marx, Karl (1818–1883) German philosopher and economist, author of *Das Kapital* and founder of Communism. See *Hume, David*.

Mason, Ned One of the Road Agents who ambushed the Metz family; gunned down in the thoroughfare by Wild Bill (and Seth Bullock).

Mason, Tom Road agent, one of those who slaughtered the Metz family; shot to death in

Saloon #10 by Wild Bill before he acts on a plan to murder his brother's killer.

Mather, Cotton (1663-1728). Stern Puritan theologian to whom Alma compares Miss Isringhausen in "Requiem for a Gleet."

Mayor In "No Other Sons or Daughters" E. B. becomes Deadwood's first mayor.

McCall, Jack Played by Garret Dillahunt. Lowlife gambler who kills Wild Bill Hickok by shooting him in the back.

McDonald, Bryan Writer of "Mr. Wu," "The Whores Can Come."

McKinnon, Ray (1961-) *Deadwood* actor, playing Reverend Smith.

McRaney, Gerald (1948-) *Deadwood* actor, playing George Hearst.

McShane, Ian (1942-) *Deadwood* actor, playing Al Swearengen.

Merrick, A. W. Played by Jeffrey Jones. Editor and publisher of the *Deadwood Pioneer*.

Metz Family Squarehead (Norwegian) family slaughtered by road agents as they leave Deadwood to return to Minnesota in "Deadwood."

Metz, Sofia Played by Bree Wall. Flathead girl, the only survivor of the slaughter by road agents of her family, later adopted and cared for by Alma Garrett.

Milch, David (1945-) Writer of "Deadwood," "A Lie Agreed Upon."

Minahan, Dan Director of "Suffer the Little Children," "Mr. Wu", "Advances", "None Miraculous." Has also directed episodes of *Six Feet Under*, *The L Word*, and *Commander in Chief* and written the screenplay for *I Shot Andy Warhol* (1996).

"Mr. Wu" *Deadwood* Episode (1.10). The one in which Bullock laments becoming health commissioner; Wu storms into the Gem and reports a dope theft; Merrick proposes establishment of the "Ambulators"; Claggett's bagman, Adams, arrives; Al drowns Jimmy Irons in the bathhouse for his dope theft and delivers the body to Wu (and his pigs).

Montana Territory (later state [1889]) from which Sol and Bullock journey to Deadwood. Rumored to be interested in annexing Deadwood.

"Montana" Wild Bill Hickok's nickname for Seth Bullock, who came to Deadwood from Montana, where he had served as a marshal.

Montgomery Ward In "No Other Sons or Daughters," a piano arrives for the Gem, ordered from this mail order company.

Moon, Philip (1961–) *Deadwood* actor, playing Lee.

Morrow, Victoria Writer of "Complications," her first television script.

N

Naked Maja, The A copy of this painting by Francisco Goya is prominently displayed in the Bella Union.

Nebraska Pussy In "The Trial of Jack McCall" Cy Tolliver uses the prospect of experiencing this delicacy as reason for Joey to journey to Fort Kearney to acquire smallpox vaccine.

"New Money" *Deadwood* Episode (2.3). The one in which Wolcott arrives; Al's condition worsens; Maddie reveals her intentions with Wolcott; E. B. tries to sell Wolcott Hickok's last letter, and Wolcott parlays the scam into manipulating E. B. into becoming his propagandist; Alma offers to buy the Grand Central; Trixie takes up bookkeeping; Wolcott visits the Chez Ami.

No. 10 Saloon A seedy drinking and gambling joint, owned by Tom Nuttall. Hickok is killed there by Jack McCall.

"No Other Sons or Daughters" *Deadwood* Episode (1.9). The one in which talk of annexation perplexes Al; Magistrate Claggett arrives and demands bribes and brings news of a warrant against Al; E. B. acquires Hickok's last letter; Rev. Smith's condition deteriorates; the camp leaders form a government (Farnum as mayor); Tolliver and Eddie Sawyer argue; Jane leaves the camp; Bullock tells Alma about his wife and son.

Nuttall, Tom Played by Leon Rippy. Owner and proprietor of the No. 10 Saloon.

O

Olyphant, Timothy (1968–) *Deadwood* actor, playing Seth Bullock.

Omundson, Timothy (1969–) *Deadwood* actor, playing Brom Garret.

P

Parker, Molly (1972-) *Deadwood* actress, playing Alma Garret.

Paulson, Sarah (1975-) *Deadwood* actress, playing Miss Isringhausen.

Peaches The canned snack-of-choice at public gatherings (e.g. the meeting to discuss response to the plague) at the Gem.

Persimmon Phil One of the road agents who slaughtered the Squareheads on their way out of Deadwood, killed by Al in order to guarantee his silence ("Deep Water").

Phlegm Respiratory system mucous Wild Bill must "get ... situated" (according to Jane) before speaking with Alma Garret ("Here was a Man").

Pigs Al (and others) take their dead bodies to Deadwood's Chinatown for disposal eaten by Wu's very hungry pigs.

Pinkerton Detective Agency This American security firm, founded in 1850, sends Miss Irsinghausen to Deadwood in an attempt to acquire Alma's wealth for her late husband's family.

"Plague" *Deadwood* Episode (1.6). The one in which Bullock is ambushed by an Indian (who he kills in a brutal fight); Al finds out about Trixie's deception with Alma; Jane learns she is immune to the plague; Charlie finds an injured Bullock; the camp's leaders meet at the Gem, eat peaches, and decide to send riders to secure vaccine and set up a plague tent in Chinatown, staffed by Doc, Jane, and Rev. Smith.

Plague, the Deadwood must deal with smallpox in several first season episodes.

Poker Card game played at the Gem, the Bella Union, Saloon #10, and elsewhere. Wild Bill is murdered by Jack McCall while at the poker table, holding the famous "deadman's hand."

Putnam, George (1948-) Writer of "No Other Sons or Daughters." Has also written for *NYPD Blue* and *Murder One*.

Putting a Stink on One's Johnson Having sex, specifically with a prostitute.

R

"Reconnoitering the Rim" *Deadwood* Episode (1.3). The one in which the Bella Union opens, to Al's shock; Hickok beats McCall at poker; Utter leaves for Cheyenne; Bullock and Star buy a lot from Al and Bullock starts building the store; Dority throws Brom off a cliff (witnessed by Ellsworth).

"Requiem for a Gleet" *Deadwood* Episode (2.4). The one in which Al's condition becomes life-threatening; Wolcott and Ellsworth have a confrontation; Alma fires Isringhausen; Dority slits Crop Ear's throat; Jarry and Carrie (the Chez Ami whore) arrive; Dority confesses Al's weakness to Adams; Ellsworth advises Alma to discount the swirling rumors; Cochran contemplates treatment of Al; Trixie mourns Al and enlists Dority in a promise to burn down the Gem if he dies; Denver agrees to a bank; Al passes his stones without the need for Doc to operate; Wolcott is quick on the trigger with Carrie.

Richardson E. B.'s imbecilic flunky at the Grand Central. Frequently the silent interlocutor of Farnum's rants.

Rippy, Leon *Deadwood* actor, playing Tom Nuttall.

Road Agents Robbers in Deadwood, Al's henchmen, who attack travelers journeying to and from the camp.

Russ, William (1950–) *Deadwood* actor, playing Otis Russell.

Russell, Otis Played by William Russ. Alma's scheming, debt-ridden, "no account" father.

S

"Same Dead Roach in the Same Damn Biscuit" Vermin found by Charlie in the food at the Grand Central ("Deep Water"). "It stuck to his position," Wild Bill notes.

Sanderson, William (1948–) *Deadwood* actor, playing E. B. Farnum.

Sarnoff, Elizabeth Writer of "Here Was a Man," "Suffer the Little Children," "New Money," "Amalgamation and Capital." Also wrote for such series as *NYPD Blue* and *Crossing Jordan*, and, as of Fall 2005, *Lost*.

Sawyer, Eddie Played by Ricky Jay. Long-time assistant of Cy Tolliver's at the Bella Union, in charge of the gambling operations.

Shepherd's Pie A "dish originating in England that consists of a bottom layer of minced (ground) lamb in gravy covered with mashed potato and a layer of cheese ... baked in an oven" (from Wikipedia), served at the Grand Central, where it sometimes contains offal ("Requiem for a Gleet").

Shill, Steve Director of "Jewel's Boot is Made for Walking," "New Money," and "Something Very Expensive," and writer of "Something Very Expensive." Also director of a wide variety of both British and American television series (*EastEnders, The Bill, The Sopranos, Law & Order, Law & Order: SVU, Law & Order: Criminal Intent, The Wire, Carnivale, Rome, Invasion, Night Stalker*).

Slippery Dan Deadwood citizen, killed when Dan Dority impales him on deer antlers in "A Lie Agreed Upon," Part 2.

Smallpox "An acute, highly infectious, often fatal disease caused by a poxvirus and characterized by high fever and aches with subsequent widespread eruption of pimples that blister, produce pus, and form pockmarks" (Dictionary. com). The disease breaks out in Deadwood in Season One.

Smith, Adam (1723–1790) Scottish economist and moral philosopher, whose *The Wealth of Nations* was a key text in the development of capitalism. See *Hume, David*.

Smith, Rev. H. W. Played by Ray McKinnon. Deeply spiritual minister, afflicted by seizures until he is euthanized by Al.

"Sold Under Sin" *Deadwood* Episode (1.12). The one in which General Crook and his troops arrive; Al warns Claggett about pursuing the warrant against him; Doc delivers Jewel's new boot; Alma's father demands she pay his debts; Bullock beats Russell senseless in the Bella Union; Con Stapleton kills a Chinese man and Bullock removes his badge; Tolliver seeks the assistance of General Crook to fight "lawlessness"; Bullock and Alma have sex for the first time; Al takes Rev. Smith's life; Adams slits Claggett's throat; Bullock agrees to be the "fucking sheriff."

"Something Very Expensive" *Deadwood* Episode (2.6). The one in which Al returns to work; Chinese whores arrive; Alma proposes founding a bank; Jarry, furious at Tolliver, flees town; Trixie encourages a bewildered Ellsworth to marry the pregnant Alma; Al begins negotiation with Isringhausen; Bullock chastises Steve for his rabble-rousing; Tolliver begins to threaten Wolcott with blackmail; Wolcott murders Doris, Maddie, and Carrie; Con and Leon trash *The Pioneer*; Steve takes out revenge on Bullock's horse; Charley secrets the still living Chez Ami whores out of town.

South Dakota Midwestern American state (it attained statehood in 1889), where Deadwood is located.

Spitting in Your Hand A Deadwood means of sealing a deal, as when Brom Garret buys his gold claim ("Deadwood").

Squareheads Deadwood slang for Norwegians.

Stapleton, Con Played by Peter Jason. Shit-heel who serves briefly as Deadwood's first sheriff.

Star, Sol Played by John Hawkes. Seth Bullock's Austrian Jewish partner, with whom he comes to Deadwood to open a hardware store.

Star and Bullock's Hardware Store New Deadwood establishment built (on a plot

purchased from Al) and owned by Sol Star and Seth Bullock.

Steve Deadwood resident who provokes the mob against Comissioner Jarry ("Complications") and later the Nigger General and ejaculates on Bullock's horse after being reprimanded by the sheriff.

Stubbs, Joanie Played by Kim Dickens. Lead whore of the Bella Union, who opens her own bordello (the Chez Ami) in Season Two.

"Suffer the Little Children" *Deadwood* Episode (1.8). The one in which Dority kills a man on behalf of Flora Anderson; E. B. wants to kill Alma and Bullock; news of a treaty with the Indians arrives; Flora and Joanie spend the night together; smallpox shots are given; Ellsworth confirms Alma's gold strike; Tolliver kills Miles and demands that Joanie kill Flora.

Swearengen, Al Played by Ian McShane. Intimidating, powerful owner of the Gem Saloon and Deadwood's leading entrepreneur.

T

Taylor, Alan (1965–) Director of "Here was a Man" and

"Requiem for a Gleet." A prolific HBO director (*Oz, Sex and the City, The Sopranos, Six Feet Under, Carnivale, and Rome*) as well as episodes of *Homicide, The West Wing, Now and Again, Keen Eddie,* and *Lost.*

Thoroughfare, the Frequently used Deadwood lingo for the street, the main road.

Tobolowsky, Stephen *Deadwood* actor, playing Commissioner Hugo Jarry.

Tolliver, Cy Played by Powers Boothe. Sinister owner of the Bella Union.

"Trial of Jack McCall, The" *Deadwood* Episode (1.5). The one in which Al arranges a swift trial for Hickok's killer; Alma struggles with her drug withdrawal; Bullock agrees to investigate the Garret claim; Tolliver has Andy Cramed left for dead in the woods, where Jane finds him; Trixie fails to keep Alma addicted; Rev. Smith presides at Hickok's funeral; McCall is found innocent; Bullock sets out after McCall.

Trixie Played by Paula Malcomson. A whore at the Gem and Al's paramour; in Season Two she becomes Sol Star's apprentice and lover.

U

Utter, Charlie Played by Dayton Callie. Wild Bill Hickok's "manager" and friend, who opens a shipping business in Deadwood.

V

Van Patten, Timothy (1959–) Director of "Childish Things." Has been an occasional actor and a prolific HBO director (*Sex and the City, The Sopranos, The Wire, Rome*). Has also directed individual episodes of *Homicide, Touched by an Angel, Central Park West, Now and Again, Ed, Keen Eddie, Into the West.*

Vance, Pruitt Taylor (1960–) *Deadwood* actor, playing Mose Manuel. His numerous roles in film and television have included *Wild at Heart* (1990), *JFK* (1991), and *Monster* (2003).

W

Wall, Bree *Deadwood* actress, playing Sofia Metz.

Watson, Clell Horse thief Bullock faces down an angry mob to hang "under color of law" in Montana before leaving for Deadwood.

Weigert, Robin (1974–) *Deadwood* actress, playing Calamity Jane.

Welliver, Titus (1961-)
Deadwood actor, playing Silas
Adams. Had previously appeared
in other Milch series like *NYPD
Blue* and *Brooklyn South.*

"Whores Can Come, The"
Deadwood Episode (2.11). The
one in which William Bullock
dies from his injuries; the
burning of dead Chinese whores
infuriates Wu; Martha Bullock
decides to leave the camp; most
of the town, including the
Gem's whores, attend William's
funeral (Andy Cramed
officiating); Alma accepts
Ellsworth's offer of marriage.

Wilkes-Barre Pennsylvania town
Tom Nuttall was forced to leave
because of violations of the fire
code.

Wolcott, Francis Played by
Garret Dillahunt. Psychopathic,
impotent advance scout for
George Hearst, who murders
several prostitutes (including
Maddie) and hangs himself at
the end of Season Two.

Worth, Jody Writer of
"Reconnoitering the Rim,"
"Bullock Returns to the Camp,"
"A Lie Agreed Upon," Part 2,
"E. B. Was Left Out." Also
wrote episodes of *Hill Street
Blues* and *NYPD Blue.*

Wu, Mr. Played by Keone
Young. Leader of Deadwood's
Chinatown and Al Swearengen's
accomplice.

Y

Yankton South Dakota city, the
original capital of the Dakota
Territory.

Yellow, the See *Color, the.*

Young, Keone *Deadwood* actor,
playing Wu.

NOTES

Introduction

1. "Except to the extent I reenact certain aspects of my father's nature, I think it's closer to the truth to say Sipowicz's personality is more like my dad's" (Milch 149).

2. A complete list of Milch's award nominations can be found at <http://imdb.com/name/nm0586965/awards>.

3. "Is it strange for you, knowing that you have such a huge following of cops in New York who love [*NYPD Blue*], and you coming from this history of heroin abuse and time spent in jail? Is it kind of weird for you?" Laura Schiff asked the "Phi Beta Cop" (Longworth) Milch, who acknowledges "I was a criminal" and answers "No":

   A good cop would be a good criminal. And cops understand criminals, and if it weren't for the fact that they're criminals they're probably more comfortable with them than with anybody else. The reason criminals confess to cops is because they trust cops. Because they understand cops better, and cops understand them better. Lawyers are bullshit. A cop knows where the crime began, he knows what was in the guy's mind. I can show you confessions where the criminals, many of whom have been beaten, as they answer the district attorney's questions, before every answer they look to the cop and trust the cop as what *they* should say. And they're not wrong. A criminal can tell a story and wind up doing two years, and he can tell the same story and wind up doing life. (10)

4. John Belluso, Regina Corrado, Sara Hess, Ricky Jay, Victoria Morrow, George Putnam, and Steve Shill authored one episode each; Malcolm MacRury and Bryan McDonald have written two, Ted Mann did three, and Elizabeth Sarnoff and Jody Worth are credited with four episodes each.

5. As Milch himself notes (as have several set visitors and actors), he "doesn't write scenes; he dictates them, the lines subsequently appearing on a large computer monitor in front of him. He'll often repeat sentences sometimes shuffling and rejiggering the words in the show's early American, profane patois until he gets the rhythm right" (Wolk 69).

6. Milch is alluding to lines attributed to director Billy Wilder (Singer 195).

7. Milch attributes these words to Kekule, but he would appear to be alluding to the oft-quoted observation of another nineteenth-century scientist, Louis Pasteur, who said that "Where observation is concerned, chance favours only the prepared mind" (Knowles).

8. Perfectly capturing *Deadwood*'s water-cooler public fame, a *New Yorker* cartoon shows a road sign on which we read "DEADWOOD 25----- MILES."

9. "For me," Milch has insisted, "democracy is a patent delusion. It's an ideal, but this society is far from democratic, nor can it be. The idea in America, even as the Declaration of Independence was put forward—'We hold these truths to be self-evident that all men are created equal'—that was bullshit" (Schiff 6).

Chapter 1

1. This essay is indebted to my colleague and fellow *Deadwood* enthusiast David Ellison of the School of Arts, Media and Culture at Griffith University for his comments on an earlier draft. It is dedicated to Dan the barman at the Governor's Club, Madison Concourse Hotel who alerted me to *Deadwood*'s brilliance during my stay in 2004, and who rivals Al himself in his wit and wicked savvy.

2. Charles Darwin's account of "sports" in *The Origin of Species* refers to plants and does not quite tally with Milch's reading.

3. Jacobs, "*Amour Fou*: Violence and Therapy in *The Sopranos.*"
4. Ian McShane, <http://www.skyone.co.uk/programmes/deadwood/interview.aspx>.
5. David Ellison email correspondence.

Chapter 2

1. This irony is not lost on him as he describes the political climate emerging from the turmoil of the 1960s with the "leading edge of reaction ... the Christian Right, with views on sex and on the position of women by no means remote from those described in *Horrors* [*of the Half-Known Life* his earlier book]" (xxxvi). (It should be noted that he was writing at the time of Bill Clinton's impeachment following his sexual shenanigans with a White House intern and not during George W. Bush's dodgy rise to prominence.) And yet, there is a certain echo of contemporary anxieties contained in his statement that of all the repercussions the most "salient has been the opposition to women's right to abortion." With the current battle raging in America over women's reproductive rights and the selection of John Roberts, as the country's most powerful judge being "the first major test of abortion rights for the Supreme Court in the guise of Ayotte v. Planned Parenthood of Northern New England" (Lerner 2005). And with the possibility of the Roe v. Wade ruling being rattled, if not overturned entirely, there is not much to choose between the ideologies being discussed here. It also reveals the pertinence of reclaiming nineteenth-century sexual mores in the twenty-first century.

Chapter 3

1. A. W. Merrick and his partner W. A. Laughlin actually faced near-catastrophe as they transported their printing equipment the almost 400 miles from Colorado to Deadwood, though not because of vandalism. One of the wagons overturned between Cheyenne and Fort Laramie, spilling the printing equipment and type to the ground. There is something about picturing grown men scouring the ground to collect lead type in the middle of the wilderness that is simultaneously pathetic,

comic and heroic. Merrick set up their office when reaching Deadwood as Laughlin was too sick to work, and because the floor of the log cabin they used turned to mud when it rained, he had to set up the printing equipment in a tent on the slope above the cabin (Dary, 93–4).

Chapter 4

1. Milch has said that "one of the things that really drew me to the story was the fact that Deadwood had no law. I had been writing shows, mostly cop shows which had to do with the intersection of law and order or the failure to intersect [like *Hill Street Blues*, *NYPD Blue*, and *Murder One*] and I was interested in what it would be like to examine a society where there was order more or less, but no law whatsoever" (David Milch, Commentary, "Deadwood," 1.1). This commentary and all of the quotes from the first season of *Deadwood* come from *Deadwood: The Complete First Season* DVD box set.

2. Swearengen's preoccupation with Wild Bill and his attempt to have him killed may well refer to the theory that Hickok "was murdered because he was considered to be a threat to the lawless element that feared that he might become city marshal" (Rosa 196), a very real possibility inasmuch as he "had a reputation for being a crusader who 'cleaned towns up'" (Ames 150) and may have been "hoping for an offer of a marshal's job" (Parker 196). According to this theory, a group of gamblers in Deadwood put McCall up to the murder; in his second trial, McCall even "alleged that a gambler named John Varnes had hired him to [do the deed]" (Rosa 201).

3. Although writer Elizabeth Sarnoff gives Bill this line in Episode 4, it has actually been attributed to Calamity Jane. As an aging Jane, in search of income, signed on for stage shows that exploited her reputation as a product of "the Wild West," she complained to cowboy, friend, and author "Teddy Blue" Abbott, "Blue, why don't the sons of bitches leave me alone and let me go to hell my own route?" (Walker 214).

4. Rosa states that there is some debate about "Wild Bill's so-called vagrant status" and that some did consider him "a 'worthless bummer'" (187).

5. Timothy Olyphant, who plays Bullock in the series, agrees that Hickok and Bullock are "cut from the same cloth" (*Deadwood*: Interviews).

6. Rosa points out that, "hearsay played a great part both in promoting reports of violence and in the efforts to contain it" (146) and that both the press and the local governments were willing to perpetuate, augment, and exploit the reputation of Wild Bill in order to maintain order among the people. While he was indeed involved in shootouts, Wild Bill was still a product of this myth-making machine, and Rosa argues that there is some disparity between the legend of "Wild Bill, the gunfighter," and the reality of Hickok, the man.

7. Bullock's friendship with Hickok is almost certainly fictional. According to Monica Mehta, "Seth Bullock rode into Deadwood Aug. 1, 1876, one day before Wild Bill was killed ... so it's likely they never met, as they did on the show" (Mehta).

8. Carradine, who was also Buffalo Bill to Jeff Bridges' Hickok in the 1995 film *Wild Bill*, plays the gunfighter in the HBO series and researched the role prior to the filming of the show.

9. Olyphant believes that Hickok and Bullock have a "sort of father-son relationship" on the show (*Deadwood*: Interviews).

10. Hickok did work briefly in Buffalo Bill's Theatrical Troupe, between 1873 and 1874, but Ames agrees that he "couldn't act worth a damn" (147).

11. Again, Milch and his writers may be drawing from history and/or legend here. As Rosa explains, "rumors ... circulated after Wild Bill's death, claiming he had several times stated that Deadwood would be his last camp" (195-6). Bill's eyesight was also beginning to fail him, "perhaps," according to Walker, "from untreated gonorrhea" (208), and this fact might have led the declining gunfighter to doubt his chances for the future.

12. In his commentary on Episode 4, Carradine states that, initially, "we had designed a voiceover where you hear me speaking the words that I had just written to my wife." Instead, Wolcott reads the letter (or a portion of it) to the prostitute Carrie in Season 2's "Complications" after buying it from Farnum: "Agnes, darling, if such should be we never meet again, while firing my last shot I will gently breathe the name of my wife Agnes, and with wishes even for my enemies, I will

make the plunge and try to swim to the other shore" (2005). Clearly, the letter does suggest, as Rosa notes, "that he did indeed have a premonition of his impending demise" (Rosa 196) and that he knew, from his life as a gunfighter, that his death would be violent and bloody.

13. Carradine states that he played it that way so that the audience would know "that he saw it coming."

14. In the "Imaginative Reality" documentary that accompanies the Season 1 DVDs, Milch notes that the Mexican with the severed Indian head "was an extraordinary and never explained coincidence" that took place shortly after Hickok's murder and that it works, both historically and cinematically, as a way to "distract the populace from any spiritual unease [by giving] them a more convenient object upon whom to focus and accommodate their anxieties."

15. The episode ends with musician Mark Lee Scott's song "Fallen From Grace."

16. Milch and his writers seem to be playing around with some kind of spiritual metaphor in the show. "Alma" Garret's name, for example, refers to the soul, and Swearengen frequently calls the moral Bullock "his holiness." That "his holiness" loves "the soul" and that Alma tries to offer Bullock "absolution" ("Bullock Returns to Camp," 1.7) from his obligation to her, an obligation Hickok is largely responsible for, seem, as examples, to lend themselves to this kind of interpretation.

17. During his short time in Deadwood, General Crook also asks Bullock to consider the position: "in a camp where the Sheriff can be bought for bacon grease, a man, a former marshal, who understands the danger of his own temperament, he might consider serving his fellows" ("Sold Under Sin," 1.12).

18. Russell, an unrepentant gambler who would unabashedly take advantage of his daughter's newfound wealth, is Alma Garret's father. Defending her and her claim from his plans, Bullock viciously beats him up at the Bella Union at the end of Season 1 before sending him home.

19. Along these lines, Milch states, in the "Imaginative Reality" documentary, "I would hurry to say that I don't find Swearengen a villain; I find him one more of what we all are, which is a fallen

creature. ... The first creature who crawled out of the primordial ooze had either a first, middle, or last name of Swearengen."

20. The portrayal of Hickok himself has also changed dramatically over time. As Donald F. Glut and Jim Harmon note, the 1950s television show *Wild Bill Hickok*, produced during the era of *The Cisco Kid* and *Tom Mix*, featured a "handsomely stalwart" Wild Bill and his sidekick "Jingles." Though Bill was generally modest, Jingles was quick to remind people that Hickok was "The bravest, strongest, fightingest U.S. marshal in the whole West!" (176).

21. Bianculli, incidentally, also connects the shock of Dillon's loss to Janet Leigh's death in *Psycho*, although he points out that this took place "[f]ive years before Alfred Hitchcock stunned movie-goers by killing off [his] heroine" ("Holy 'Gunsmoke'!").

Chapter 7

1. There are several reasons for this shift in style and function: the increasing clout in the 1950s of Hollywood labor unions, which demanded more onscreen recognition, the filmmaker's self-conscious desire to signal his/her "artistic" aspirations (Alfred Hitchcock being the most obvious), and the need to compete with the already graphically oriented world of television (King).

2. See Johansson, "Homeward Bound: Those *Sopranos* Titles Come Heavy."

3. The TNT miniseries, *Into the West* (2005), which tells the story of westward expansion through the interlinked narratives of the Wheeler family of Virginia and the Lakota tribe of the Great Plains, used the image of the wheel as its central thematic and visual motif.

4. *Deadwood* acknowledges this convention by having the new eastern schoolmarm, Mary Stokes, replete with starched white collar and dark suit, flee Deadwood one day after her arrival, terrified by what she has seen there.

5. I use the term "Indian" here because it reflects the terminology used in the classic Western.

6. According to Thomas Schatz, the integration of these opposing forces, usually taking the form of a heterosexual marriage, is a narrative

pattern found in genres like the musical, domestic melodrama and screwball comedy (35).

7. The ubiquity of the horse in *Deadwood*'s opening credits prompted Ian McShane, on the DVD commentary for Season One to remark "What, the horse doesn't get a credit?"

8. The figure of the wild horse makes a significant appearance in Season Two ("Amalgamation and Capital," 2.9), when he breaks loose from an attempted castration and tramples William Bullock to death.

9. *Deadwood*'s creator, David Milch, claims that he chose to base his series in Deadwood because "Everything was accelerated there. Two years before [the show starts] there was literally not a white person, and in two years they had telephones. You watched American society going on at warp speed" (quoted in Wolk).

10. To quote James Poniewozik's review of the series in *Time*, "HBO dramas rework popcorny genre formats (the cop drama, the Mob flick) with dark, even cynical themes: that institutions are corrupt, that people and systems and families will screw you over, that heroes are never entirely heroic or villains alone in their villainy" (66).

11. Ian McShane explains that, in *Deadwood*, "Nobody is a complete baddie or goodie... Nobody wears a black or white hat. It's convenience, practicality, opportunity" (quoted in Wolk).

Chapter 9

1. Broad comparisons between Dickens, or other nineteenth-century serialists, and television dramas are not unfamiliar, of course. But Dickens' publishing methods are much more explicitly similar to HBO's publishing methods than to those of the commercial networks. Consider these facts: the fact that viewers pay directly for HBO programs, rather than receiving them at no cost over the air; the fact that viewers pay on a regular, monthly basis; the fact that each season runs for a set number of consecutive episodes, undisturbed by out-of-sequence repeats; the fact that the episodes are free of advertising breaks, which not only interrupt the flow of story but create artificial dramatic peaks and valleys. All of these characteristics of HBO (and other premium-channel networks) directly mirror the manner in

which readers would have purchased and consumed monthly numbers of *Our Mutual Friend*. Even HBO's habit of repeating new episodes multiple times, on multiple HBO channels, during the episode's one-week window echoes the multiple formats that Dickens' novels often adopted. Dickens' 1859 decision to publish *A Tale of Two Cities* simultaneously in weekly serial and monthly numbers, numbers that reissued the installments of the preceding weeks in the old green cover (Patten 272–3), looks a lot like HBO's decision to repeat some serial episodes in widescreen on the main HBO channel and some in cropped full frame on HBO2. In short, we need to be rigorous in how we connect serial fiction, especially in its heyday, with current incarnations, distinguishing blurry parallels from more precise ones.

2. Jennifer Hayward also lingers on this moment from the novel, in her book on seriality. Her interests, however, lie in general thematic preoccupations of social conditions and class (44–5) rather than on the very conditions of reading and reception that the first paragraph illustrates.

3. Taxidermy appears as a curious leitmotif in the second season of *Deadwood* as well, from the mounted bear that Con Stapleton finds "melancholy," to the deer head that Richardson worships as Alma Garret's familiar, to the Indian head (not actually embalmed) that Al totes around. The metaphor of the recycled body, perhaps as a description of the old/new machine of serial fiction, appealed to Dickens and Milch alike. Even more precisely, the brandishing of parts of animals or people offers one more simile for the work of part-publication, or serial fiction.

4. Another possible reason for the Hayes reference might be the additional opportunity it affords to connect the old and the new, for the 2005 audience of *Deadwood*. Hayes, like the recently reappointed George W. Bush, was brought to office in one of the nation's most contested elections. Aside from the mere suggestion that history repeats itself, the two elections speak to *Deadwood*'s central interest in the sources and complications of American democracy and society.

5. It is worth mentioning that the second season contains a serial within a serial, as the first two episodes, which unfold in uninterrupted time, are presented as a two-part story, "A Lie Agreed Upon."

6. A number of critics have discussed the telegraph as a new nineteenth-century technology that raised questions for the practice of fiction and poetry. None, however, specifically considers the telegraph's relationship, as either apparatus or language, to serial fiction. For three recent examples, see McCormack, Menke, and Otis.

7. The character of Andy Cramed offers another kind of return-with-a-difference in the second season. An associate of Tolliver's who brings the pox to camp, is left to die in the woods, and then recovers from his illness, Cramed is missing from the end of the first season to the antepenultimate episode of the second season, when he reappears as a preacher, reformed from his former hustling days. The role of minister had itself been unoccupied since the end of the first season, when Reverend Smith, in the last stages of a debilitating brain tumor, received a mercy killing at the hands of Al Swearengen. If Dillahunt's double act asks us to compare unlike roles, the fusion of gambling sharp and man of God stages another version of old and new combined.

8. A self-referential joke along the lines of Farnum's speculation about whether people used obscenities in the past may be found at the moment when Wolcott, recovering from his pummeling at the hands of Charlie Utter, asks Doc Cochran to seek out his assailant, and ask him to pay a call. "If I deliver the message," asks Cochran cautiously, "will there be a renewal of the violence?" "Oh, I hope not, doctor," Wolcott replies. "I didn't do well in the original." Garret Dillahunt's invocation of "the original," especially an original that does not end up faring very well, might well be interpreted, by experienced telegraph operators, as an allusion to the tribulations of Jack McCall.

Chapter 10

1. John Cawelti's popular "generic transformation" theory offers some sort of explanation for this shift toward self-reflexivity. However, this theory is ultimately unsatisfying as it ignores historical context, among other things. For a more involved discussion, see Jim Collins' "Genericity in the Nineties" in *The Film Cultures Reader*, ed. Graeme Turner (New York: Routledge, 2002).

2. An exception would of course be Ford's 1939 biopic *Young Mr. Lincoln*, starring Henry Fonda as the future president.

Chapter 11

1. This point is reasserted later in the episode when Trixie returns to Swearengen's room and Swearengen says, "Since last our eyes were upon each other, lo, I hope you've earned me five dollars." Trixie also simply says, "No," before closing the shutter doors to "their" room, reifying it as a place belonging exclusively to them just as her refusal to earn through whoring likewise implies that exclusivity. Swearengen's lack of complaint about this refusal is similarly telling.

2. Note, too, how Tolliver's "alien-ness" to the organism of the community throughout the first season. In "No Other Sons or Daughters" (1.9), Eddie Sawyer, one of Tolliver's employees, comments following one of the town organizational meetings, "Why didn't you volunteer for something at that meeting? Why didn't you put your hand up? Might've kept you from bein' such an evil cocksucker." Tolliver's refusal to join the "body" of the camp signals him as the truest villain of *Deadwood*.

3. This prayer and Swearengen's asphyxiation of Smith all occur in the season's final episode, "Sold Under Sin" (1.12).

Chapter 12

1. Even before *American Tabloid*, Ellroy's disturbing and provocative "L.A. Quartet," which consisted of *The Black Dahlia*, *The Big Nowhere*, *L.A. Confidential*, and *White Jazz*, indulged this irreverent mixture of nostalgia and disgust at the pretenses of American boomtowns like Los Angeles. In a sense, Milch's *Deadwood* is the spiritual inheritor of this fictional project to unearth truths about our communities and our history that we might rather see remain buried. It is obvious too that Milch and company have taken plenty of inspiration from Pete Dexter's excellent 1986 novel *Deadwood*, a National Book Award winner of which Jonathan Franzen has said: "If you want to call [Dexter's] *Deadwood* a Western, you might as well call *The House of*

Mirth chick lit" (quoted in Dexter, cover). Many thanks to our friend Bob Legnini for putting us on to this book, which only recently came back into print, and for his hospitality on our journey West.

2. In William Locklear's "The Celestials and the Angels: A Study of the Anti-Chinese Movement in Los Angeles to 1882," a possible explanation for the epithet "Celestial" is offered: "This was one of several popular terms of reference to the Chinese and appears to have been second only to 'John Chinamen' in usage. In California it was frequently used to ridicule the 'obviously non-Celestial' Chinese immigrant. The term probably derived from 'Celestial Empire,' an Occidental name for China" (Locklear 255). It is indeed difficult to account for the term with any certainty, and no doubt context played a very large role in its deployment, as its uses on the show amply demonstrate. It is also plausible that the term was sometimes used to express genuine bafflement at the seductive exoticism of a people who were both close neighbors and cultural aliens, granting that the "exoticism" here was as much imposed on the Chinese as it may have been cultivated by them to various ends.

3. As is true for so much of what we've learned about Deadwood's Chinatown in our research, we are genuinely indebted to historian Jerry Bryant and to archaeologist Rose Estep Fosha, who took time to meet with us and answer our many questions when we visited Deadwood in August 2005. They have proverbially forgotten more about Deadwood's real history than most of us will ever know; what they have remembered, unearthed, and shared with us has proven invaluable. That they do their work with such humanity, passion, and respect for their long-dead subjects is exemplary. For more on their efforts, please see the longer online version of this chapter on the website dedicated to this collection. There one can find extensive commentary on the historical traditions surrounding the real Chinese of Deadwood. The conclusions of this more complete historical study are born out of our own research and a recent visit to Deadwood itself, where we tried to flesh out the picture of the town's Chinese community.

4. This of course alludes to the important work of the late Edward Said, whose classic and controversial study *Orientalism* discusses how the

West must literally invent and continually manipulate its vision of whatever counts as "Eastern" (be it Arabic, Asian, or so on). Said's most significant claim about Orientalist discourse is that it is about everything *but* the East; instead, cultures play out their own traumas, preoccupations, and cultural anxieties in the conceptual crucible afforded by subject peoples (or at the very least, peoples who exist at a remove and at the economic and political pleasure of more powerful rivals). A fair question here is whether Milch's *Deadwood* subverts Orientalism, or merely repackages it in an edgier and more hip vehicle; the answer may well be a little of both.

5. We would like to credit and thank Cristi H. Brockway (aka "turtlegirl 76") for her outstanding efforts in transcribing every line from the first two seasons of the production; her hard work can be found and downloaded at <http://members.aol.com/chatarama>. Our quotations from the series are drawn from these transcripts and from our own crosschecking upon repeated viewings. We would also like to thank our friend David Perry for his shrewd and witty insights into *Deadwood*.

6. While Mr. Lee enjoys Al's cautious respect and the backing of some powerful new players in Deadwood, he nonetheless remains a target for resentment, not only from Mr. Wu, but also from Tolliver's buffoonish underlings, Leon and Stapleton. At one point, the articulate and mannered Lee is dismissed by them as a "glorified fuckin' monkey," although even they later acknowledge him to be the superior pimp, one "better suited than us in every fuckin' aspect of the task, fluent in both languages and don't mind standing in the filth" (2.19).

7. This is the title of episode 2.21, and it is clearly an overriding theme for the second season, both in terms of the economic destiny of Deadwood and of the effects of industrial capitalism on the town's moral landscape and frontier values.

8. We are grateful to all the posters on the "Mr. Wu" thread on hbo. com's official *Deadwood* forum, most especially the great Keone Young. Since the show first aired, he has been a tireless respondent to *Deadwood* fans. The dignity Young has brought to what could easily be a truly hackneyed role is admirable; the insights that he brings to the role are equally so. For another perspective, consider historian Liping Zhu, who recounts the following incident: "In 1896, when a

white man attempted to pull the queue of a Chinese man for fun, the targeted man immediately knocked his attacker down and kicked him into submission, which a newspaper editor said 'served him exactly right.' The editor went on to comment, 'It is more than likely that Englewood Jimmie fully understands that he cannot take liberties with a Chinaman's queue'" ("Ethnic Oasis" 28). It is curious to contrast Wu's autonomous decision to cut his queue with the strenuous and equally autonomous *defense* of the queue on the part of this historical resident of Chinatown.

Chapter 14

1. The attention to period detail that David Milch, a veteran of quality TV shows like *NYPD Blue* (1993–2001) and *Hill Street Blues* (1981–1987), lavishes on the town of Deadwood is remarkable; and indeed few television series or films exhibit such fidelity to historical record. Given this verisimilitude, the series stands in marked contrast to such big budget studio films like Cecil B. DeMille's *The Plainsman* (1937), starring Gary Cooper as Wild Bill Hickok and Jean Arthur as Calamity Jane, and Poverty Row oaters like *Deadwood Pass* (1933), a Depression-era B-film focusing on the exploits of Robert Leroy Parker, better known as "Butch Cassidy." Of course, these are not the only motion pictures to play loose with the facts about the famous lives and events in this South Dakota town, but are just two among several dozen fictionalized accounts about Wild Bill, Calamity, and other famous personalities (such as George Armstrong Custer, Wyatt Earp, Bat Masterson, Buffalo Bill Cody, Sitting Bull, and Crazy Horse) who—like Cassidy's notorious partner, Harry Longbaugh (aka the Sundance Kid)—passed through Deadwood at some time or other. Other examples (some of which were partially shot in the Dakota Badlands) include: *The Deadwood Coach* (1924); *Badlands of Dakota* (1941); *Bad Man of Deadwood* (1941); *North from the Lone Star* (1941); *Wild Bill Hickok Rides* (1942); *Overland to Deadwood* (1942); *The Texan Meets Calamity Jane* (1950); *Jack McCall Desperado* (1953); *The Lawless Eighties* (1957); *Deadwood* (1965); *Deadwood '76* (1965); and *Red Tomahawk* (1967).

2. The only expletive spoken more frequently in the series is "fuck" (a word that is not anachronistic, but dates back to the Middle Ages). Jeff Kay, a blogger with the West Virginia Surf Report, has kept a running tally of the number of times the expletive is uttered on the show. The number crunching provided by this Scranton, Pennsylvania native, who tracks the word's per-minute usage, has drawn the attention of conservative radio and Internet personalities such as Rush Limbaugh and Matt Drudge (of "The Drudge Report"). See: "The F-Man Returns," *Broadcasting & Cable*, Vol. 35, no. 9 (May 9, 2005), 6.

3. In the same episode, there is a reference to a "prick stunt" that was performed by a character named Bummer Dan, who—we learn in a passage of dialogue—has pulled his penis out to urinate on another character, Harry Young, a bartender at Nutall's saloon who promptly shot the sprinkler.

4. Immediately after *Deadwood*'s premiere, several contributors to HBO's message board for the series railed against the repeated use of words like "fuck" and "cunt." For instance, one contributor named "Cinaet" found the profanity-sprinkled dialogue "absolutely pathetic" and admits to having switched off the program after the first ten minutes. Another contributor, "macon55," expressed a similarly shocked reaction on March 22, 2004, writing, "It seemed like every other word was [profane]." However, a few commentators have pointed out that these self-righteous reactions to the filthy language of *Deadwood*— besides illustrating just how puritanical Americans often are in their "distaste for profanity"—point toward an unwillingness to acknowledge other, more terrifying, aspects of the series, including what Erica Stein refers to as its "gratuitous, shameless, inaccurate violence." By focusing almost exclusively on the word "cock" and its colorful cognates, detractors have been able to ignore the capacity for violence within us all, thus safely relegating the show's troubling depictions of torture, lynching, and rape (not to mention images of recently murdered teenagers being fed to Mr. Wu's pigs) to the distant past. See: Erica Stein, "Profanity Detractors Miss the Boat on HBO's *Deadwood*," *Cornell Daily Sun* (April 2, 2004).

5. Besides the real-life Nat Love, there was a fictional character bearing the name of "Deadwood Dick" who became popular in the USA from

1877, when dime novelist Edward L. Wheeler wrote the first of several dozen books about a Black Hills Robin Hood. Love was among many boastful cowboys who claimed to be the inspiration of Wheeler's creation, which went on to inspire numerous plays and melodramas in the 1890s. A 1940 motion picture serial apparently named after Nat Love, *Deadwood Dick*, actually has nothing to do with the real-life exploits of the African-American cowboy. In fact, this fifteen-chapter potboiler from Columbia is—like many Westerns made in Hollywood during the classical studio era—largely divorced from historical record. Nevertheless, like David Milch, who deals with Wild Bill Hickok's death in the fourth episode of his series, the producers of *Deadwood Dick* managed to undercut audience expectations by having the US marshal-turned-gambling addict (played by veteran character actor Lane Chandler) killed in the opening minutes, thus shifting emphasis away from the legendary hero and toward a broad array of fictional characters, including a masked terrorizer of the town known as "The Skull" and the titular protagonist, a newspaper editor who, by the end of chapter three, has avenged Hickok's death by sending Jack McCall to an early grave at the bottom of a deep gorge.

6. William Nathaniel Banks, "History in Town: Deadwood, South Dakota," *Antiques* (July 2004), 96–105.

7. Truly trailblazing types, Al Swearengen and Dan Dority, we learn in episode three ("Reconnoitering the Rim"), made their way to Deadwood six months prior to everyone else, chopping down trees and building the Gem in anticipation of the business to come.

8. Just as E. B. Farnum must scrub his floorboards to get the blood out, so too must Jewel, in "Suffer the Little Children," work on her hands and knees over a similar stain—her action beginning and ending the episode in a manner that lends structure and meaning to events in between.

9. Notably, the name "Sofia" comes from the Greek word meaning wisdom.

10. This is just one of the many racial or ethnic epithets used in the series to refer to recently immigrated foreigners.

11. Brian Lambert, "HBO's *Deadwood*: violent, vulgar and very hard to resist," *The Standard-Times* (March 21, 2004): C1.

12. In the same scene, Trixie is immediately called upon to "milk" Al's prick to get the "gleet" out.

13. This is something perhaps best illustrated in a homoerotic scene from Howard Hawks's *Red River* (1948), which shows Montgomery Clift's Matthew Garth sizing up his shooting abilities against a fellow cowpoke played by John Ireland—the two of them fondling each other's guns while Walter Brennan's improbably named Groot Nadine spies on them from behind a bush. A more overt reference to the "gun as penis" metaphor occurs in a scene from Stanley Kubrick's *Full Metal Jacket* (1987). Following nighttime shots of the Marines going to bed with their rifles, there is a scene of the men marching *sans* uniforms (in just their underwear) and grabbing their crotches to the telltale, singsong lyrics, "This is my rifle! This is my gun! This is for fighting! This is for fun!"

14. Similar female appropriations of this male-encoded piece of hardware occur in such lovers-on-the-run road movies as *Gun Crazy* (1949) and *Bonnie and Clyde* (1967), which both culminate with images of women being violently punished. Classic romances and films *noir* like *Casablanca* (1942) and *Double Indemnity* (1944) feature women who momentarily take possession of guns and threaten to shoot their lovers, but ultimately are unable to usurp phallic power and end up collapsing, teary-eyed, into men's arms. Similarly, in the 1950 musical western *Annie Get Your Gun*, the agency of the pistol-packing woman is safely contained within a heterosexual union.

BIBLIOGRAPHY

Adams Banner Fall 2004 (5.4): 1.4.

Adams Museum and House. *The Reality Behind the Romance: A Historical Guide to 1876 Deadwood.* Deadwood, SD: Adams Museum and House, 2004.

Aikman, Duncan. *Calamity Jane and the Lady Wildcats.* New York: Henry Holt and Company, 1927.

Ames, John. *The Real Deadwood.* New York: Chamberlain Bros., 2004.

Anderson, Grant K. "Deadwood's Chinatown." Dirlik, ed. *Chinese.* 415–28.

Armitage, Susan. "Through a Woman's Eyes: A New View of the West." Armitage and Jameson. 9–18.

___ and Elizabeth Jameson, eds. *The Women's West.* Norman: U Oklahoma P, 1987.

Banks, William Nathaniel. "History in Town: Deadwood, South Dakota." *Antiques* July 2004: 96–105.

Barker-Benfield, G. J. *The Horrors of the Half-Known Life: Male Attitudes toward Women and Sexuality in Nineteenth-Century America.* London: Routledge, 2000.

Barris, Alex. *Stop the Presses! The Newspaperman in American Films.* South Brunswick, NJ: A.S. Barnes and Company, 1976.

Bazin, André. "The Western: Or the American Film Par Excellence." *What is Cinema?* Vol. 2. Trans. Hugh Gray. Los Angeles: U California P, 1971. 140–148.

Beaumont, Thomas. "Kerry: Bush should bend in Iraq." *Des Moines Register* 9 March 2003. Accessed November 20, 2004. <http://www.dmregister.com/news/stories/c4789004/20687439.html>.

Beck, Ulrick, Anthony Giddens, and Scott Lash. *Reflexive Modernization: Politics, Tradition and Aesthetics in the Modern Social Order.* Cambridge: Polity Press, 1994.

Bell, Daniel. *The Coming of Post-Industrial Society: A Venture in Social Forecasting.* New York: Basic Books, 1999.

Belton, John. *American Film/American Culture.* 2nd Ed. New York: McGraw-Hill, 2005.

Benjamin, Walter. "Theses on the Philosophy of History." *Illuminations: Essays and Reflections.* Ed. Hannah Arendt. New York: Schocken Books, 1968. 253–64.

Bennett, Estelline. *Old Deadwood Days.* New York: Charles Scribner's Sons, 1935.

Bianculli, David. "*Deadwood* Comes Alive." *New York Daily News* 6 May 2004. Accessed 9 July 2005 <http://www.nydailynews.com/entertainment/story/190528p-164794c.html>.

___. "Holy 'Gunsmoke'!: 50th ann'y of a legend." *New York Daily News* 10 Sept. 2005. Accessed 10 Sept. 2005 <http://www.nydailynews.com/entertainment/ent_radio/story/344922p-294476c.html>.

___. "There's no deadwood in this cast." *New York Daily News* 4 March 2005. Accessed 8 July 2005 <http://www.nydailynews.com/entertainment/story/286479p-245286c.html>.

Billard, Mary. "Cashing In On the Past." *The New York Times* 30 April 2004: F1, F3.

Black Hills Visitor Magazine, Fall 2005: <http://www.blackhillsvisitor.com/main.asp?id=14&cat_id=30244>.

Blotner, Joseph. "Telephone Interview With David Milch" (Sept. 2, 1988). Unpublished typescript in Robert Penn Warren Collection, Western Kentucky University Library.

Böhnke, Michael. "Myth and Law in the Films of John Ford." *Journal of Law and Society* 28.1 (2001): 47–63.

Boles, David. "David Milch's Active Imagination." *Go Inside* 17 May 2002. <http://goinside.com/02/5/milch.html>.

Brian, Denis. *Pulitzer: A Life.* New York: John Wiley & Sons, 2001.

Brown, Jessie and A. M. Willard. *The Black Hill Trails: A History of the Struggles of the Pioneers in the Winning of the Black Hills.* Ed. John T. Milek. Rapid City: Rapid City Journal Company, 1924.

Bryant, Jerry and Rose Estep Fosha. Interview conducted by the authors (Wright & Zhou), Deadwood, SD, 4 August 2005.

Butler, Anne M. and Ona Siporan. *Uncommon Common Women: Ordinary Lives of the West.* Utah State U P: Logan, Utah, 1996.

Carter, Bill. "HBO, Looking at 'Deadwood,' Sees Cavalry Riding to Rescue." *New York Times* 16 June 2004: E3.

___. "Town Without Pity: How the West Was Run." *The New York Times.* 21 March 2004: 13.4.

Caruth, Cathy. *Unclaimed Experience. Trauma, Narrative and History.* Baltimore: John Hopkins U P, 1996.

Castells, Manuel. *The Rise of the Network Society,* 2nd ed. Oxford: Blackwell Publishers, 2000.

Cawelti, John. *The Six-Gun Mystique.* Bowling Green: Popular Press, 1971.

Collins, Jim. "Genericity in the Nineties." *The Film Cultures Reader.* Ed. Graeme Turner. New York: Routledge, 2002. 276–89.

Connelley, William Elsey. *Wild Bill & His Era.* New York: The Press of Pioneers, 1933.

Corkin, Stanley. "Cowboys and Free Markets: Post-World War II Westerns and US Hegemony." *Cinema Journal* 39.3 (2000): 66–91.

Cox, Harvey. "The Purpose of the Grotesque in Fellini's Films." *Celluloid and Symbols.* Ed. John C. Cooper and Carl Skrade. Philadelphia: Fortress, Press, 1970. 92–101.

Coxe, Margaret. *Claims of the Country on American Females,* Vol. 1. Columbia: Isaac N. Whiting, 1942.

Crane, Stephen. "The Bride Comes to Yellow Sky." 1898. *The Bedford Introduction to Literature.* 6th ed. Ed. Michael Meyer. Boston: Bedford/St. Martin's, 2002. 251–58.

Crawford, Lewis F. *Rekindling Camp Fires.* North Dakota: Capital Books Co., 1926.

Creeber, Glenn. "Confessions of a Text Addict: Television & Textual Analysis." *Critical Studies in Television: Scholarly Studies for Small Screen Fiction* 1 (Spring 2006).

Dary, David. *Red Blood & Black Ink: Journalism in the Old West.* New York: Alfred E. Knopf, 1998.

D'Alessandro, Anthony. "'Deadwood' Delivery Man." *Variety* 16 July 2005: A4.

"*Deadwood* Transcripts: Seasons One and Two". 2005. Transcribed by Cristi H. Brockway. <http://members.aol.com/chatarama/>.

Dexter, Pete. *Deadwood*. 1986. New York: Vintage Books, 2005.

Dickens, Charles. *The Letters of Charles Dickens*. Madeleine House and Graham Storey, eds. Oxford: Clarendon Press, 1965–2002.

____. *Master Humphrey's Clock* (1840–41). Gimbel Collection, Beinecke Library, Yale University.

____. *Our Mutual Friend*. London: Penguin, 1997.

Dirlik, Arif. "Introduction: Mapping the Chinese Presence on the U.S. Frontier." Dirlik, ed. *Chinese*. xv–xxxvi.

____, ed. *Chinese on the American Frontier*. Pacific Formations: Global Relations in Asian and Pacific Perspectives. Lanham, MD: Rowman & Littlefield, 2001.

Ellroy, James. *American Tabloid*. New York: Ballantine, 1995.

Elsaesser, Thomas. "Postmodernism as Mourning Work." *Screen* 42 (2001): 193–201.

Etulain, Richard W. "Calamity Jane: Creation of a Western Legend." *Calamity Jane: A Study in Historical Criticism*. Ed. Roberta Beed Sollid. Montana: Montana Historical Society Press, 1995: 149–63.

Fabian, Ann. "History for the Masses: Commercializing the Western Past." *Under an Open Sky: Rethinking America's Western Past*. Eds. William Cronon, George Miles, and Jay Gitlin. New York: Norton, 1992: 223–38.

Feeney, Matt. "Talk Pretty." *Slate*, May 21, 2004. <http://www.slate.com/id/2100950/>.

Fiedler, Leslie. *Love and Death in the American Novel*. Cleveland, OH: World Publishing, 1962.

"The F-Man Returns." *Broadcasting & Cable* 35.9 (9 May 2005): 6.

Fosha, Rose Estep. "The Archaeology of Deadwood's Chinatown: A Prologue." *Ethnic Oasis: The Chinese in the Black Hills*. Ed. Liping Zhu and Rose Estep Fosha. Pierre, SD: SD State Historical Society Press, 2004. 44–68.

Glut, Donald F., and Jim Harmon. *The Great Television Heroes*. Garden City: Doubleday, 1975.

Good, Howard. *Outcasts: The Image of Journalists in Contemporary Film*. Metuchen: Scarecrow Press, 1986.

Grego, Melissa. "HBO makes series deal for Milch's *Deadwood*." *Daily Variety* 7 Jan. 2003: 21.

Haskin, Pamela. "Saul, Can You Make Me a Title?" *Film Quarterly* 50.1 (1996): 10–17.

Havilresky, Heather. "The Man Behind 'Deadwood'." Salon.com 17 July 2005. <http://archive.salon.com/ent/feature/2005/03/05/milch/>.

Hayward, Jennifer Poole. *Consuming Pleasures: Active Audiences and Serial Fictions from Dickens to Soap Opera*. Lexington: University Press of Kentucky, 1997.

"HBO: Deadwood—Davis Guggenheim." HBO Deadwood Website. 23 November 2004. <http://www.hbo.com/deadwood/cast/interviews/davisguggenheim.shtml>.

Holland, Deb. "Actor: Realities of Wild West Sobering." *Deadwood Discovered* 9 July 2005 <http://www.deadwooddiscovered.com/articles/2005/06/23/hbo/ deadwood925.prt>.

Hoppenstand, Gary. "Gone With the Western." *The Journal of Popular Culture* 38.1 (2004): 1–4.

Horney, Karen. *Feminine Psychology*, New York: Norton, 1993.

http://laststagetodeadwood.nexuswebs.net/swearingen.html.

http://www.hbo.com/deadwood/behind/therealdeadwood.shtml (2005).

http://www.legendsofamerica.com/WE-DeadwoodHBO.html (2003–2005).

http://www.legendsofamerica.com/WE-GemSaloon.html (March 2005).

Hueston, Ethel. *Calamity Jane of Deadwood*. Indianapolis: Bobbs-Merrill Company, 1937.

"Interviews: Timothy Olyphant." HBO Deadwood Website. 7 July 2005 <http://www.hbo.com/deadwood/cast/interviews/timothyolyphant.shtml>.

Jacobs, Jason, "*Amour Fou*: Violence and Therapy in *The Sopranos*." *The Contemporary Television Series*. Ed. Michael Hammond and Lucy Mazdon. Edinburgh: Edinburgh U P, 2005.

Jameson, Elizabeth. "Women as Workers, Women as Civilizers: True Womanhood in the American West." Armitage and Jameson 145–64.

Johansson, David. "Homeward Bound: Those *Sopranos* Titles Come Heavy." *Reading* The Sopranos: *Hit TV from HBO*. Ed. David Lavery. London: I.B.Tauris, 2006: 27–36.

Keats, John. *Selected Poetry and Letters.* Ed. Richard Harter Fogle. NY: Rinhart Editions, 1969.

Kegley, Charles W., Jr. and Gregory A. Raymond. "Preventive War and Permissive Normative Order." *International Studies Perspectives* 4 (2003): 385–94.

Khatchadourian, Raffi. "East Meets (Wild) West." *Smithsonian Magazine* March 2005: 25.

Kinder, Marsha. "Music Video and the Spectator: Television, Ideology and Dream." *Film Quarterly* 38. 1 (1984): 2–15.

King, Emily. "Taking Credit: Film Title Sequences, 1955–1965." *Typotheque* 28 June 2005 <http://www.typotheque.com/site/article.php?id=88>.

Knowles, Elizabeth, ed. *The Oxford Dictionary of Quotations.* New York: Oxford U P, 2003.

Koestler, Arthur. *The Act of Creation.* 1964; rpt. London: Arkana, 1989.

Lambert, Brian. "HBO's *Deadwood*: violent, vulgar and very hard to resist." *The Standard-Times* 21 March 2004: C1.

Lavery, David. "The Soul of Andy Sipowicz: Depth of Character and the Depth of Television." PopPolitics.com (March 2001): <http://www. poppolitics.com/articles/2001-06-11-sipowicz.shtml>.

Lawlor, Mary. *Recalling the Wild: Naturalism and the Closing of the American West.* New Brunswick: Rutgers U P, 2000.

Lawson, Mark. "The West Has Never Been Wilder." *The Guardian* 20 September 2004. G2: 17.

Lee, Bob, ed. *Gold, Gals, Guns, Guts: A History of Deadwood, Lead, and Spearfish, 1874–1976.* 1976. Pierre, SD: SD State Historical Society Press, 2004.

Lejeune, Anthony. "The Rise and Fall of the Western." *National Review* 31 Dec 1989: 23–26.

Lerner, Sharon. "Here Comes John Roberts, There Goes Roe v. Wade." 29 September 2005: <http://www.villagevoice.com/news/ 0549,news,70631,2.html>.

Locklear, William R. "The Celestials and the Angels: A Study of the Anti-Chinese Movement in Los Angeles to 1882." *Anti-Chinese Violence in North America.* Ed. Roger Daniels. The Asian Experience in North America: Chinese and Japanese. New York: Arno Press, 1978. 239–56.

Longworth, James L., Jr. "David Milch | Phi Beta Cop." *TV Creators: Conversations with America's Top Producers of Television Drama*. Syracuse: Syracuse U P, 2000. 89–102.

___. *TV Creators: Conversations with America's Top Producers of Television Drama*, Volume 2. Syracuse: Syracuse U P, 2002.

Lusted, David. *The Western*. London: Pearson Longman, 2003.

Martel, Ned. "Resurrecting the Western To Save the Crime Drama." *The New York Times*. 21 March 2004: 34.

McClintock, John S. *Pioneer Days in the Black Hills: Accurate History and Facts Related by One of the Early Day Pioneers*. Ed. Edward L. Senn. 1939. Norman, OK: U Oklahoma P, 2000.

McCormack, Jerusha Hull. "Domesticating Delphi: Emily Dickinson and the Electro-Magnetic Telegraph." *American Quarterly* 55:4 (December 2003). 569–601.

McMurty, Larry. *Buffalo Girls: A Novel*. New York: Simon and Schuster, 1990.

Mehta, Monica. "*Deadwood*: History Lesson." *Entertainment Weekly* 9 April 2004: 18.

Menke, Richard. "Telegraphic Realism: Henry James's *In the Cage*." *PMLA* 115:5 (October 2000). 975–90.

Milch, David and Bill Clark. *True Blue: The Real Stories Behind* NYPD Blue. NY: Morrow, 1995.

Motley, Clay. "'It's a Hell of a Thing to Kill a Man': Western Manhood in Clint Eastwood's *Unforgiven*." *Americana: The Journal of American Popular Culture* (Spring 2004). Accessed November 27, 2004. <http://www.americanpopularculture.com/journal/contents.htm>.

Murphy, Mary. "The Private Lives of Public Women: Prostitution in Butte, Montana, 1817–1917." Armitage and Jameson 193–206.

Myers, John. *Print In A Wild Land*. Garden City, NY: Doubleday, 1967.

Nyhuis, Philip. "David Milch's *Deadwood*." *Buffalo Spree Magazine Online*. January 2, 2005: <http://www.buffalospree.com/archives/2005_0102/010205Milch.html>.

Oldenburg, Ann and Kitty Bean Yancey. "Popular 'Deadwood' livens up South Dakota namesake." *USA Today* 3 May 2004: Life 01d.

Otis, Laura. "The Other End of the Wire: Uncertainties of Organic and Telegraphic Communication." *Configurations* (2001), 9:181–206.

Parker, Watson. *Deadwood: The Golden Years.* Lincoln: U of Nebraska P, 1981.

Patten, Robert L. *Charles Dickens and His Publishers.* Oxford: Clarendon Press, 1978.

Poniewozik, James. "True Grit." *Time* March 2004: 66.

Ray, Robert B. *A Certain Tendency of the Hollywood Cinema, 1930–1980.* Princeton: Princeton U P, 1985.

"The Real Deadwood." HBO Deadwood Website 5 Sept. 2005. <http://www.hbo.com/deadwood/behind/therealdeadwood.shtml>.

Reiter, Joan Swallow. *The Old West: The Women.* New York: Time-Life Books. 1978.

Riegel, Robert. "Review of Sollid's *Calamity Jane.*" *Montana: The Magazine of Western History* 9 January 1959: 63-4.

Robinson, Forrest G. "The New Historicism and the Old West." *Old West–New West: Centennial Essays.* Ed. Barbara Howard Meldrum. Moscow, Idaho: U of Idaho P, 1993. 74-96.

Rosa, Joseph G. *Wild Bill Hickok: The Man & His Myth.* Lawrence, Kansas: Kansas U P, 1996.

Sabin, Edwin Legrand. *Wild Men of the Wild West.* New York: Thomas Y. Cromwell, Co, 1929.

Said, Edward W. *Orientalism.* New York: Random House, 1978.

Saunders, John. *The Western Genre: From Lourdsburg to Big Whiskey.* London: Wallflower, 2001.

Scarry, Elaine. *The Body in Pain: The Making and Unmaking of the World.* New York: Oxford U P, 1985.

Schatz, Thomas. *Hollywood Genres: Formulas, Filmmaking and the Studio System.* New York: Random House, 1981.

Schiller, Herbert I. *Communication and Cultural Domination.* New York: International Arts and Sciences Press, 1976.

Singer, Mark. "The Misfit: How David Milch Got from *NYPD Blue* to *Deadwood* by Way of an Epistle of St. Paul." *The New Yorker* 14 & 21 February 2005: 192-205.

Slotkin, Richard. *Gunfighter Nation.* New York: HarperPerrenial, 1992.

Sollid, Roberta Beed. *Calamity Jane: A Study in Historical Criticism.* Montana: Montana Historical Society Press, 1995.

Sontag, Susan. *Illness as Metaphor; and AIDS and Its Metaphors.* New York: Picador/Farrar, Straus and Giroux, 1989.

Starr, Paul. *The Creation of the Media: Political Origins of Modern Communications.* New York: Basic Books, 2004.

Stein, Erica. "Profanity Detractors Miss the Boat on HBO's *Deadwood.*" *The Cornell Daily Sun* 2 April 2004: xx.

Sturken, Marita. *Tangled Memories: The Vietnam War, The AIDS Epidemic and the Politics of Remembering.* Berkeley and Los Angeles: U of California P, 1997.

Sulentic, Joe. *Deadwood Gulch: The Last Chinatown.* Deadwood, SD: Deadwood Gulch Art Gallery, 1975.

Tompkins, Jane. *West of Everything: The Inner Life of Westerns.* New York: Oxford U P, 1992.

Toms, Don. *Tenderloin Tales: Prostitution, Gambling, and Opium on the Gold Belt of the Northern Black Hills, 1876–1915.* Pierre, SD: State Publishing Company, 1997.

Turner, Frederick Jackson. *The Frontier in American History.* New York: Dover, 1996.

United States National Security Council. *National Security Strategy.* Accessed November 24 2004. <http://www.whitehouse.gov/nsc/nss.html>.

Walker, Dale L. *The Calamity Papers: Western Myths and Cold Cases.* New York: Tom Doherty Associates, 2004.

Ward, Josiah M. "Calamity Jane as a Lady Robin Hood." *The Literary Digest* 14 November 1925: 46–7.

Warren, Robert Penn. *The Collected Poems.* Ed. John Burt. Baton Rouge: Louisiana State U P, 1998.

___. "Democracy and Poetry." *Southern Review* NS 11 (Winter 1975). 1–28.

___, ed. *Selected Poems of Herman Melville.* New York: Random House, 1970.

Warshow, Robert. "The Westerner." *The Immediate Experience: Movies, Comics, Theatre, and Other Aspects of Popular Culture.* Cambridge: Harvard U P, 2001. 105–24.

Webster, Frank. *Theories of the Information Society,* 2nd edition. London: Routledge, 2002.

Welter, Barbara. "The Cult of True Womanhood, 1820–1860." *American Quarterly* 18 (Summer 1966): 151–74.

Wheeler, Edward L. *Deadwood Dick's Doom; or, Calamity Jane's Last Adventure.* 1899?: <http://www.sul.stanford.edu/depts/dp/pennies/texts/wheeler_toc.html>.

Wolfe, Mark S. *Boots on Bricks: A Walking Tour of Historic Downtown Deadwood.* Deadwood, SD: Deadwood Historic Preservation Commission, 1996.

Wolk, Joshua. "How the West is Run." *Entertainment Weekly* 11 Mar 2005: 66–70.

Wright, Judith Hess. "Genre Films and the Status Quo." *Film Genre Reader.* Ed. Barry Keith Grant. Austin: U of Texas P, 1986. 41–9.

Wright, Will. *Sixguns & Society: A Structural Study of the West.* Berkeley: U of California P, 1975.

Young, Keone. Email to the authors (Wright & Zhou), 15 September 2005.

Zhu, Liping. *A Chinaman's Chance: The Chinese on the Rocky Mountain Mining Frontier.* Niwot, CO: U P of Colorado, 1997.

___. "Ethnic Oasis: Chinese Immigrants in the Frontier Black Hills." *Ethnic Oasis: The Chinese in the Black Hills.* Ed. Liping Zhu and Rose Estep Fosha. Pierre, SD: SD State Historical Society Press, 2004. 3–43.

Film and Television

All the King's Men (Robert Rossen, 1949).

All the King's Men (Stephen Zaillian, 2006).

Annie Get Your Gun (George Sidney, 1950).

Bad Man of Deadwood (Joseph Kane, 1941).

Beverly Hills Buntz (television series, 1987–1988).

Big Apple (television series, 2001).

Bonanza (television series, 1959–1973).

Bonnie and Clyde (Arthur Penn, 1967).

Boogie Nights (Paul Thomas Anderson, 1997).

Buffy the Vampire Slayer (television series, 1997–2003).

Calamity Jane (David Butler, 1953).

Capital News (television series, 1990).

Carnivale (television series, 2003–2005).

Casablanca (Michael Curtiz, 1942).

Cosby Show, The (television series, 1984–1992).

Dances with Wolves (Kevin Costner, 1990).

Deadwood (television series, 2004–).

Deadwood '76 (James Landis, 1965).

Double Indemnity (Billy Wilder, 1944).

Dr. Quinn, Medicine Woman (television series, 1993–1998).

Duel in the Sun (King Vidor, 1946).

Fellini: I'm a Born Liar (Damian Pettigrew, 2002).

Forty Guns (Samuel Fuller, 1957).

Freaks and Geeks (television series, 1999–2000).

Friends (television series, 1994–2004).

Full Metal Jacket (Stanley Kubrick, 1987).

Great Train Robbery, The (Edwin S. Porter, 1903).

Gun Crazy (Joseph H. Lewis, 1949).

Gunsmoke (television series, 1955–1975).

Harvey Girls (George Sidney, 1946).

High Plains Drifter (Clint Eastwood, 1973).

Hill Street Blues (television series, 1981–1987).

House (television series, 2004–).

Into the West (television series, 2005).

Jack McCall Desperado (Sidney Salkow, 1953).

Lawless Eighties, The (Joseph Kane, 1957).

Left Handed Gun, The (Arthur Penn, 1958).

Long Riders, The (Walter Hill, 1980).

Lovejoy (television series, 1986–1994).

Man Who Shot Liberty Valance (John Ford, 1962).

McCabe and Mrs. Miller (Robert Altman, 1971).

My Darling Clementine (John Ford, 1946).

North from the Lone Star (Lambert Hillyer, 1941).

NYPD Blue (television series, 1993–2005).

Open Range (Kevin Costner, 2003).

Outlaw Josie Wales, The (Clint Eastwood, 1976).

Overland to Deadwood (William Berke, 1942).

Pale Rider (Clint Eastwood, 1985).

Plainsman, The (Cecil B. DeMille, 1936).

Psycho (Alfred Hitchcock, 1960).

Red River (Howard Hawks, 1948).

Red Tomahawk (R. G. Springsteen, 1967).

Ride the High Country (Sam Peckinpah, 1962).

Rome (television series, 2005–).

Sexy Beast (Jonathan Glazer, 2000).

Shane (George Stevens, 1943).

Six Feet Under (television series, 2001–2005).

Sopranos, The (television series, 1999–2007).

South Park (television series, 1997–).

Stagecoach (John Ford, 1939).

Texan Meets Calamity Jane, The (Ande Lamb, 1950).

Tombstone (George P. Cosmatos, 1993).

Unforgiven (Clint Eastwood, 1992).

Wild Bill (Walter Hill, 1995)

Wild Bill Hickok (Clifford Smith, 1923).

Wild Bill Hickok Rides (Ray Enright, 1942).

Wild Bunch, The (Sam Peckinpah, 1969).

Winchester '73 (Anthony Mann, 1950).

Wire, The (television series, 2002–).

Wyatt Earp (Lawrence Kasdan, 1994).

X-Files, The (television series, 1993–2002).

INDEX